KV-476-808

Performance Interventions

Series Editors: Elaine Aston, University of Lancaster, and Bryan Reynolds, University of California, Irvine

Performance Interventions is a series of monographs and essay collections on theatre, performance, and visual culture that share an underlying commitment to the radical and political potential of the arts in our contemporary moment, or give consideration to performance and to visual culture from the past deemed crucial to a social and political present. *Performance Interventions* moves transversally across artistic and ideological boundaries to publish work that promotes dialogue between practitioners and academics, and interactions between performance communities, educational institutions, and academic disciplines.

Titles include:

Alan Ackerman and Martin Puchner (*editors*)
AGAINST THEATRE
Creative Destructions on the Modernist Stage

Elaine Aston and Geraldine Harris (*editors*)
FEMINIST FUTURES?
Theatre, Performance, Theory

Maaike Bleeker
VISUALITY IN THE THEATRE
The Locus of Looking

James Frieze
NAMING THEATRE
Demonstrative Diagnosis in Performance

Lynette Goddard
STAGING BLACK FEMINISMS
Identity, Politics, Performance

Alison Forsyth and Chris Megson (*editors*)
GET REAL: DOCUMENTARY THEATRE PAST AND PRESENT

Leslie Hill and Helen Paris (*editors*)
PERFORMANCE AND PLACE

D.J. Hopkins, Shelley Orr and Kim Solga
PERFORMANCE AND THE CITY

Amelia Howe Kritzer
POLITICAL THEATRE IN POST-THATCHER BRITAIN
New Writing: 1995–2005

Marcela Kostihová
SHAKESPEARE IN TRANSITION
Political Appropriations in the Post-Communist Czech Republic

Jon McKenzie, Heike Roms and C. J. W.-L. Wee (*editors*)
CONTESTING PERFORMANCE
Emerging Sites of Research

Ramón H. Rivera-Servera and Harvey Young
PERFORMANCE IN THE BORDERLANDS

Mike Sell (*editor*)
AVANT-GARDE PERFORMANCE AND MATERIAL EXCHANGE
Vectors of the Radical

Melissa Sihra (*editor*)
WOMEN IN IRISH DRAMA
A Century of Authorship and Representation

Performance Interventions
Series Standing Order ISBN 978-1-4039-4443-6 Hardback
978-1-4039-4444-3 Paperback
(*outside North America only*)

You can receive future titles in this series as they are published by placing a standing order. Please contact your bookseller or, in case of difficulty, write to us at the address below with your name and address, the title of the series and the ISBN quoted above.

Customer Services Department, Macmillan Distribution Ltd, Houndmills, Basingstoke, Hampshire RG21 6XS, England

Avant-Garde Performance and Material Exchange

Vectors of the Radical

Edited by

Mike Sell
Associate Professor, Indiana University of Pennsylvania

First published 2011 by
PALGRAVE MACMILLAN

Palgrave Macmillan in the UK is an imprint of Macmillan Publishers Limited,
registered in England, company number 785998, of Houndmills, Basingstoke,
Hampshire RG21 6XS.

Palgrave Macmillan in the US is a division of St Martin's Press LLC,
175 Fifth Avenue, New York, NY 10010.

Palgrave Macmillan is the global academic imprint of the above companies
and has companies and representatives throughout the world.

Palgrave® and Macmillan® are registered trademarks in the United States,
the United Kingdom, Europe and other countries.

ISBN: 978–0–230–24134–3 hardback

This book is printed on paper suitable for recycling and made from fully
managed and sustained forest sources. Logging, pulping and manufacturing
processes are expected to conform to the environmental regulations of the
country of origin.

A catalogue record for this book is available from the British Library.

Library of Congress Cataloging-in-Publication Data

Avant-garde performance and material exchange : vectors of the
radical / edited by Mike Sell.
   p. cm.—(Performance interventions)
Includes bibliographical references and index.
ISBN 978–0–230–24134–3 (alk. paper)
   1. Experimental theater – Political aspects. 2. Experimental theater –
Social aspects. 3. Performing arts – Political aspects. 4. Performing arts –
Social aspects. 5. Avant-garde (Aesthetics) I. Sell, Mike, 1967–

PN2193.E86A93 2011
792.02'2—dc22   2010034429

10 9 8 7 6 5 4 3 2 1
20 19 18 17 16 15 14 13 12 11

Printed and bound in Great Britain by
CPI Antony Rowe, Chippenham and Eastbourne

Contents

Part III Divergences

Acknowledgements

Anthologies are always collaborations, so many thanks are due. Though it is in very different form now, this book began as a special issue of *Works and Days* in 2002. That issue was made possible by *Works and Days* general editor David Downing, Dean Brenda Carter (now retired) of Indiana University of Pennsylvania's College of Humanities and Social Sciences, the IUP Faculty Senate, Graduate Assistant Patrick Clark, research assistant Tony Leon, English department administrators Esther Beers and Jackie Rohrabaugh, and Mona Baker, James Sosnoski, and Lawrence Venuti. Also important to that project were writers who contributed essays that didn't make it into this version of the project, but whose work was inspirational: Seth Baumrin, David Callaghan, Grant Farred, David William Foster, Bina Toledo Friewald, Carol Motta, Bill Mullen, Kunio Nakamura, Ilka Saal, and Sehnaz Tahir Gürçaglar. The English Department at IUP is my academic home; in addition to providing everyday support, it, the Graduate Program in Literature and Criticism, and CHSS provided funds for the 2009 conference I co-organized with Eric Meljac and Melissa Lingle-Martin for the IUP English Graduate Organization/Graduate Student Association – the hosts for the roundtable that became the afterword to this book. Many of the essays in this collection first saw light at the annual American Society for Theatre Research conference; my thanks to the many conference organizers, seminar participants, and seminar co-chairs, particularly Kimberly Jannarone. Sarah Bay-Cheng's essay originally appeared in *Theatre Journal* in a special issue edited by Jean Graham-Jones. Special thanks go to the contributors, several of whom have been with this project since the very beginning, and especially Alan Filewod, Jean Graham-Jones, James Harding, and Kimberly Jannarone, who all provided pertinent criticism of my work as writer and editor. This project was inspired by my dad, Tom Sell, who first drew my attention to the role of epidemiology in the policing of dissident subcultures and first told me the story of the garden jazz concerts held at the Lexington Narcotics Hospital. My work is no use at all without Kate, Dylan, River, and Brando.

Notes on Contributors

Mike Sell is Associate Professor of English and faculty member of the Graduate Program in Literature and Criticism at Indiana University of Pennsylvania, where he teaches modern drama, performance and theatre studies, critical theory, the Black Arts Movement, and the avant-garde. He is author of *Avant-Garde Performance and the Limits of Criticism* (2005) and *The Avant-Garde: Race Religion War* (2010). He has written articles on avant-garde drama, theatre, and performance appearing in *Theatre Survey*, *Theatre Journal*, *African American Review*, *TDR*, and in anthologies published by University of Michigan, Cambridge, Oxford, Columbia, and Blackwell presses. He edited *Ed Bullins: Twelve Plays and Selected Writings* (2006) and was editorial adviser for the avant-garde and aesthetic movements sections of *The Columbia Encyclopedia of Modern Drama* (2007).

Sarah Bay-Cheng is Associate Professor of Theatre at the University at Buffalo, where she conducts research in avant-garde theatre and film, modernist drama, and intermediality in performance. She is a co-founder of the Intermedia Performance Studio, which produces live-digital hybrid performances in virtual reality, and she teaches performance theory in the Department of Media Study. Bay-Cheng's books include *Mama Dada: Gertrude Stein's Avant-Garde Theater* (2005) and the forthcoming *Poets at Play: An Anthology of Modernist Drama*. She is currently working on a book-length study of the twentieth-century performing body across media.

Laura Edmondson is an Assistant Professor at Dartmouth College. She is the author of *Performance and Politics in Tanzania: The Nation on Stage* (2007). Her articles on East African performance have appeared in *Theatre Journal*, *Theatre Research International*, and *TDR*, as well as in the anthologies *The Performance Arts in Africa: A Reader* (2002) and *Violence Performed: Local Roots and Global Routes of Conflict* (Palgrave Macmillan 2008).

Alan Filewod is Professor of Theatre Studies at the University of Guelph. His books include *Collective Encounters: Documentary Theatre in English Canada* (1987), *Performing "Canada": The Nation Enacted in the Imagined Theatre* (2002), and, with David Watt, *Workers' Playtime: Theatre and the*

Labour Movement since 1970 (2001). He is a past president of the Association for Canadian Theatre Research and of the Association for Canadian and Quebec Literatures and is a former editor of *Canadian Theatre Review.*

Patricia Gaborik is an independent scholar and fellow of the American Academy in Rome, where she held the Paul Mellon Postdoctoral Rome Prize in Modern Italian Studies in 2005–6. A specialist in early twentieth-century Italian theatre, she is the author of essays in *Modern Drama, Metamorphoses, National Theatres in a Changing Europe* (Palgrave Macmillan 2008), and the forthcoming *Atlante storico della letteratura italiana*. Gaborik is currently completing *Watching the Moon and Other Plays*, a volume of plays by Massimo Bontempelli in English translation.

Jean Graham-Jones is Professor of Theatre at the Graduate Center of the City University of New York, where she currently serves as Executive Officer of the PhD Program in Theatre. An expert on Argentinian theatre and performance, she is the author of *Exorcising History: Argentine Theater under Dictatorship* (2000) as well as the translator and editor of *Reason Obscured: Nine Plays by Ricardo Monti* (2004) and *Buenos Aires in Translation: Recent Argentinian Plays* (2008). Graham-Jones is a former editor of *Theatre Journal*, and her articles have appeared in, among other journals, *Theatre Survey, Theatre Journal, Theatre Research International, Latin American Theatre Review, Gestos,* and *The Journal of Beckett Studies.*

James M. Harding is Professor of English at the University of Mary Washington and a former editor of *Theatre Survey*. His most recent book *Collage Enactments/Engendered Vanguards* is forthcoming. His previous publications include the anthologies *Not the Other Avant-Garde: On the Transnational Foundations of Avant-Garde Performance* (2006), which he co-edited with John Rouse, and *Re-Staging the Sixties: Radical Theaters and their Legacies* (2006), co-edited with Cindy Rosenthal. He is the editor of *Contours of the Theatrical Avant-Garde: Performance and Textuality* (2000) and author of *Adorno and a Writing of the Ruins: Essays on Anglo-American Literature and Culture* (1997). His articles have appeared in the journals *Theatre Survey, Theatre Journal, Modern Drama, TDR,* and *PMLA,* among others.

Andrea Harris is Assistant Professor of Dance at University of Wisconsin-Madison, and the author of essays in *Interrogating America through Theatre and Performance* (Palgrave Macmillan, 2006) and *Dance Discourses* (2007), as well as the editor of *Before, Between, and Beyond: Three Decades of Dance Writing*, a collection of writings by Sally Banes (2007). Dr. Harris has been on the dance faculties of Texas Christian University, the University of Oklahoma, and the Universidad de las Américas, and has performed with companies including the Martha Graham Dance Company and Li-Chiao Ping Dance.

Kimberly Jannarone is Associate Professor of Theater Arts at the University of California, Santa Cruz. She has published essays on Artaud, Alfred Jarry, and Surrealism in *Theatre Journal*, *Theatre Survey*, *French Forum*, *New Theatre Quarterly*, and *The Exquisite Corpse: Chance and Collaboration in the World's Most Popular Parlor Game* (2009). Her essay "The Theater Before Its Double: Artaud Directs in the Alfred Jarry Theater" won the 2006 Gerald Kahan Scholar's Prize for best essay in theatre studies by a younger scholar, awarded by the American Society for Theatre Research. Jannarone has reviewed avant-garde and experimental performance for *Modernism/Modernity*, *Theater Survey*, *Theatre Journal*, and *TDR*. Her book *Artaud and His Doubles* is forthcoming. Jannarone has directed works by Samuel Beckett, Maria Irene Fornes, and Caryl Churchill.

Esther Kim Lee is Associate Professor in the Department of Theatre and the Asian American Studies Program at the University of Illinois, Urbana-Champaign. She is the author of *A History of Asian American Theatre* (2006), which received the 2007 Research Award for Outstanding Book-length Study in Theatre Practice and Pedagogy given by the Association for Theatre in Higher Education. Her research specialities include Asian-American theatre, ethnic theatre, transnational theatre, and performance theory.

Siyuan Liu is Assistant Professor of Theatre at the University of British Columbia. He has published research articles on twentieth-century Chinese and Japanese theatre in *Theatre Journal*, *TDR*, *Asian Theatre Journal*, and *Text & Presentation*.

Cindy Rosenthal is Associate Professor of Drama and Dance and Director of Women's Studies at Hofstra University. She co-edited *Restaging the Sixties: Radical Theatres and their Legacies* (2006) with James Harding and *Living on Third Street: Plays of the Living Theatre 1989–1992* (2008) with Hanon Reznikov. Current projects include *Ellen Stewart Presents: Posters and Chronicles from the Archives of La Mama Experimental Theatre*, a monograph analyzing Ellen Stewart's life and work through oral histories and poster art (forthcoming) and *The Rise of Performance Studies: Rethinking Richard Schechner's Broad Spectrum*, co-edited with James Harding (Palgrave Macmillan, forthcoming). Dr. Rosenthal received her BA in English and Drama from Tufts University and her PhD in Performance Studies from New York University. She is a founding member of the Bread Loaf Acting Ensemble in Middlebury, Vermont.

Graham White is Reader in Drama and Creative Practice at Roehampton University, London, UK. His work has appeared in *TDR*, *Theatre Research International*, *Theatre Survey*, and *New Theatre Quarterly*, amongst others. He is a playwright, and his adaptations of Laurence Sterne's *Tristram Shandy* and Franz Kafka's *Amerika* have recently been broadcast by BBC Radio. He is currently working on a project on the place of theatricality and performance in the workings of tribunal justice.

Praise Zenenga teaches in the Africana Studies Program at the University of Arizona at Tucson. Dr. Zenenga's teaching and research areas include Africana Theatre and Dance Aesthetics, and Theatre for Social Change and Development. He has published on masculinities, censorship, avant-gardism, and protest theatre in Zimbabwean theatre.

Introduction
Vectors of the Radical
Mike Sell

A "vector of the radical" is a kind of thing, a thing that moves and interacts with the people and places it encounters. Wherever they move, such things catalyze change, radical change. This is the kind of change that goes to the roots of a society ("roots" being the etymological origin of the term "radical"). Wherever vectors of the radical travel, change happens that alters basic ideologies, social relations, attitudes, beliefs, values, behavior, or cultural practices.[1]

The *process* of change is as fascinating and significant as *what* is changed. Indeed, entire eras can be understood as the consequence of the vector process. Modernity, for one, might be understood as a vast, continually contested global system produced by a rapidly expanding and intensifying infrastructure that enabled goods, labor, and ideology to move in unprecedented ways, radically altering local conditions of self, community, and historical being.[2] This expansion and intensification, which linked both the far-flung and intimate spaces of our collective lives, continues today in our moment of cargo containers, virtual meeting rooms, and iPods. Radical modernism – that spirit of absolute revolt against the conditions and institutions of modern life that we associate especially with the avant-garde – is both a producer and product of this circulation system. The vectors of radical modernism move within this broader system of circulation. This mutually transformative, motile, and situational relationship between radical modernism (as both belief system and cultural practice) and the various circulatory systems of the modern era is the central concern of this collection of essays.

Complicating our understanding of how vectors of the radical shape modernity is the fact that they are both a *form* of praxis and a *medium* for praxis. We might consider the different paths a play script might travel: furtively tucked into a satchel at an airport terminal, published in a state-sponsored academic journal, performed for a secret audience in a private living room or before dignitaries arrayed in a gilded opera house, displayed on an evidence table at a criminal trial, proudly carried to a political rally, or appended to an e-mail. Depending on the circulation path, the script would serve varied functions: a script to guide a theatrical production, a literary text for reading, a doorway onto happenings elsewhere in the world, a catalyst for an exclusive cultural event – a *form* of praxis. But it might also serve the role of a symbolic object – a sign of a sign, as Roland Barthes might put it.[3] For example, the play might be read as a symbol of support for a social movement, physical evidence for attorneys, or an object of scorn and abuse from torturers. In that case, it would be a *medium* for praxis.

Further complicating matters, vectors of the radical occasionally alter the very conditions of exchange that enabled them to be there in the first place. The secret living-room performance might inspire a different way of thinking about performer/audience relations or a creative collaboration that leads to a new political party or a manifesto for a cultural movement that leads to an alteration of the very social conditions that catalyzed the living-room performance. A trial involving the play might lead to censorship, arrests, pressure on publishers, the withdrawal of funding from academic departments, and so on, dampening the circulation of the text.

A vector of the radical need not only be a thing, however; a person can be a vector, too. Though we must take care when designating living beings as things, there is no doubt that a person has thing-like qualities: a body that moves through space, a mouth that projects messages, eyes and ears that take in information. The body, as with all vectors of the radical, is both a form of praxis and a medium for praxis. It is inevitably governed by complicated exchange rules – courting rituals, hygiene practices, immigration and naturalization laws, incarceration, etc. This is no more true than when the body-vector crosses cultural, ideological, or social boundaries. Bodies-in-movement are especially useful to study when we wish to learn about vectors of the radical, which is why this book is about forms of live art, particularly theatre and performance, art forms that depend on the body in motion. The writers in this collection explore how bodies move in dances, plays, concerts, demonstrations, street performances, and other kinds of live art; doing so, they suggest different ways to understand modernity.

Language is also important. In *Poetry of the Revolution: Marx, Manifestos, and the Avant-Gardes*, one of the few book-length studies of radical vectors and their impact on modernity, Martin Puchner traces the impact of manifestos on global modernity. Following the *Communist Manifesto* as it crosses geopolitical and linguistic boundaries, he shows that the manifesto is modern not just because of its message, but precisely because it is part and parcel of modern transportation and translation methods.[4] In this spirit, Jean Graham-Jones writes in her section introduction to this book that translation "has never been the simple 'carrying across' from one language to another as the word's etymology might suggest, nor do the standard categories of translation, adaptation, and versioning accurately account for translation practices' inherent complexities." The three essays she introduces focus on very different kinds of translational activity: the translation of text from one spoken and written language to another, the translation of page to stage, and the appropriation and misuse of ideological codes and performative repertoires.

Fortunately, Puchner's book isn't entirely alone. Anna Balakian's precocious 1984 compilation *The Symbolist Movement in the Literature of European Languages* initiated the trend towards global, exchange-oriented models of the avant-garde, a trend continued in the Summer 1999 issue of *The Stanford Humanities Review*, edited by Joy Conlon and Esther Gabara; by Timothy O. Benson's *Central European Avant-Gardes: Exchanges and Transformations, 1910–1930* (2002); *Not the Other Avant-Garde: The Transnational Foundations of Avant-Garde Performance*, edited by James Harding and John Rouse (2006); and by the writers in Duane Corpis and Ian Fletcher's recent special issue of *Radical History Review*, devoted to transnational avant-garde movements of the last century. Since then, the field of avant-garde studies has witnessed an expansive treatment of the space, as scholars investigate the history and significance of the avant-garde in virtually all areas of the world. These suggest a different way of thinking of the kinds of cultural radicalism that have abetted and been catalyzed by the larger forces of modernity. Doing so, they have contributed to the labors of Simon Gikandi, Charles Pollard, Laura Doyle, Benedict Anderson, Laura Winkiel, and others who are dismantling the homogeneous, linear concepts of modernity that have dominated academic study until recently.[5] Susan Stanford Friedman would likely applaud the writers in this anthology for the way they "move from singularities to pluralities of space and time, from exclusivist formulations of modernity and modernism to ones based in global linkages, and from nominal modes of definition to relational ones."[6]

The writers in this collection explore a diverse range of vectors. Siyuan Liu, for one, focuses on the international community of anarchists and socialists assembled around the linguistic and theatrical translations of

Leopold Kampf's otherwise forgettable play *On the Eve* (1906). Taking a more formalist approach, Sarah Bay-Cheng ponders a single page from Tristan Tzara's now classic *Le Coeur à Gaz*, showing how it resists the exchange processes of both theatre – stage design, blocking, enunciation, gesture – and literary translation and publication. Other contributors discuss artists, performance repertoires, and non-dramatic texts such as journals, ideas, and ideologies. While such diversity of topics is a necessary part of any vectors-based analysis, it can be a bit dizzying. To provide some counterbalance, I've organized the essays into three sections – intersections, translations, and divergences – that describe, in broad terms, some of the more significant ways that vectors of the radical move and transform. These are introduced by James M. Harding, Jean Graham-Jones, and Alan Filewod, respectively, each of whom have special expertise in that kind of vectoral motion and change.

Another counterbalance is, of course, our collective interest in the *avant-garde*. But what does "avant-garde" mean? That isn't an easy question to answer. For one, it's a notoriously promiscuous word, trafficked by professors, hedge-fund marketers, and strip-mall piercing gurus alike. Even a rigorous use can lead to varied meanings, as is apparent in Praise Zenenga's essay on avant-garde theatre in Zimbabwe, where we find it used to designate the formally experimental, the politically radical, those in the lead, a historical European tendency, and a canon of theatrical techniques. Zimbabwean theatre culture is not unique in this semantic diversity. Further complicating matters, recent scholarship has greatly expanded the field of avant-garde studies, calling into question many of our assumptions about what it means to be "vanguard."[7] That's the case in these pages, too; all the essays attempt to meaningfully complicate our understandings of the avant-garde in one way or another, and all provide critical perspectives on the avant-garde. As Kimberly Jannarone puts it in the afterword, "They re-look at important historical events and ask, what does this make us think about the avant-garde? How are we interpreting these moments through ideological frameworks? What do they mean to us that might not be political in the way we want them to be?"

As much as we hope to expand our understandings of the avant-garde and sustain a spirit of criticism towards all things designated "avant-garde," we share several assumptions. First and fundamentally, we believe that the avant-garde *challenges power* and that such a challenge is as varied as power itself. Every avant-garde challenges power somewhere, sometime, with somebody. A vanguard is a situation, a singular conjunction of people, ideas, and things.[8] Indeed, one of the more important contributions of the avant-garde to our society is a more sophisticated understanding of how power works, whether it be the mechanical power of the internal combustion engine or the interpersonal power unleashed by the feminist/civil rights mantra "the personal is political." Second, to be avant-garde, one must be a *minority*. The avant-garde is *different* – it paints differently, dances differently, lives differently, thinks differently. Such difference isn't always a choice. One can certainly choose to be avant-garde, as is the case with the U.S. theatre activists in Uganda and Rwanda criticized by Laura Edmondson or the modernist choreographers and rabble-rousing Futurists in Patricia Gaborik and Andrea Harris's essay. But just as surely, one can be forced to be avant-garde, as with the dissident theatre artists in contemporary Zimbabwe discussed by Zenenga. Regardless of the causes of their vanguardism, they are both minorities. Avant-gardes can be elite minorities: the technocrats advocated by Henri de Saint-Simon back in the 1820s, for example. Avant-gardes can be down-pressed, degraded, subaltern minorities, such as the Rastafarian community, the women of Fortaleza de la Mujer Maya (a women's collective in Chiapas, Mexico), or the queer activists of ACT-UP.[9] Whatever the case and for whatever the reason, vanguards take an *anti-majority stance* and, in so doing, gain forms of power, perspective, and productivity that are unavailable to the majority. And they often suffer for doing so.

Third, to challenge power, the avant-garde must work with and within *culture*. Culture is the medium of the avant-garde. "Culture," however, is another contentious and complex term, as Terry Eagleton points out. But we can keep our definition fairly broad and avoid the worst of the mess. Eagleton suggests "the complex of values, customs, beliefs, and practices which constitute the way of life of a specific group,"[10] to which I'd add "attitudes." As with power, the avant-garde has often been the creator of and inspiration for new sorts of cultural "complexes."[11] The Black Arts Movement (BAM), for example, produced a new market for African-American art and literature and a community of scholars, critics, and business people to support and sustain it. Guinea-Bissau won its independence from fascist Portugal by waging a cultural revolution, a struggle led by Amilcar Cabral who understood that a successful colonial operation required the control of culture and a successful anti-colonial movement required the most nuanced calibration of tradition and the new.

Together, these three criteria suggest the following definition:

The avant-garde is a minority formation that challenges power in subversive, illegal, or alternative ways, usually by challenging the routines,

*assumptions, hierarchies, and/or legitimacy of existing political and/or
cultural institutions.*

This definition isn't elegant or perfect. It is unwieldy with freelance
vanguardists like Elsa von Freytag Loringhoven, Terayama Shūji, or
Stanislaw Witkiewicz. And while it reflects the centrality of power, culture, and minority, it fails to account for a fourth criterion of particular
importance to this anthology:

To be avant-garde is to perform.

Foregrounding performance in our definition is no small matter. There
are certainly canonical avant-garde performances – the premiere performance of Alfred Jarry's *Ubu Roi* (1896); Stravinsky and Nijinsky's *Le
Sacre du Printemps* (1913); the raucous Futurist *serate* (c.1910); Picasso,
Satie, Cocteau, and Massine's *Parade* (1917); the Cabaret Voltaire (1916) –
but, the lion's share of attention in avant-garde studies has fallen to the
"objective arts": painting, sculpture, and so on. That's understandable;
performance is ephemeral and difficult to document. It involves the
critic in imaginative and affective activity that goes against the grain of
conventional scholarship and criticism.[12]

But the problem is deeper than that: the very terms of avant-garde
theory are patently biased against performance. Michael Fried's highly
influential 1967 essay "Art and Objecthood" is ostensibly a critique of
minimalism and a cry for a renewed commitment to radical form, but is
based in a prejudice against all performance-based art forms, essentially
one more anti-theatrical screed, Puritanism in modernist guise. Peter
Bürger doesn't mention a single performance in *Theory of the Avant-
Garde* (1968), despite the fact that he views Dada as central to any
definition of "avant-garde." Yet it has long been assumed that the most
radical dimension of Dada was performance. And Dada was born as a
cabaret! The one theatre artist he mentions is Bertolt Brecht (no Dadaist,
he), but what Brecht *did* in the theatre isn't. Rosalind Krauss's groundbreaking *The Originality of the Avant-garde and other Modernist Myths*
(1985) doesn't say a word about theatre or performance, suggesting that
originality means the same thing for everybody. It doesn't. Originality
is one thing for painters and photographers, entirely another for theatre
artists, playwrights, and performers.

RoseLee Goldberg first exposed the anti-performance bias in 1979.
Subsequently, performance has been well treated by Kristine Stiles,
Judith Butler, Elin Diamond, Sue-Ellen Case, Richard Schechner, Sally

Banes, James Harding, John Rouse, Rebecca Schneider, and many others. But the bias remains in the field more broadly. In terms of circulation, what we see now is a one-way flow; those in performance-based fields are expected to know Matei Calinescu and Bürger and to keep up with developments in other media. But those who work in the "objective" arts (painting, poetry, and so on) don't feel the same pressure to know our work. A more dynamic flow of ideas is needed. This anthology hopes to contribute to that flow.

The advantages are clear. The turn to performance provides a more balanced understanding of the media used by vanguardists and a better understanding of how avant-gardes challenge power. As we know, avant-gardes always challenge power *in situation*, which means that they must *enact* that challenge, *practice* that challenge, *display* their difference, *announce* their authority, *demonstrate* their relationship to the masses, *enact* their rebelliousness. In other words, avant-gardes *perform* their challenge. So, we agree with Harding and Rouse that "our understanding of avant-garde performance is compromised by being filtered through theories that fail to recognize, let alone conceptualize, the avant-garde gesture as first and foremost a performative act."[13]

Theatre and performance studies provide time-tested tools for understanding such acts. Theatre scholars, particularly those with an interest in dramatic literature, often explore the interface between literature and performance, the ways written texts become something else through different modes of enactment. Performance studies scholars do similar things with the interzones between larger cultural texts – ideology, media, and so on – and individual and group enactments of them. Both are attentive to the social, historical, material, and institutional dimensions of art, human behavior, and social organization. They are able to, in Jannarone's words, "go to the event itself, to all its material detail, as much as we can reconstruct, and see how untidy the event really is and how inadequate the narratives and interpretations we have really are ..."

Most of the contributors in this book consider performance primarily in an aesthetic sense: Gaborik and Harris write about ballet, Bay-Cheng about a play, Graham White about punk concerts, Zenenga about many kinds of theatre. But some of the chapters focus on performance more in terms of Eagleton's "cultural complexes." Alan Filewod tracks performance strategies borrowed from Stalin's USSR and Mao's China through the sectarian *sturm und drang* of the 1960s Canadian ultra-Left. Some do both, as White does with racist punk, Zenenga with the mercurial political climate of Zimbabwe, Cindy Rosenthal with the Living Theatre in Brazil, and Gaborik and Harris with Cold War liberalism.

All of the contributors demonstrate that there is a "social life of things," as Arjun Appadurai puts it.[14] The things that people make move – or are kept secured from motion. By following the performative paths of things, we can draw a map of the material infrastructure of a society's beliefs, values, and attitudes. Doing so, we are able to acquire "a series of glimpses of the ways in which desire and demand, reciprocal sacrifice and power interact to create ... value in specific social situations," as Appadurai writes.[15] In this spirit, Rosenthal examines a transformative moment in the history of the Living Theatre, when they abandoned the conventional pathways of the international theatre festival circuit to collaborate with poor and working-class people in Brazil. Their "value" as artists changed when the way they moved and the places in which they moved changed – which is why they found themselves in a Brazilian jail. In her fascinating discussion of the funerals, monuments, and obituaries that marked the passing of Fluxus trickster and video artist Nam June Paik, Esther Kim Lee describes the very different value his creative dissidence holds for the arts community in the U.S. and for finance capitalists in South Korea. As she shows, Paik has become a valuable commodity in two very different social situations – two distinct "signs of a sign."

As I hope I've made clear, the fundamental goal of this anthology is to expand the scope of avant-garde studies: *where*, *when*, and *what* we study. However, one of the challenges of such an expansionist approach is that it severely taxes the knowledge of a single scholar. There is simply more to know than any one scholar can hope to cover. Equally important, one of the necessities of this expansionist approach is, in my opinion, a willingness to decenter scholarly authority and promote debate. If we are going to expand, then we must avoid accusations of scholarly imperialism. To help address these two issues, I've asked James M. Harding, Jean-Graham Jones, and Alan Filewod to write section introductions that address common issues and questions in the three essays that comprise their respective sections, but that also allow them to raise questions that are distinctly theirs, concerning subject matter about which they have unique expertise.

There's another reason I invited them to contribute. Each has significantly shaped my understanding of the avant-garde, theatre, drama, and performance, pressing me to recognize the ways in which the avant-garde is materially altered as it moves across cultural, ideological, and geopolitical terrains. Lest I give the suggestion that such shaping was without disagreement or debate, the anthology concludes with a transcript of a roundtable I hosted at Indiana University of Pennsylvania in the summer of 2009. I asked James, Jean, and Alan to read all the essays in the collection and comment critically upon them, identifying assumptions and tracing possible paths for future research. As with their section introductions, their comments demonstrate a ready willingness to debate and disagree. We were joined in that lively discussion by Kimberly Jannarone. Her presence was due to her special role in the genesis of this anthology. This book began many years ago as a special issue of the journal *Works and Days*. It had a very different form and focus then; while the concept of vectors of the radical was at its center, the essays concerned a much narrower time span – the 1960s – and were far broader in terms of discipline and media. Though I had always intended to return to the collection, it was not until I began collaborating with James, Jean, Alan, and Kimberly – the latter, in particular, when we co-chaired an American Society for Theatre Research working group on the subject of vectors of the radical – that this new iteration became possible. The roundtable is, therefore, both a gesture of thanks and a concrete effort to sustain the critical dialogue that helped this collection of essays evolve.

Of course, to truly understand vectors, we need more than case studies, discussion, and debate; indeed, we need to consider the full history of the avant-garde. Unfortunately, there isn't space to provide a full discussion of that.[16] However, we can visit a few moments and hint at the broader impact of material exchange on the avant-garde. According to Matei Calinescu, the word "avant-garde" was first used by French literary critics in the 1600s, though its military sense was centuries older.[17] But the term was of little significance until the early 1800s, when it became a favorite of Henri de Saint-Simon, the entrepreneurial socialist best known for his declaration, "New meditations have proved to me that things should move ahead with the artists in the lead, followed by the scientists, and that the industrialists should come after these two classes."[18] This is a very kind gesture to pay to the arts, but distracts from the scientists and industrialists on the team. Saint-Simonians planned and propagandized the epic public projects of modernity: a "chunnel" between England and France, canals and railroad systems networking continents. Further, Saint-Simonianism was *lingua franca* for modernity's administrators. They dominated three of the key institutions in the French school system: the École de Médecine de Paris, the École Polytechnique, and the École Supérieure de Guerre. They literally built the French empire – and trained other nations who aspired to similar power.[19] Thus, the avant-garde is deeply implicated in technocracy, colonialism, and the capitalist state. It is a child of the modern market.

But the theory and practice of the avant-garde weren't guided by technocratic imperialists only. In the 1820s, a dissident subculture emerged in the working-class and red-light districts of Europe's capitals, a scruffy, slang-slinging, outré, mouthy bunch prone to hyperbolic claims about their artistic vision, imaginative independence, and sexual prowess. These were the "bohemians." They lived and worked in urban enclaves of multiculturalism, countercultural safe zones for the outcast and abject, for people with no security, but plenty of *esprit* and audacity: single mothers, immigrants, refugees, sex workers, the disabled, the chronically ill, and artists. Not incidentally, bohemian neighborhoods were (and are) free zones for the expression of alienation and identity – and launching pads for public displays of impertinence in cushier neighborhoods and public gathering places.[20] In essence, "bohemias" are alternative cultural markets comprised of multiple and shifting social networks, informal economies, and intercultural exchange routes. Thomas Crow, however, has convincingly argued that bohemian neighborhoods function as informal research-and-development centers for capitalist societies.[21]

Saint-Simonianism and bohemianism are the two most important influences on the development of the European avant-garde tradition – and they show us how deeply material exchange has shaped the avant-garde. What isn't as apparent, however, is how situational, how contingent and local, these exchanges are. If the avant-garde is a "movement," it is a movement that goes in many different directions. Zenenga provides perhaps the best example, describing three distinct forms of material exchange that have shaped radical performance in Zimbabwe: (1) colonialist exchange between Europeans and black Africans in the interest of promoting Eurocentrism; (2) postcolonialist exchanges that are more egalitarian in nature; and (3) intracultural exchanges between and within African nations, especially among black Africans. He lets us understand the relationship of European and Zimbabwean avant-gardes as a case of multiple, overlapping, but always intensely situated vectors.

Bürger has shown that the moments when artists and critics turn their attention to the way art moves are often moments when they change their ideas about what the avant-garde is. In *Theory of the Avant-Garde*, he argues that the late nineteenth-century art-for-art's-sake movement, in its quest for transcendent aesthetic experience, essentially abdicated control over the galleries, dealers, auction houses, journals, and academies that circulated their work. This fatally compromised their ability to articulate an effective politics, though it did allow a "full unfolding of the phenomenon of art" and an expanded "cognition of that field."[22]

Learning their lesson, the Dadas made those institutions an explicit target of their art. Marcel Duchamp entered a toilet into an art show to tweak the pomposity and hypocrisy of self-proclaimed progressive artists, art critics, and art dealers. Other vanguardists attempted to "eliminate the antithesis between producer and recipient" of art[23]: Tristan Tzara cut a newspaper article into bits and reassembled it at random; the Surrealists invented games that allowed multiple people to collaboratively create poetry and visual art without being aware of what the others were doing and without controlling the outcome of the process.

We can trace from these a rich tradition of *infrastructure* or *circulation art* which takes institutional critique directly to the structural mechanisms that enable it. Concrete poetry, minimalism, performance art, digital and other "new media" have turned what allows their art to move into the very subject of their art. Ray Johnson, for one, explored the formal, social, and creative possibilities of mail. His one-man "New York Correspondance [sic] School" distributed collages, drawings, performance instructions, and modified found objects. The mail served Johnson as an instrument of delivery and display; one opened a letter or rifled through a stack of mail and discovered the work. It also provided him entrance into the enclaves of high culture; he got his mail art into the Museum of Modern Art's collection by exploiting loopholes in its curatorial rules.[24] A different approach to critically engaging the infrastructure of art can be seen in the works of the WochenKlausur collective. They propose concrete, short-term social projects to international art shows and state and municipal grant organizations to improve the lives of people. WochenKlausur projects have helped significant numbers of immigrants, refugees, the unemployed, and youth.[25] A more ambitious project was launched by the artists and critics of the Black Arts Movement (c.1964–1975). Working to counter centuries of economic, political, and cultural oppression, these African-American artists created institutions to promote the production of Afro-centric culture. The Black Arts Repertory Theatre/School, Free Southern Theatre, Black House, and others promoted independent Black art, in part, by controlling the circulation of their cultural products. Many had their own printing presses or special relations with independent presses. Black artists like Sonia Sanchez and scholars like Donald Warden fought on another "circulation front," fighting for Black Studies programs to halt the academic circulation of racist representations of black people.

The BAM was not unique in this respect; the academic institutions of avant-garde studies are deeply intertwined with the art and artists of the avant-garde. This is so in part because of institutional connections – avant-garde artists have often been employed by or affiliated with the institutions that tell the story of the avant-garde; they share social spaces with those who study and market their work. Critics and artists are often friends, lovers, and family members.[26] They are part of what critic Paul Mann has called a "discursive economy" of "reviewing, exhibition, appraisal, reproduction, academic analysis, gossip, and retrospection." This economy impacts the avant-garde at all kinds of levels.[27] That's easy to see when Graham White shows the things that British scholars have *not* written about 1970s punk, particularly the nasty racist who was at every seminal punk concert, founded white power punk, and continues to inspire racists around the world. Edmondson levels a devastating critique at academic performance practitioners (including herself) in her account of two post-genocide performances in Rwanda and Uganda. She suggests that academic preconceptions about the politics of performance may actually block meaningful communication between the powerful and the powerless.

Another academic entanglement concerns this collection's key word. "Vector" comes from the academic field of epidemiology, where it is used to describe disease agents that don't *cause* but *spread* disease. Fleas living on rats were vectors of bubonic plague in the 1300s; tainted ground beef is a regular vector of food poisoning in the U.S. today. Epidemiology is a specifically modernist field, the love child of modern hygiene, nutrition science, civil planning, and sociology. It is an ethnocentric discipline, tangled with ideas about subjectivity, history, and technocracy that helped build European hegemony. They did this in part by disciplining the avant-garde. The French medical corps helped invent the field of epidemiology. They did this to improve the health and hygiene of the people of colonized Algeria. Their surveys of the kitchens and toilets also identified the incipient vanguards among them. Max Nordau's *Degeneration* (1892), the very first book-length study of the avant-garde, describes it as a kind of contagious vermin, part airborne toxin and social predator. He was a disciple of the pioneering criminologist Cesare Lombroso, who interpreted crime as a public-health issue. Reactionary U.S. politicians in the 1950s followed Lombroso's lead, too, subverting the avant-garde jazz community by criminalizing the drugs the musicians and their fans preferred. Essentially the same thing happened in the 1990s to the international rave community. But, as compromised as it may be, the word "vectors" best captures what we're trying to describe here – the social movement of catalytic agents.

Avant-garde movements move and so do their creations. Studying the material exchanges that make up avant-garde performance history, we can continue the important work of writing (and rewriting) the history of radical cultural production. The history of the avant-garde is not the one we find in the history books. The stories we've exchanged for the last half century or so, as inspiring as they have been, need to be put away and others given a chance to travel and transform.

Notes

1. Carol Rosenthal suggested these parameters in her Indiana University of Pennsylvania English Honors Seminar project, spring 2009.
2. The idea of modernity being the consequence of global movement is not new. See, for example, Paul Gilroy's *The Black Atlantic: Modernity and Double Consciousness* (Cambridge, MA: Harvard University Press, 1993) and Arjun Appadurai's *Modernity at Large: Cultural Dimensions of Globalization* (Minneapolis: University of Minnesota Press, 1996).
3. Roland Barthes, *Mythologies*, trans. Annette Lavers (London: Paladin, 1972).
4. Martin Puchner, *Poetry of the Revolution: Marx, Manifestos, and the Avant-Gardes* (Princeton, NJ: Princeton University Press), 1.
5. Simon Gikandi, *Writing in Limbo: Modernism and Caribbean Literature* (Ithaca, NY: Cornell University Press, 1992); Charles W. Pollard, *New World Modernisms: T. S. Eliot, Derek Walcott, and Kamau Brathwaite* (Charlotte: University of Virginia Press, 2004); Laura Doyle and Laura Winkiel (eds), *Geomodernisms: Race, Modernism, Modernity* (Bloomington: Indiana University Press, 2005).
6. Susan Stanford Friedman, "Periodizing Modernism: Postcolonial Modernities and the Space/Time Borders of Modernist Studies," *Modernism/Modernity* 13.3 (2006): 426.
7. Works in this trend would include Barrett Watten, *The Constructivist Moment: From Material Text to Cultural Poetics* (Middletown, CT: Wesleyan University Press, 2003); Rachel Blau DuPlessis, *Genders, Races, and Religious Cultures in Modern American Poetry, 1908–1934* (Cambridge: Cambridge University Press, 2001); Kimberly Jannarone, *Artaud and His Doubles* (Ann Arbor: University of Michigan Press, forthcoming); and Mike Sell, *The Avant-Garde: Race Religion War* (Kolkata, India: Seagull Books, 2010).
8. For discussion of the challenges facing the avant-garde vis-à-vis the spectacle, see the works of the Situationist International collected in *The Situationist Inernational Anthology*, ed. and trans. Ken Knabb (Detroit: Bureau of Public Secrets, 2007).
9. For more on minority, see the chapter on race in Sell, *The Avant-Garde: Race Religion War*.
10. Terry Eagleton, *The Idea of Culture* (Oxford: Blackwell, 2000), 34.
11. For more on the "cultural turn" of the avant-garde, see Mike Sell, "Bohemianism, the 'Cultural Turn' of the Avant-Garde, and Forgetting the Roma," *TDR: The Drama Review* 51.2 (T194) (Summer 2007): 41–59.
12. See Erika Fischer-Lichte, *The Transformative Power of Performance: A New Aesthetics*, trans. Saskya Iris Jain (New York and London: Routledge, 2008).
13. James M. Harding and John Rouse, Introduction, *Not the Other Avant-Garde: The Transnational Foundations of Avant-Garde Performance* (Ann Arbor: University of Michigan Press, 2006), 1.

14. Arjun Appadurai (ed.), *The Social Life of Things: Commodities in Cultural Perspective* (Cambridge: Cambridge University Press, 1988).
15. Ibid., 4.
16. And, unfortunately, no good general introduction. Useful sources include Matei Calinescu, *Five Faces of Modernity: Modernism, Avant-Garde, Decadence, Kitsch, Postmodernism* (Durham: Duke University Press, 1987); Donald Drew Egbert, *Social Radicalism and the Arts: Western Europe* (New York: Alfred A. Knopf, 1971); RoseLee Goldberg, *Performance Art: From Futurism to the Present* (New York: Thames and Hudson, 2001); Max Nordau, *Degeneration* (Lincoln: University of Nebraska Press, 1968); and Renato Poggioli, *Theory of the Avant-Garde*, trans. Gerald Fitzgerald (Cambridge, MA: Harvard University Press, 1981).
17. Calinescu, *Five Faces of Modernity*, 97–100.
18. Quoted in ibid., 102.
19. Patricia M. E. Lorcin, "Imperialism, Colonial Identity, and Race in Algeria, 1830–1870: The Role of the French Medical Corps," *Isis* 90.4 (Dec. 1999): 653–679 (658).
20. Mary Gluck, "Theorizing the Cultural Roots of the Bohemian Artist," *Modernism/Modernity* 7.3 (2000): 351–378.
21. Thomas Crow, "Modernism and Mass Culture in the Visual Arts," in *Modernism and Modernity*, ed. Benjamin H. D. Buchloch et al. (Nova Scotia: Nova Scotia College of Art and Design, 1983).
22. Peter Bürger, *Theory of the Avant-Garde*, trans. Michael Shaw (Minneapolis: University of Minnesota Press, 1984), 17.
23. Ibid., 53.
24. See interviews with Chuck Close and Clive Philpot in *How to Draw a Bunny*, dir. John Walter and Andrew Moore (Palm Pictures, 2000).
25. See *WochenKlausur: Sociopolitical Activism in Art*, ed. Wolfgang Zinggl, trans. C. Barber (New York: Springer, 2001).
26. See Mike Sell, Introduction, *Avant-Garde Performance and the Limits of Criticism: Approaching the Living Theatre, Happenings/Fluxus, and the Black Arts Movement* (Ann Arbor: University of Michigan Press, 2008); Sally Banes, "Institutionalizing Avant-Garde Performance: A Hidden History of University Patronage in the United States," in *Contours of the Theatrical Avant-Garde*, ed. James M. Harding (Ann Arbor: University of Michigan Press, 2000); Fred Orton and Griselda Pollock, *Avant-Gardes and Partisans Reviewed* (Manchester: Manchester University Press, 1997); Diana Crane, *The Transformation of the Avant-Garde: The New York Art World, 1940–1985* (Chicago: University of Chicago Press, 1987); and Joan Marter (ed.), *Off Limits: Rutgers University and the Avant-Garde, 1957–1963* (New Brunswick, NJ: Rutgers University Press, 1999).
27. Paul Mann, *Theory-Death of the Avant-Garde* (Bloomington: Indiana University Press, 1991), 5–6.

Part I
Intersections

1
Introduction

James M. Harding

Walter Benjamin may be best known to scholars of the avant-garde because of his writings on Brecht, Surrealism, and art in the age of mechanical reproduction, but it is worth considering whether his value to those interested in the history and theory of the avant-garde might lie elsewhere: in his theories of history, for example. One might focus, in particular, on the seventh of Benjamin's fifteen "Theses on the Philosophy of History," where he famously argues that "there is no document of civilization which is not at the same time a document of barbarism."[1] There is much in Benjamin's assertion that intersects with the often militant anti-cultural sentiments of the historical avant-garde, especially sentiments like those coming from vanguard artists who were profoundly disillusioned by how impotent the great accomplishments of European culture proved to be in the face of the bellicose nationalisms that fueled the First and Second World Wars. Indeed, if that impotence did not signal a kind of direct cultural complicity with the destructive forces of nationalism and, hence, of what proved to be its own kind of barbarism, it indicated a vulnerability to easy appropriation into the sustaining ideologies of those same forces, a vulnerability that, however indirect, amounted to complicity as well. In this respect, the historical avant-garde's anti-cultural sentiments laid the foundation for a wide range of provocations and gestures that, while now enshrined as (anti) art, originally had profound ideological affinities with Benjamin's own assertion linking the appearance of civilization with instances of barbarism. At a conceptual level, this affinity forms a kind of intersection where the confluence of politics, art, and ideals offers a fitting introduction to the essays in this section.

The significance of that intersection and of the link that it provides to the essays by Gaborik and Harris, Edmondson, and Rosenthal necessitate a recognition that Benjamin's assertion about the barbarous undercurrent to the documents of civilization is not so much a critique of the impotence of established culture as it is a lament about history's vanquished and about historical perspective. Though never explicitly stated, there is in Benjamin's lament a call for histories no longer written from the vantage point of the victors. Indeed, commenting on this same lament, Theodor Adorno suggests that Benjamin was both questioning why "history had hitherto been written from the standpoint of the victor" and arguing that history "needed to be written from... [the standpoint] of the vanquished." It needed to "address itself," Adorno added, to "what might be called the waste products and blind spots that have escaped" the accepted narratives of history.[2]

Interestingly enough, when Benjamin finished writing his "Theses on the Philosophy of History" in 1940, much of the so-called historical avant-garde could be counted among the vanquished – scattered as they were in exile, having fled Germany and Europe while the fascists shut down their performance spaces, burned their books, and exhibited their works as examples of "degenerate art." Inasmuch as the vanguard constitutes one of the many vectors of the radical, this movement into the ranks of the vanquished marks an important but largely unexplored intersection. That intersection is the meeting ground for what we might call the "vanquished vanguard."

Keeping an eye towards this intersection, one might legitimately argue that Benjamin's call for a history written from the standpoint of the vanquished implicitly includes a call for a radically different history of the vanguard, and I would suggest here not only that Benjamin's call potentially situates the radical vanguard within a completely different vector, but that this call also echoes through the essays by Gaborik and Harris, Edmondson, and Rosenthal. Indeed, the essays in this section demonstrate the ways that historians can revolutionize the extant histories of the avant-garde by simply considering the spaces where the corresponding trajectories of the vanguard and the vanquished intersect and become one and the same. Such considerations possess a particular significance, it seems to me, given the tendency among scholars to celebrate the artistic vanguard's successes at politically inspired artistic innovation while disregarding its failures to bring about actual artistically inspired political change. Critical celebration of artistic innovation is a sorry consolation prize for political defeat.

Critical though this last observation may seem, it is in fact very close to what I would argue are the defining but largely unacknowledged building blocks of the avant-garde itself – building blocks that Rosenthal identifies, for example, in her account of the Living Theatre's disastrous trip to Brazil and that Edmondson discovers by problematizing her own recent work as a theatre practitioner and activist in Uganda and Rwanda. Both of these examples remind us that the building blocks of the avant-garde are always multi-sided: innovation is always tied to the experimental, which, in turn, is tied to risk, which, in turn is tied to potential success and potential failure.

Indeed, I would go so far as to suggest that, collectively, the essays in this section ask us to consider a history of the experimental arts that is always at an intersection where the celebrated spoils of the victors converge with an equitable accounting of experimental failure and defeat. Although it is easier to document that which is celebrated than it is to document that which fails to capture immediate critical attention, it is only at the intersection of these two related vectors that critical scrutiny of the criteria for celebration is possible. It is also at that intersection where we can recognize some of the genuine value that Benjamin's seventh thesis on the philosophy of history has for our conceptual understanding of the histories of the avant-garde.

When seen through the critical lens of Benjamin's arguments, previous histories of the vanguard not only appear decisively one-sided and biased towards the victors, but in this bias they also betray a mentality that is both deferential to established authority and inclined towards a subtle ideological affirmation not of a vanguard sensibility, but of a conceptual reaffirmation of the values embraced within the status quo. As Benjamin himself notes, "Empathy with the victor invariably benefits the rulers."[3] Following this line of thought, I would suggest that the radical histories of the vanguard will always remain unwritten until they too are written from the standpoint of the vanquished and of those who, in daring to experiment, have failed. What radical history, we might ask by way of example, did Renato Poggioli elide in his classic *Theory of the Avant-Garde* when he argued,

> When Fascism and Nazism fell, no avant-garde work created in secret and silence, through the years when the spiritual life of two great European nations was suffocated by the tyranny and oppression of those two regimes, came to light. From now on we cannot believe that other masterpieces exist, unless perhaps those once visible and misunderstood... [In] the modern world we cannot help doubting the existence of manuscripts closed in chests, paintings hidden in attics, statues stashed away in kitchens.[4]

Here the focus on "masterpieces" – which, it is worth noting, is a focus on the very traditional notions of art and accomplishment that the historical avant-garde opposed – eclipses the profoundly important work of those who toiled unsuccessfully amid tyranny and oppression, but who were vanguard nonetheless. Ironically, their erasure is history's own validation of their credentials among the anti-institutional currents of an avant-garde that shunned the deference to author/ity implied in the embrace of author/ship, that rejected the institutions of art in favor of the strategic ephemerality of provocation and gesture, and that circumvented easy appropriation through the elusiveness of unscripted improvisation.

Some awareness of that reverberation echoes through the three essays in this section, and there is perhaps no greater sense of continuity between them than the sense in which they begin to explore the waste products, the failed experiments, and the defeats that are very much a part of the evolving history of anything we might call avant-garde.

Of the three essays, Gaborik and Harris's is least interested in this notion of failure, but their essay does remind us that the scholarly fixation on the successes of fascist Futurism has discouraged the kind of analysis that links Italian-style Futurist aesthetics with the neo-liberalism of U.S. artists like George Balanchine. All the essays point us towards the largely uncharted historical and discursive territory emerging from international and transnational histories of the avant-garde, and at least two if not three of the essays embrace a global perspective that is clearly conscious of how histories of the avant-garde that privilege the European or U.S. vanguards incline towards the victors rather than the vanquished and reinforce First World cultural prerogatives. What these essays thereby suggest is that to write the histories of the avant-garde from the standpoint of the vanquished vanguard – to address the "waste products" or "blind spots" that remain discarded or overlooked in the extant histories of the avant-garde – generally demands a critical journey beyond the cultural borders of Europe and the U.S.

If Benjamin's arguments on history and the vanquished point us towards one shape that such models might take, the need to explore the overlapping spaces of the vanquished, the victorious, and the vanguard becomes all the more pressing, I would suggest, in light of the critique of Benjamin that Patricia Gaborik and Andrea Harris formulate towards the end of their essay on George Balanchine and Futurism. Gaborik and Harris's essay has a two-fold argument. First of all, they demonstrate that, despite a reputation for having made a distinctly "American" contribution to ballet, George Balanchine in fact owed a great debt to the aesthetics of Italian Futurism. Second, they then challenge interpretations that reduce Italian Futurism to a variant of fascism – an interpretation that, in the final section of their essay, they attribute to Walter Benjamin. This attribution is a rather odd moment in the essay since it is based upon Benjamin's critique in "The Work of Art in the Age of Mechanical Reproduction" not of Futurism per se but of Filippo Marinetti's manifesto in praise of the Italian fascists' colonial enterprise in the Second Italo-Abyssinian War – the war that Benjamin refers to as the "Ethiopian colonial War,"[5] the war in which Marinetti fought as an armed fascist volunteer. Although the Ethiopians never surrendered, the victors and the vanquished in this war were clear: Haile Selassie was driven into exile and the Italian fascists imposed a brutal colonial regime.

Benjamin's critique of Marinetti, written while Benjamin was in exile in Paris, culminates in what Gaborik and Harris rightly identify as his famous distinction between the fascist introduction of aesthetics into politics (e.g. Marinetti) and the communist politicizing of art (e.g. Brecht). This distinction came at a time when Britain was still pursuing a course of appeasement, the United States was wrapped up in isolationism, and the only viable source of resistance to fascism's otherwise unchecked rise to power was coming from communist circles. But, in the larger context of Benjamin's essay, this is a secondary matter. The dynamic that he posits as that which remains after the loss of aura is not limited to a binary between fascism and communism. The dynamic he proposes is one in which all art has been reduced to politics. The critical question that thus emerges for every work of art is: Whose interests does the politics of the work serve? In other words, who does it support as victors and who does it leave among the vanquished?

That this question has no clear orientation towards Right or Left is vividly demonstrated in the final two essays in this section, Laura Edmondson's "Confessions of a Failed Theatre Activist" and Cindy Rosenthal's "The Living Theatre's Arrested Development in Brazil." Both essays are striking for the profound attention that they devote not to a history of experimental innovation or accomplishment, but rather to a history of experimental failure among activist artists whose seemingly progressive agendas slip into an inadvertent affirmation of Western privilege and cultural dominance when those agendas move from the U.S. into Africa and South America, respectively. While Edmondson recounts her own work as a theatre activist among former children soldiers in Uganda and Rwanda during the first decade of the twenty-first century, Rosenthal recounts the work of the Living Theatre among Brazil's poor and disenfranchised in the early 1970s. What unites these two essays is that they both describe moments of theatre activism that culminate in a failure of seemingly radical politics – a failure that ultimately precipitates an arguably more radical confrontation with the governing hierarchical dynamics of the activists' own subject positions.

For Edmondson, that confrontation involves a recognition of how her work as a U.S. theatre activist working among former children soldiers in Uganda (a literally vanquished vanguard), rather than transforming the world, tended to reinscribe "the existing order ... dividing the world between Northern benefactors and Southern victims." For the members of the Living Theatre, as Rosenthal notes, that confrontation came with their arrest and imprisonment while trying to work among Brazil's poor and disenfranchised, and it resulted from the realization that the very U.S. passports that they denounced in works like *Paradise Now!* protected them while their Brazilian colleagues were tortured and, in at least one instance, murdered. Indeed, the privileged status granted through their passports may very well have fueled the hostility and brutality unleashed on their Brazilian comrades.

Somehow amid these failures, we find trace elements of vanquished vanguards. Rosenthal writes at length about Judith Malina's decision, after her release from prison, to censor her own journal entries so as to protect activist/artist friends in Brazil who might be compromised and endangered by the publication of her writing. Acknowledgement of that self-censorship, even four decades later, points to the historical shadows where the vanquished and the vanguards coexist, only tenuously protected from the risks that they incur in the blending of politics and art. Their history is that of a vanguard vanquished but not defeated.

Notes

1. Walter Benjamin, "Theses on the Philosophy of History," in *Illuminations*, ed. Hannah Arendt, trans. Harry Zohn (New York: Schocken Books, 1968), 256.
2. Theodor Adorno, *Minima Moralia*, trans. E. F. N. Jephcott (New York: Verso, 1974), 151.
3. Benjamin, "Theses," 256.
4. Renato Poggioli, *Theory of the Avant-Garde* (Cambridge, MA: Harvard University Press, 1968), 100–101.
5. Walter Benjamin, "The Work of Art in the Age of Mechanical Reproduction," in *Illuminations*, 241.

2

From Italy and Russia to France and the U.S.: "Fascist" Futurism and Balanchine's "American" Ballet

Patricia Gaborik and Andrea Harris

Twelve actors create geometric spatial patterns. They utter "tètètè" or "ftftft." Rhythmically, repetitively, mechanically, they move their arms forward, their torsos stiffly back and forth. Others rotate their arms like levers, over and over, from the shoulder socket. Moving as a single unit, they mimic a rotary printing press.

A man propels himself through space; he juts his pelvis forward and lunges, his foot in forced arch. He arches so far that his back is parallel to the floor below. He chases three women, who shift into one hip, the lines of their torsos echoing the precise angles of the set while they dance, first classical, then music-hall steps. Their marionette doubles drop from above. Colorful geometric flats swivel to transform the scene through which they dance. Shadows and cinematic projections play.

Six men in metal and plastic jump, bend, twirl. Personifying "rulers, triangles, and circles,"[1] they come together into a rigid double line; lunges, forced arches, and extended arms in front, forward bends in back, they form a car. It carries the lead dancer to his lover, a cat changed into a woman. In shiny satin and plastic cones for tutu and ears, the dancer-cat is multiplied in triplet on the set: translucent plastic complexes, large, black rectangles with circular eyes, a big toy cat, too. The dancers move through and with their geometric world as exuberant lights set the industrial materials of costume and set in motion.

Geometrical spatial patterning. Onomatopoeia. Simultaneity. Multiplied, mechanical bodies. Interpenetration of human and environment. Emulation of the cinema and music hall. We are in the realm of

23

Futurist performance, and the pieces described above represent diverse manifestations of the Futurist experiment. The first, Giacomo Balla's 1914 *Macchina Tipografica*, was the painter's first attempt at theatrical production. An embodiment of early Futurist machine idolatry, its goal was the human imitation of a modern machine. The second, *Le Marchand de Coeurs*, one of the ballets staged by Enrico Prampolini's *Théâtre de la Pantomime Futuriste*, opened in Paris in 1927, extolling the virtues of the machine age in a total theatre that would "abandon mimicry in design – because this is merely superficial – and [to] enter into the domain of architecture – because this is concerned with depth."² The third is *La Chatte*, created by Diaghilev's Ballets Russes in 1927. It fuses the Futurist visions of the other two pieces, creating architecture out of dancers while devising choreography and bodies infused with syncopated dynamism and mechanical power. Its choreographer was George Balanchine.

This isn't to say that you'll find references to Futurism in scholarly works on Balanchine, nor characterizations of him as a Futurist choreographer. For U.S. dance scholars, Balanchine "Americanized" ballet with a bold and original neoclassicism marked by speed, dynamism, athleticism, plotlessness, and vocabulary from popular culture. This style has come to be seen as quintessentially American, personifying the spirit of democracy and expressing "American character at its best."³ Yet, these trademarks characterized Balanchine's style long before he arrived in America. Moreover, they were less innovations than emblems of a broader modernization of ballet in Paris, one entwined with Italian Futurism, a trend in which Balanchine took part when he joined the Ballets Russes in 1924.

In the crowning of Balanchine as the American ballet master, his modernist influences have been given short shrift; his early career in Russia and Europe remains marginalized, and what has been done focuses on the émigré's "Russian roots."⁴ But Italian Futurism had a significant impact on Balanchine's work – not simply because of its ubiquitous influence on the modernist avant-garde but due to a series of collaborations and cross-fertilizations that remains unexplored until now. This is not simply a historiographic omission, but an indication of the limits of the paradigms underpinning scholarship on Futurism, theatrical and dance modernism, and larger questions about performance and politics in the twentieth century and beyond.

Futurism came to Balanchine through two routes: the Russian and the Parisian. In 1912, the Union of Youth, whose patron Levky Zheverzheyev would later become Balanchine's father-in-law and friend, published

Russian translations of Italian Futurist manifestos and, in 1913, produced Mayakovsky, Kruchenykh, and Malevich's "First Futurist Theatre Performances in Russia." When F. T. Marinetti gave lectures in Moscow and St. Petersburg in early 1914, he sparked debate among such luminaries as Malevich, Larionov, Mayakovsky, and Meyerhold (whom he had met the year before in Paris). As a budding choreographer, Balanchine breathed the "intellectual oxygen" such members of the avant-garde brought into the post-Revolution Soviet dance school.[5] Shortly before he left for Paris in 1923, the Factory of Eccentric Actors (FEKS) invited Balanchine to work with them. Inspired by the Italian Futurists' "Variety Theatre Manifesto" (published in Russia in the teens), FEKS freely mixed genres, threw in the Charleston, Charlie Chaplin, and acrobatics, and intermingled cinematic and live action. The Futurist spirit fathered by Marinetti had wed itself to the Soviet cause.[6] In short, even before Balanchine left Russia, his world was Futurist.[7]

Balanchine's compatriot, the Ballets Russes, had been in Paris since 1909, and its relationship with the Futurists was established almost as long ago as that, for in those pre-war years, Futurism spread its shockwaves far and wide. Serge Diaghilev and Igor Stravinsky (who had seen a Futurist concert in London in 1914) began to build a Futurist–Ballets Russes "alliance" that would become a major factor in the Futurist influence on Balanchine. In the months leading up to the spring 1917 season, Diaghilev and cohort (including Stravinsky, choreographer Léonide Massine, Jean Cocteau, and Pablo Picasso) settled in Rome. They spent afternoons in the Futurists' studios, evenings in Rome's sumptuous hotels or rehearsing their dances in the underground foyer of the Caffè Faraglia. One evening, Balla organized an impromptu production of *Macchina Tipografica* for Diaghilev, who considered producing it that season. Ultimately, he opted instead to commission Balla's designs for *Feu d'artifice* and those of another Futurist, Fortunato Depero, for *Le Chant du Rossignol* (which, however, never made it to the stage). On April 12, *Feu d'artifice* premiered at the Teatro Costanzi. The next day, Massine's private art collection was exhibited on site with works by Picasso, Fernand Léger, the Futurists Balla, Carlo Carrà, Gino Severini, Depero, and Ballets Russes scenographers Mikhail Larionov and Natalya Gontcharova (also in residence in Rome).

Balla's stage design for this three-minute and fifty-second piece was comprised of wedges, rectangles, cones, arcs, and spirals that were lit from inside and out. For the first (and only) time in a Ballets Russes production, there were no dancers, the human body replaced by lights and shadows flickering on and off in accompaniment to the music, creating "an expression of ever-changing dynamics to the statics of the stage."[8] This spectacle might be considered a presentation of the universe Balla and Depero described in their 1915 manifesto, where the goal was to "find abstract equivalents for all the forms and elements of the universe [...] to shape plastic complexes which we will set in motion."[9] Here, geometric shapes animated with light created the illusion that the entire stage was alive with electric motion.

Such characteristics – a fully dynamic stage space; an emphasis on technology, mechanization, and geometric angularity; the loosening of narrative structure in favor of the kinetic potential of form – were central to the reshaping of the Ballets Russes' appearance and character at the time, which critics noticed. The May 1917 edition of Pierre Albert-Birot's *SIC* proclaimed in its title, "Ballets Russes. Cubistes et Futuristes." In an article entitled "Futurist Explorations," Pierre Lerat declared that Balla "will remain the first to have forged the path; and for this he ought to be the one, in the future, ordained as the great artist and innovator."[10] Later dance scholars have acknowledged Futurism's impact on the Ballets Russes, particularly in the choreography of Massine, as summarized here by Lynn Garafola:

> If Diaghilev did not remake the Ballets Russes in the image of Futurism, his contact with the movement certainly altered the company's countenance. [...] Through his choreographic Galatea, Massine, he would incorporate into ballet the dynamism and angularity advocated by the Futurists, along with the impersonal performance style, discontinuous narrative, and studied incongruity that became trademarks of Ballets Russes modernism.[11]

Garafola does not extend her discussion beyond 1917, but historian Valerian Svetlov suggests these qualities persisted into the 1920s.[12]

Massine himself credited the Futurists for their impact on his choreography.[13] A striking example of Futurism's influence on his work is the interrelation between plastic form and movement. Classical ballet had long blended movement phrases with suspended poses, such as the ballerina's ability to end a chain of pirouettes with a balanced *arabesque* on *pointe*. But whereas such poses served to spotlight the dancer's virtuosity and line, Massine turned his attention to motion and plasticity as energetic dualities. In his 1919 essay, he explains, "I believe that in the art of the ballet we must strive to reach a synthesis of movement and form," and distinguishes himself from previous Ballets Russes choreographers precisely by this new fusion of motion and stillness.[14]

Massine's insistence on the play between motion and plastic form as a working, analytic principle, his dancers moving with sudden, explosive bursts and spurts, is a choreographic echo of the Futurists' notions of the dynamic potential of plastic forms.

Though the aesthetic elements we have discussed here – compacting and speeding up the dance phrase; emphasizing dynamic movement over narrative, representation, or psychological characterization; more angular and geometric movement forms – are said to characterize Balanchine's neoclassical "innovations" with their uniquely American stamp, such practices defined the Ballets Russes' art when Balanchine joined the company. And, given his experience in Russia, most of this was unlikely to surprise him. Moreover, in the "Futurist city" (as Marinetti called Paris), Balanchine's dance floor was one among many.

Enrico Prampolini, who earned a reputation as a great theatrical innovator, was the chief exponent of Futurist performance in the 1920s. Since the days of the first Ballets Russes/Futurist collaborations in 1917, Prampolini had admired Diaghilev, noting that the new avant-garde aesthetic in Russian choreography could not be fully explained without the participation of Picasso and the Italian Futurists.[15] Ten years later, the Italians realized their own Futurist ballet theatre, and, indeed, when the *Théâtre de la Pantomime Futuriste* had its Parisian debut, the ongoing kinship between its work and that of the Ballets Russes and Ballets Suédois was not lost on anyone: "Nothing looks more like an Italian triangle and square than a Russian or Swedish triangle and square," the *Excelsior*'s critic quipped.[16]

Prampolini sought to incorporate dance into the total theatre aesthetic that he, an architect-scenographer, had begun to devise as early as 1915 in the "Futurist Scenography and Choreography" manifesto. Prampolini's choreography strove to set an entire stage in motion: centrifugal bodies, exuberant lighting, and "electromechanical architecture" would harmonize to produce a "choreoplastic," "dynamic" rather than "static" scene. The interpenetration of man and machine described in the "Multiplied Man and the Reign of the Machine" manifesto underpinned Prampolini's theatrical vision: "Hence, we must prepare the imminent and inevitable identification of man with motor, facilitating and perfecting an incessant exchange of intuition, rhythm, instinct, and metallic discipline." This new man, "constructed for an omnipresent velocity," would extend his will beyond himself, become a ruler over time and space, and "continuously become a better aviator."[17]

What better aviator than a skilled dancer? The Pantomime Theatre aspired to a new genre in which "all the scenic elements converge in the dynamic exaltation of rhythm and the orchestration and interpenetration of visions in freedom." Space-turned-actor ("attore-spazio") and man-turned-aviator would together produce these visions in, *and of,* freedom, with a "mechanization of gesture and rhythm that is no longer contained in the decorativism of the human figure, but spins and explodes through to the edges of the scenic environment."[18] What must have attracted Prampolini to dancers was that their athleticism and skill could create a sensation – spiritual, kinetic, material – of harmonized movement between man and environment.

Prampolini's formulations aimed not to replicate but to embody the spirit of the machine; as Cinzia Sartini Blum has pointed out, Futurism's valorization of energy and discipline, its rejection of psychology, was part of a new, empowering relationship with the mechanized world. Its violence was compensatory, an extreme attempt to resolve the anxieties of life in this new environment.[19] Not subjugation to or envious imitation of the all-powerful machine, but channeling a machine-like spirit to redouble human potential. Prampolini, Ivo Pannaggi, and Vinicio Paladini identified in the machine a font of physical and spiritual inspiration: "We feel ourselves made of steel. We are machines, too, we are mechanized. We Futurists call on the machine to break away from its practical function, to rise up to the spiritual and disinterested life of art, and to become a fertile inspiration. [...] to give over its spirit, and not its external form."[20] Dance, in which "muscular audacity and resistance" were celebrated, the limits of the body overcome,[21] offered rich potential for this superhumanization of the body.

The Pantomime Theatre, which premiered twelve pieces at the Théâtre de la Madeleine on May 12, 1927, staged this relationship between man and machine. Its first season was relatively successful, though Prampolini himself only considered a handful of the pieces "Futurist" enough to be presented again on tour in 1928. Nonetheless, some ballets moved in the right direction, stripping away the gigantically geometric Futurist universe, leading to a distillation of Futurist principles – the movement of man through space as if he were one with it, the multiplication and incarnation of a machine-like spirit, the perfection of geometric form in set as well as dancer, replication of the modern world's rhythms.

The description of Prampolini's choreography as a "compromise associating classic plasticity with the rhythm and neurosis of modern times," of *"grottesco,* expressionist, classicizing, and Futurist stylization,"[22] underlines the extent to which Futurist principles still propelled avant-garde dance in the 1920s. In any case, Prampolini's clear preference was for an aesthetic best associated with Futurist mechanization, as the *Impero*'s French correspondent reported after visiting a Pantomime rehearsal: "Every now and then he would say, 'Halt! Let's start over! [...] You, accentuate those movements, which have to happen in fits and starts, like a marionette! Arms up higher!'" Other dancers looked on, he reported, warming up, an absolutely necessity given the agility required of the movements.[23] Testimony, reviews, and production photos from the first and second seasons reveal Prampolini's attempts to create all-encompassing stage pictures, where light, shadow, body, and music worked together to produce the vision and sensation of movement. Going beyond early Futurist fixation on geometric objects, Ruggero Vasari reported, Prampolini "abstracted and mechanized" objects, which for him included dancers, for in the end his real goal was to "glorify the God of the stage: Movement."[24] Futurist dance was moving away from *reproducing* machines on stage, to instead *taking inspiration from* the machine, striving to embody its power.

This was the moment of the so-called "return to order" spearheaded by Jean Cocteau and Prampolini's compatriot Massimo Bontempelli, who from Paris in 1926 launched the *Novecento*, a type of ultramodern literary classicism that called for "new myths for the modern age." Prampolini seems to have been attracted by this notion, for the Pantomime's stage was populated with a myriad of characters, from satyrs and nymphs to ideal women and their marionette doubles, from Japanese soldiers to a princess-turned-tortoise, from salamanders battling the gods to liquor bottles come to life. These characters danced and pantomimed in front of cinematic projections, within and about rotating geometric flats. They passed under phallic ladders and through tree-vulvas into industrial cityscapes. Magnificent colored lights and shadows played around them as their marionette imitations, intertwined arms, popped hips, and *pas de deux* combined not simply to give the impression of a frenzied, electric world but to transport that world into the fragile one of gesture and dance, as one critic marveled.[25] While too little evidence remains to fully analyze the Pantomime Theatre's choreographic practices, Prampolini clearly combined German Expressionist dance, music-hall movement vocabulary, machine-like motion, and pantomime with a total-theatre design in order to utilize dance to full Futurist potential.[26] Balanchine would do the reverse: utilize Futurist concepts to dance's fullest potential.

As noted, the Ballets Russes had already been transformed by its collaboration with the Futurists. As he shared the choreographic helm with Massine from 1925 to 1928, Balanchine's work displayed the Futurist bent that had become part of the company's signature. One of his first pieces was an *entr'acte* inspired by Marinetti's *Le basi*, in which the curtain was raised only high enough to see the dancers' feet.[27] It's little wonder then that, during this coming-of-age period, critics described characteristics in Balanchine's choreography similar to those in Massine's work with the interwar Ballets Russes, as well as those found in Prampolini's choreography: a whole-stage dynamism, "rhythmic pantomime,"[28] technological elements like "dancing backcloths,"[29] "pictorial gymnastics [and] grotesque and angular movements,"[30] a "wild exaggeration and mockery of the Classical School."[31] Despite a critical tendency to sideline the early works as "less familiar Balanchine,"[32] Ballets Russes dancers Alexandra Danilova and Alicia Markova point to the continuity between the European and U.S. phases of his career, insisting that Balanchine's early ballets, particularly *Le Chant du Rossignol* (1925) and *La Chatte* (1927), are integral to understanding his evolving choreographic style.[33]

Most striking about *La Chatte* was the set, created by Russian sculptors Gabo and Pevsner: a series of transparent plastic circles, cones, curves, rhomboids, and rectangles supported by shiny metal frames. Glossy black oilcloth augmented the set's reflective quality.[34] Three images of the cat – a vertical structure with a box-shaped head and arched plastic tail, a large, dark rectangle with two circular eye-holes, and a furry toy cat who peeks out of one of these circles – echoed the human ballerina-Cat, whom Gabo dressed in similar high-tech materials: a plastic skirt over her classical tutu, plastic leggings, and a transparent bonnet with two large conical projections as ears. Production photos show the dancers manipulating and passing through the set pieces. As they danced, rays of light glinted off their costumes, tracing the lines of their movement through space and transforming them into "mobile components complementing and interacting with the set."[35] Reviewers were struck both by the ballet's "inauguration of the era of constructed décor" and the dancers' achievement of Balanchine's "plastic" creation.[36] Movement and design worked together to set the entire stage to shimmering motion.

As Nesta Macdonald points out, the Ballets Russes' interest in the scenographic use of high-tech materials, dynamic lighting, and cinematographic effects explored eleven years prior in Balla's *Feu d'artifice* is revealed again in *La Chatte*.[37] Further, the ballet demonstrates the development of early Futurist efforts to shatter the static stage, as here, the dancers' movements serve as the catalyst for scenic dynamism. Whereas, in *Feu d'artifice*, the stage was mobilized by the play of electric lights on static forms, in *La Chatte*, the energy produced by the human body in motion is the force that unites costume, set, and dancer and brings the total stage to life. That is, *La Chatte* epitomizes the machine-spirit and interpenetration of man and environment, going beyond even the wartime Futurists' achievements. "The metamorphosis wrought by M. Diaghilev, his choreographist, and scenic designers is wider than that from cat to lady," wrote one critic. "They have transposed the young man, his companions, and their background into a mathematical pattern. [The dancers] move as though they belonged to a theory of ballistics."[38] London *Vogue* cheered, "This new choreography [...] invites us to admire the machinery by which man achieves the plentitude of power, *suggesting rather than materialising* the infinite possibilities of which that machinery is capable."[39] These effects were produced in part by amplifying the athletic physicality of the classical vocabulary – the Cat's pyrotechnic leaps and *tours en l'air* – as well as by bodies counterbalanced in architectural structures – six dancers forming a large pyramid, for example. However, critics had noted the use of such acrobatic, music-hall conventions in Balanchine's, as well as others', choreography for years. In these accounts of *La Chatte*, they describe something more significant: performers' bodies transformed into machine-like entities. In a way that echoed Prampolini's call for Futurist performance to physically capture the spirit of the machine, Balanchine drew its essence into his choreography.

This distillation of the Futurist machine aesthetic into the dancer's body to produce a more dynamic stage space is the exact characteristic that U.S. ballet critics take to be quintessentially "American." Not long after Balanchine's migration to the U.S., his fast, spatially expansive, dynamic, and powerful ballet, freed from the constraints of narrative or representation, was said to symbolize the American "pioneer urge for speed, progress, and change."[40] Lincoln Kirstein, the impresario who brought the choreographer to the U.S., proudly designated "our classicism (in the American Century)" in mechanical terms: it "is measured by syncopated, interrupted, discontinuous rhythms, and serial forms"; its "shapes are abrupt, asymmetrical"; and, in its movement qualities, "[t]oes have a trip-hammer beat; the whole body finds a piston's pulsation."[41] As recently as 2008, Alistair Macaulay wrote of how the Balanchine dancer's rhythmic precision, "blazing energy," and "full-toned audacity" were "startling to European eyes and an embodiment of American character."[42] The Futurists' vision of mechanized man, streamlined, superpowerful, and tuned to the rhythms of modernity, is, in this discourse, transmuted into very loaded notions of "American."

Balanchine's dancers strove for greater mastery of space through ever-more virtuosic bodily control. Heightening discipline, compounding energy, continuously taking up more space in less time, they internalized the empowerment that the spirit of the machine could bring to man. Nowhere is this more evident than in *Agon* (New York City Ballet, 1957). Balanchine said *Agon* was "more tight and precise than usual, as if it were controlled by an electronic brain."[43] As Kirstein describes it:

> Impersonalizations of arms and legs into geometric arrows (all systems "go") accentuates dynamics in a field of force; dancers are magnetized by invisible commands according to logical but arcane formulas.[44]

Agon (whose name is the Greek word for "contest") evokes an edgy, agitated feeling in part through the counterpoint of music and movement, but largely because the ballet continuously fractures, rebuilds, and refractures spatial configurations. The dancers are like atomic bundles of energy, human incarnations of Balla and Depero's "essential force-lines of speed" that manipulate and reconfigure the viewer's perceptions of the space.

Throughout many of the ballet's twelve short movements, multiple groups of dancers, executing precise, repetitive, identical movements, dart across the stage at sharp angles. Although they move in canon, their uneven rhythm creates the effect of gears moving in opposition. As more and more dancers join the groups, the bodies multiply and dynamism intensifies. Dancers fly through space with expansive leaps, lunges, and lurches, but sudden freezes, abrupt reverses, and syncopated, staccato isolations constantly interrupt these forward-driving propulsions. Even as clusters of dancers join together in sculptural shapes, such stillnesses shatter almost instantly, sending bodies scattering through space like "the pieces of glass in a kaleidoscope"[45] (an interplay of plastic form and motion reminiscent of Massine). At moments, the frenetic pace slows to showcase the classical vocabulary, but even here, archetypal academic positions, transformed into ever-shifting formal patterns of triangular *passés* and right-angled *arabesques*, emphasize the body's geometric and mechanistic capacities. As women step boldly onto *pointe*, one leg slicing to full extension in a single beat, the classical movements "turn their limbs into force vectors."[46] Male dancers suddenly and repeatedly propel into the air, taking off without any noticeable preparation to hover for an instant like a photograph captured in real time. Dancers leap, jump, lunge to the floor, rise, extend their legs, and balance on- and off-center like bullets, defying gravity and time, their limbs rebounding in constant motion. This choreography, which activates the entire stage space, not just the dancers on it, realizes Prampolini's "attore-spazio" vision, in which the stage space itself comes alive. Prampolini and Balanchine, it seems, both worshiped the god of movement.

Kirstein, the theoretical proponent of American neoclassicism, arguably initiated the explicitly politicized discourse that would make Balanchine into the mastermind behind the new American ballet and turn his neoclassical style into the "legitimate reflection of a democracy." The choice of a future ballet style, Kirstein wrote, "ultimately depends [...] on which political or economic system has the best bet in America."[47] Comparing Balanchine's dances to IBM computers in their "streamlined metal boxes"[48] and attributing the "athleticism, speed, extrovert energy, the reckless dynamism in its syncopation and asymmetry, and as well a kind of impersonal mastery" of his style to "the force of the rhythm of New York,"[49] Kirstein places the capitalist production of America's democracy at the heart of his formulation. From the sleek design of the world's most modern technological commodities to the pulse of Wall Street, Balanchine's ballets had all the qualities that made the U.S. distinct from its others: Europe's fascists and Russia's communists.

The critical establishment of Balanchine's ballet as emblematically American was a radical aesthetic shift in U.S. ballet history that emerged in tandem with the post-Second World War rhetoric of liberalism, which centered on the belief that the American free market system represented a successful form of capitalism that could solve social problems through increased production and economic growth.[50] Not unlike the Futurists' answer to the unsettling changing world around them, this rhetoric was in part compensatory, responding to the communist threat by offering an optimistic notion of the revolutionary power of the American free market. In sharp contrast to the distrust of big business in the Roosevelt era, corporate America was now seen as the impetus for individual liberty at home and in the world.

"Our ballet style [...] is beginning to assume the tone of our time, the character of our place, and the features of our people," stated Amberg in 1949, indicating these uniquely American traits as its "native dignity," "intelligence," "uninhibited rhythm," "bodily self-confidence, and youthful stamina."[51] Moreover, while their response to the chaos and uncertainty of modern life was not lost on critics, the sense of conflict in Balanchine's ballets is transformed into harmony, order, and innovation. Despite the dancers' endless "[w]hirling, lunging, striking out [...] tugging the stage this way and that," writes Jowitt of *Agon*, the whole "resolves as boundless symmetry."[52] In 1959, Kirstein stated that Balanchine's neoclassical ballet "magnifies the meaning of liberty in disciplined dancing";[53] twenty years later he theorized American ballet's new "policy" as one in which the dancers' advanced "speed and control," "level of efficiency," and ability to move together as if one "body of interchangeable soloists" created "a democratic corps de ballet [...] without hierarchical status or fixed table of organization which could demonstrate celerity, muscularity, interplay of sportive action."[54] Turning "constructs of stressed extreme movement" into the very "meaning of liberty," neoclassical ballet resolved modernist anxiety into metaphors of a society running smoothly as an assembly line, its well-tuned individual parts cooperating for an efficient, productive whole. Not unlike Balla's *Macchina Tipografica*.

Despite these aesthetic affinities and historical continuities, scholars haven't looked to Futurism in their search for George Balanchine's roots. The reasons for the elision of Futurism's influence on Balanchine are many. First there are practical issues of scholarship: a study such as ours will be considered "interdisciplinary," a crossing of the border between theatre and dance. Futurism, too, is studied in parts and pockets and, relative to its literary and fine arts production (manifestos and painting, in particular), its many performance forms are marginalized, with dance-centered spectacle even more distant. Also, scholars and critics are often strikingly reluctant to work across other perceived boundaries, be they geographic, generic, temporal, or political. Yet, as Mike Sell points out, "The avant-garde has tended not to honor the kinds of categorical and institutional boundaries respected by its critics and scholars."[55] Thinking of Balanchine, *the* American neoclassicist, in relationship to the Futurists requires a practical and imaginative leap over virtually all such borders.

Of these, the political boundary is perhaps the most insurmountable because it has been legitimated by a philosophical tradition that responded to the horrors of the interwar period, persevered throughout the Cold War, and today leaves us theorizing in its shadows. The dominant figure here is Walter Benjamin, whose famous thesis, in which he contrasts the aestheticization of politics (i.e. fascism) to the politicization of aesthetics (i.e. communism), haunts contemporary criticism in diffuse and diluted forms. As Gerhard Richter puts it, "Today Benjamin's ghosts are legion. But because they are everywhere, who could speak of them?"[56] In his seminal essay, "The Work of Art in the

Age of Mechanical Reproduction," Benjamin contended that the modern capabilities of technical reproduction had destroyed the work of art's aura, detaching it from its ritualistic function and making it available for political use. Herein were multiple progressive possibilities, but great danger as well, for "the logical result of Fascism is the introduction of aesthetics into political life," and all such attempts "culminate in one thing: war."[57] Benjamin builds his argument against fascist nihilism by quoting F. T. Marinetti as if he were fascism's ideologue and as if fascism and Futurism were one and the same: "*'Fiat ars – pereat mundus,'* says Fascism, and, as Marinetti admits, expects war to supply the artistic gratification of a sense perception that has been changed by technology. This is evidently the consummation of *'l'art pour l'art.'* "[58] Here both Futurism and fascism are reduced to purposeless, empty destruction, and simple synonyms.

Benjamin's ghost quietly lurks almost everywhere Futurism appears (or doesn't). One sees constantly the theoretical and philosophical welding of Futurism to fascism, and few serious attempts to make sense of the Futurist movement and its specific, complicated place in the history of the avant-garde.[59] By reading fascism back onto all of Futurism, scholars have turned everything Futurist fascist. Futurist proclamations like, "Hunger and poverty disappear. The bitter social question, annihilated. [...] Ended now is the need for wearisome and debasing work" (from the "Electrical War" manifesto) are offered as propagandistic catch-phrases of a movement whose concern is, in the words of one scholar, an "amoral exaltation of action for its own sake [...] Again one can see how this easily communicated ideal foreshadowed Fascism's cult of action and drive."[60] In such Benjaminian readings of Futurism, the artistic movement is cordoned off as the aesthetic manifestation of a deviant politics, Futurism and fascism together remaining that evil other against which art of the Left will fight.

In Benjamin's contrast between aestheticized politics and politicized aesthetics, we find a series of comfortable and ordering binaries – Left/Right, revolutionary/reactionary, subversive/submissive – that reverberate through subsequent theories of the avant-garde and gird performance studies of the modernist period. However, when it comes to analyzing Futurism in performance, we might take to heart Franca Angelini's observation that, for the Futurists, "between the will to destruction and theatre, theatre wins,"[61] and look at what that theatre actually produced. When we think about the consecration of Balanchine's neoclassicism as "the American ballet," Benjamin's ghosts seem even ghostlier, for though Benjamin hasn't played much of a role in dance criticism, they lurk even here. Despite the personal relationships and aesthetic congruities between Italian Futurism and Balanchine, they are neatly fixed by scholars on opposite sides of the nebulous political–aesthetic divide:

Futurism = fascist nihilism
Balanchine's neoclassicism = capitalist productivity

By now, it should be clear that the canonization of George Balanchine as the maestro of a new American ballet form required decades of rhetorical somersaulting in which artistic ideals and elements produced on the Futurist stages of Rome, St. Petersburg, Paris, and Monte Carlo, and seen, reworked, and elaborated by Balanchine before and after his arrival on the glittering streets of New York are reformulated as intrinsic to American character. Naturally, these somersaults could only be turned if the words "Rome," "Futurist," "fascist," "St. Petersburg," "constructivist," "communist," "Paris," "cubist," and "European" were first wiped from the dance floor. Otherwise, why would we not have recognized that such inherently productive, "American" qualities (of society as well as dance) were the same as those celebrated by those "fascist Futurists"?

Benjamin's equation offered hope when there was little to be found, but it has failed to stand the test of time. "The past seven decades have shown that almost none of Benjamin's central predictions have proven to be right," Hans Ulricht Gumbrecht and Michael Marrinan admit, pointing out that the mystical aura of original art has "conquered the field of art's technical reproduction" rather than disappearing and that film has failed to become a critical medium for the masses.[62] In turn, it becomes difficult to accept the aesthetics-versus-politics paradigm as relevant in modern culture. Indeed, the case of Futurism and Balanchine renders his thesis untenable even for the historical moment to which he applied it – his own. In the end, the Futurism–Balanchine connection, whether its initial phase of pan-European collaboration or the later construction of Balanchine as the American ballet master, is just one of myriad pieces of history that belie the German philosopher's claims, claims that contemporaries like Antonio Gramsci, who declared Marinetti a revolutionary, may well have contested, had they known his work.[63]

European criticism on Balanchine has better remembered his past. In Italy and France, for instance, Balanchine is widely understood as a post-Diaghilev artist who took the modernist aesthetic with him to the U.S. Balanchine is hailed as a legendary twentieth-century ballet choreographer, but his American oeuvre is seen as the final phase of a career launched under the auspices of the Ballets Russes. His neoclassicism is, in turn, seen as a continuation of the style he developed during the *rappel à l'ordre* of his Parisian days. In U.S. dance discourses, however, the idea that Balanchine's neoclassical ballet is the distinctively American development of a formerly Russian Imperial form remains chronic. This is a "politicization of aesthetics" on the part of U.S. dance scholars that has created a great American ballet master, but has done little to map the international penetration that made modernism, Futurism, and the neoclassical ballet the revolutionary forms that they were. Recently reflecting on Balanchine's legacy, Alastair Macaulay speaks of the early years of the New York City Ballet, writing, "Balanchine was a classicist, a radical, a romantic, a modernist, an avant-gardist, and he also loved to watch *Charlie's Angels* and *Wonder Woman* on television." Quintessentially American – is that the suggestion, once again? It may be, for in the end, Macaulay's article is a celebration of the fact that "Balanchine is now a global phenomenon." But it seems to us that he always was.

Notes

1. Critic in *The Sphere*, quoted in Nesta Macdonald, *Diaghilev Observed by Critics in England and the United States, 1911–1929* (New York: Dance Horizons, 1975), 346.
2. Quoted in Günter Berghaus, *Italian Futurist Theatre, 1909–1944* (Oxford: Clarendon Press, 1998), 450.
3. Deborah Jowitt, *Time and the Dancing Image* (Berkeley: University of California Press, 1988), 274.
4. See Margaret Thompson Drewal, "Constructionist Concepts in Balanchine's Choreography," *Ballet Review* 13.3 (Fall 1985): 42–47; Marilyn Hunt, "The Prodigal Son's Russian Roots: Avant-Garde and Icons," *Dance Chronicle* 5.1 (1982): 24–49; Robert Johnson, "White on White: The Classical Background of *Apollon Musagète*," *Ballet Review* 13.3 (Fall 1985): 48–55; and Giora Manor, "Before Balanchine: Kasyan Goleizovsky's Russian Revolution – Part One," *Dance Magazine* (Jan. 1989), 56–60, and "Part Two," *Dance Magazine* (Feb. 1989), 60–64.
5. Yuri Slonimsky, "Balanchine: The Early Years," *Ballet Review* 5.3 (1975–1976): 14.
6. Anatole Lunacharsky, *Teatro e rivoluzione* (Rome: Samonà e Savelli, 1968).
7. See Vladimir Pavlovič Lapšin, *Marinetti e la Russia* (Milan: Skira, 2008); Claudia Salaris, *La Roma delle avanguardie dal futurismo all'underground* (Rome: Riuniti Editore, 1999) and *Storia del futurismo* (Rome: Editori Riuniti, 1985); Edward Braun, "Futurism in the Russian Theatre, 1913–1923," in *International Futurism in Arts and Literature*, ed. Günter Berghaus (Berlin: Walter de Gruyter, 2000), 75–99; and Frantisek Deák, "Two Manifestos: The Influence of Italian Futurism in Russia," *The Drama Review* 19.4 (Dec. 1975): 88–94.

8. Quoted in Berghaus, *Italian Futurist Theatre*, 256.
9. Umbro Apollonio (ed.), *Futurist Manifestos* (Boston: MFA, 1973), 197.
10. In *Europa* 1 (March 1975): 109. Unless otherwise noted, all translations are our own.
11. Lynn Garafola, *Diaghilev's Ballets Russes* (Cambridge, MA: Da Capo Press, 1998), 81–82.
12. Valerian Sveltov, "The Diaghileff Ballet in Paris," *The Dancing Times* (Dec. 1929): 274.
13. Léonide Massine, *My Life in Ballet* (London: Macmillan, 1968), 107.
14. Léonide Massine, "On Choreography and a New School of Dancing," *Drama* 1.3 (Dec. 1919): 69.
15. Enrico Prampolini, "I valori dell'allestimento scenico e i Balli Russi," *I Novissimi* 3.1 (Apr. 9, 1917).
16. "Théâtre de la Madeleine; La Pantomime Futuriste," *Excelsior* (May 13, 1927), Rome: Fondo Prampolini, Series 5, folder 115.
17. F. T. Marinetti, *Teoria e invenzione futurista* (Milan: Arnaldo Mondadori Editore, 1968), 256.
18. From a publicity write-up by Prampolini, "La Pantomima Futurista," probably from the 1928 Italian tour, here a slight modification of parts of the excerpt translated in Berghaus, *Italian Futurist Theatre*, 450. Original in Raffaele Carrieri, *La Danza in Italia, 1500–1900* (Milan: Editoriale Domus, 1946), 85.
19. Cinzia Sartini Blum, *The Other Modernism: F. T. Marinetti's Futurist Fiction of Power* (Berkeley: University of California Press, 1996), 52.
20. Quoted in Enrico Crispolti, "Pittura, Scultura, Architettura e Ambientazioni futuriste a Roma," in *Il futurismo a Roma*, ed. Giovanni Antonucci et al. (Rome: Istituto di Studi Romani, 1978), 60.
21. Silvana Sinisi, "In Italia, la danza e il balletto moderni dal futurismo a Milloss. I. La danza futurista," in *La danza moderna. I fondatori*, ed. Elisa Vaccarino (Milan: Skira, 1998), 75.
22. Giovanni Lista, *Lo spettacolo futurista* (Firenze: Cantini, 1991), 23–24.
23. "A Parigi con Enrico Prampolini e Silvio Mix," Rome: Fondo Prampolini, Series 5, folder 115.
24. *Città Futurista*, June 1929, Rome: Fondo Prampolini, Series 5, folder 115.
25. Quoted in Berghaus, *Italian Futurist Theatre*, 459.
26. Patrizia Veroli discusses Prampolini's inspirations in "The Futurist Aesthetic in Dance," in *International Futurism*, ed. Günter Berghaus (Berlin: Walter de Gruyter, 2000), 443–445. Darrell Wilkins notes the extent to which the Ballets Russes mixed styles and genres. See "La modernità, la danza, e l'avanguardia parigina dal primitivismo alla 'moderna classicità,'" in *La danza delle avanguardie. Dipinti, scene e costumi da Degas a Picasso, da Matisse a Keith Haring* (Milan: Skira, 2005), 113–121.
27. Veroli, "The Futurist Aesthetic in Dance," 438.
28. André Levinson, "Les Ballets Russes. Pastorale," *Comoedia* (May 31, 1926): 1.
29. "The Russian Ballet. La Pastorale," *The Times* (June 29, 1926): 14.
30. "The Russian Ballet. The Song of the Nightingale," *The Times* (July 19, 1927): 12.
31. André Levinson, "Crisis in Ballets Russes," in *André Levinson on Dance: Writings from Paris in the Twenties*, ed. Joan Acocella and Lynn Garafola (Hanover, NH: Wesleyan University Press, 1991), 67.

32. Garafola, *Ballets Russes*, 138.
33. Kenneth Archer and Millicent Hodson, "Balanchine's Twenties," *Ballet-tanz* (Jan. 2004): 75.
34. W. A. Propert, quoted in Martin Hammer and Christina Lodder, *Constructing Modernity: The Art and Career of Naum Gabo* (New Haven: Yale University Press, 2000), 154.
35. Hammer and Lodder, *Constructing Modernity*, 159.
36. Emile Vuillermoz, "Les Ballets Russes," *Candide* (June 2, 1927): page illegible.
37. Macdonald, *Diaghilev Observed*, 362.
38. Ibid., 346.
39. Ibid., 366 (our emphasis).
40. George Amberg, *Ballet in America: The Emergence of an American Art* (New York: Duell, Sloan and Pearce, 1949), 127.
41. Lincoln Kirstein, in *Ballet: Bias and Belief. Three Pamphlets Collected and Other Dance Writings of Lincoln Kirstein*, comp. Nancy Reynolds (New York: Dance Horizons, 1983), 376.
42. Alastair Macaulay, "Mother Ship Off Balance, Balanchine Still Soars," *New York Times* (Nov. 14, 2008): AR1.
43. Balanchine, quoted in Sally Banes, *Dancing Women: Female Bodies on Stage* (London: Routledge, 1998), 194.
44. Lincoln Kirstein, *Movement and Metaphor: Four Centuries of Ballet* (Mineola, NY: Dover, 1984), 242.
45. Beaumont on Balanchine's "abstract ballets," in "Kirstein, Balanchine, and Others," *Tempo* 17 (Autumn 1950): 11.
46. Banes, *Dancing Women*, 197.
47. Quoted in Reynolds, *Ballet: Bias and Belief*, 200.
48. Ibid., 378.
49. Ibid., 124.
50. See Andrea Harris, "Choreographing America: Redefining 'American' Ballet in the Age of Consensus," in *Interrogating America Through Theatre and Performance*, ed. William W. Demastes and Iris Smith Fischer (New York: Palgrave Macmillan, 2007), 139–155.
51. Amberg, *Ballet in America*, 127.
52. Jowitt, *Time and the Dancing Image*, 254.
53. Quoted in Reynolds, *Ballet: Bias and Belief*, 376.
54. Quoted in ibid., 124.
55. Mike Sell, *Avant-Garde Performance and the Limits of Criticism: Approaching the Living Theatre, Happenings/Fluxus, and the Black Arts Movement* (Ann Arbor: University of Michigan Press, 2008), 18.
56. Gerhard Richter, Introduction, *Benjamin's Ghosts: Interventions in Contemporary Literary and Cultural Theory*, ed. Richter (Palo Alto: Stanford University Press, 2002), 1.
57. Walter Benjamin, "The Work of Art in the Age of Mechanical Reproduction," *Illuminations*, ed. Hannah Arendt, trans. Harry Zohn (New York: Schocken Books, 1968 and 1988), 241.
58. Ibid., 242.
59. See Peter Bürger's exclusion of Futurism from his *Theory of the Avant-Garde* (Minneapolis: University of Minnesota Press, 1984). One of the few to break away from the Benjaminian paradigm is Marjorie Perloff, *The Futurist*

Moment: Avant-Garde, Avant Guerre, and the Language of Rupture (Chicago: University of Chicago Press, 1986 and 2003).

60. Judy Rawson, "Italian Futurism," in *Modernism*, ed. Malcolm Bradbury and James McFarlane (New York: Penguin Books, 1976), 244–245.

61. Franca Angelini, *Teatro e spettacolo nel primo Novecento* (Roma-Bari: Laterza, 1988 and 2004), 39.

62. Preface to *Mapping Benjamin: The Work of Art in the Digital Age*, ed. Hans Ulrich Gumbrecht and Michael Marrinan (Palo Alto: Stanford University Press, 2003), xiii-xiv.

63. Antonio Gramsci, *Selections from Cultural Writings*, ed. David Forqacs and Geoffrey Nowell-Smith, trans. William Boelhower (Cambridge, MA: Harvard University Press, 1991), 46–54.

3
Confessions of a Failed Theatre Activist: Intercultural Encounters in Uganda and Rwanda

Laura Edmondson

In the summer of 2004, I traveled to the town of Gulu in northern Uganda, proudly bearing an invitation to facilitate theatre workshops at a rehabilitation center for former child soldiers. These children had been kidnapped by the notorious Lord's Resistance Army, which terrorized the region in the longest civil war in the history of sub-Saharan Africa. In the heart of this warzone, I met another U.S. theatre artist, as eager as I was to contribute her skills. She had arranged for private workshops at another rehabilitation center in Gulu, which she invited me to observe. She led a group of fifteen teenage girls in a series of theatre exercises, working with them to use their body as a tool of expression. She was wearing a loose, flowing skirt, and, as she demonstrated the movements, all of us caught glimpses of her underwear. As members of a culture in which modest dress is a social norm, the girls giggled and whispered among themselves. These outbursts continued despite the obvious annoyance of the facilitator, who repeatedly requested their undivided attention. Although I'm fairly certain that the residents of Gulu did not see my underwear, the image of white woman as ludicrous spectacle haunted my own attempts to practice activist theatre.

Activism and the avant-garde are historic bedfellows, as Matei Calinescu and Renato Poggioli show. Calinescu links the "messianic fervors" of the avant-garde to Henri de Saint-Simon's socialist belief that artists would blaze a path towards an egalitarian society.[1] Calinescu's argument that avant-garde artists perceived themselves as constituting "the 'vanguard' in the moral history of mankind"[2] resonates with Poggioli's identification of activism as one of the "four moments" of the avant-garde. Although Poggioli qualifies his inclusion of activism as the "least important or, in any case the least characteristic" of the four moments, his description of avant-garde activism deserves attention in light of my focus on U.S. theatre activism in the twenty-first century.[3] Poggioli defines it as "the tendency of certain individuals, parties, or groups to act without heeding plans or programs, to function with any method ... for the mere sake of doing something, or of changing the sociopolitical system in whatever way they can."[4] In the context of northern Uganda in 2004, Poggioli's cynical description strikes a chord. In our inchoate desire to "do something" to help former child soldiers, the two of us were perhaps pandering to the "vanguard fantasy"[5] that art could save the world. Three years later, I received another opportunity to indulge this fantasy. In the summer of 2007, I participated in "More Life," an annual cross-cultural exchange in Uganda and Rwanda spearheaded by Erik Ehn, playwright and Dean of the School of Theatre at the California Institute of the Arts, and Jean-Pierre Karegeye, director of the Interdisciplinary Genocide Studies Center (IGSC) in Kigali.[6] These experiences would both indulge and challenge Poggioli's definition of vanguard activism.

In the first section of this essay, I draw upon my Ugandan experiences in "More Life" to question the implications of theatre activism as a means of cross-cultural exchange. Given the uncomfortable legacy of avant-garde primitivism,[7] these interventions could be viewed as a search for a new, but no less exotic terrain on which the vanguard fantasy might be staged. As addressed in the second section, however, the Rwandan portion of the program introduced me to an alternative model of theatre activism, one that troubles the hierarchies that pervade human rights and vanguard discourses alike and articulates a space of what I call, borrowing from Emmanuel Levinas, radical passivity. Despite my reservations about the "More Life" program, these experiences were instrumental in my conceptualization of a more ethical mode of activist theatre. The notion of radical passivity stands against "messianic" strategies of vanguard activism and emphasizes what James Harding calls "the moment of problematic intercultural exchange [that] belong[s] to the history of the avant-garde."[8] He notes that "highlighting that moment of contested exchange provides us with a vantage point from which we might begin to retheorize the avant-garde as a whole."[9] A Levinasian vantage point might help theatre activists shed the vestiges of avant-garde primitivism and messianism and work towards understanding the world instead of intervening to save it.

Compassionate colonialism

In a book about international humanitarian agencies in Somalia and Kenya, Jennifer Hyndman argues that a "former colonialism of derision" has been reinscribed as "a colonialism of compassion."[10] Hyndman reminds us how compassion in the guise of humanitarianism shores up the existing order by dividing the world between Northern benefactors and Southern victims. Alain Badiou articulates a distrust of humanitarianism more forcefully in his condemnation of universal human rights, which depends upon a split between "a passive, pathetic [pathétique], or reflexive subject – he who suffers," and "the active, determining subject of judgment – he who, in identifying suffering, knows that it must be stopped by all available means."[11] From this perspective, theatre activism that depends upon a separation between the helper and helped is hardly transformative. As the giggling former rebel soldiers indicate, this version of activism is routinely resisted or at least mocked.

In an introduction to a *TDR* special issue devoted to social theatre, James Thompson and Richard Schechner emphasize the idea of mutual transformation: "It ought to become a performance that can transform the practitioners, the participants, and the public's existing knowledge and experience. It ought not to just map onto or sit authoritatively above."[12] Sonja Kuftinec expands on this, noting that "theatrical encounters...highlight productive ruptures – moments of 'truths colliding' that undo the stability of what we think we know of ourselves and others."[13] Such encounters "offer the opportunities to examine our assumptions, to reconstitute the world beyond in-group and out-group, beyond a nationalized (and naturalized) 'us' and 'them.'"[14] Such reflections seek to overturn or at least unsettle "authoritative" models of theatre activism by emphasizing theatre exchange as a means of producing new forms of knowledge.[15]

Perhaps my concerns about theatre activism could be resolved simply by recasting humanitarian projects as cross-cultural theatrical exchanges that emphasize collaboration. Jacqueline Lo and Helen Gilbert describe this approach: "While there is a general desire to maintain equitable power relations between partners, the aim is not to produce a harmonious experience of theatre-making but rather to explore the fullness of cultural exchange in all its contradictions and convergences for all parties."[16] But even when we march into these international contexts armed with ideas of mutual transformation and collaboration, we might still overlook the possibility that *our presence is not wanted* or simply tolerated out of the hope that more tangible benefits are forthcoming. In specific circumstances – not all – our eagerness to use the performing arts as a forum for the exploration of trauma could be entirely misplaced.

Three years after my encounter with the civil war in northern Uganda, I visited Hope North, a resettlement center and secondary school for displaced families and former child soldiers, located just south of the Nile River. The terms of my visit were quite different from 2004; this time, I was a participant in the "More Life" cultural exchange program, of which Hope North was the final segment. Our group of U.S., Tanzanian, and Ugandan artists and students had come in response to an invitation by the founder of Hope North, Okello Kelo Sam, himself an Acholi and one of the most well-known performing artists in Uganda. Sam was keen to encourage artistic activity at Hope North and welcomed the opportunity to have us work with the schoolchildren. The situation boded well for an artistic interaction that would, in Kuftinec's terms, "reconstitute the world beyond in-group and out-group." Indeed, on the first night, the dances that the Hope North children performed turned into a celebratory dance in which we all participated. The workshops held the following day adhered to a more hierarchical structure, as the "More Life" participants taught playwriting, poetry, and hip hop. Sam, however, promptly stepped in to unsettle our positions, assigning us tasks for the evening meal: chopping wood, killing and butchering a goat, fetching water. He also declared that the "More Life" participants would play the residents of Hope North in a soccer match, which the Hope North residents proceeded to win.

The next day, the ideal of co-creation was more actively sought. Ugandan playwright and "More Life" participant Deborah Asiimwe moderated a discussion about the challenges that the Hope North students faced. Under Asiimwe's guidance, Hope North students raised a few issues that they faced at the center, chief of which was a lack of time to study for the exams scheduled for the following week. We then divided into three groups, one categorized as "optimistic" that solutions to these problems could be found, and two that were more ambivalent. Although all three groups included a mix of Hope North and "More Life" participants, a majority of the "More Life" participants, including myself, were in the "optimistic" group, evenly divided between Hope North students and us. Each group was charged to develop a performance that addressed the problems the students faced.

This technique relies upon standard notions of theatre-for-development, in which theatre is used to target specific problems within the community. What ensued, however, was a tribute to the creativity of the Hope North students, who seized the opportunity to target *us*, the "More Life" participants, as the problem. Our group leader, a student named Owen, assigned us roles in a play that showed that entertaining the visitors and providing them with food and water interrupted their study time. The enthusiasm for this production was palpable among both students and visitors. We gleefully created scenes in which the Hope North students were forced to carry massive amounts of water for the shower and flush toilet that was in the VIP hut (where some of the more senior members of "More Life" were staying), and we also parodied the exhausted students forcing themselves to dance at the evening bonfire. I felt as if I was participating in a textbook example of how theatre can produce unique knowledges and break down hierarchies. It was exhilarating.

Then we broke for lunch. Visitors and students ate separately. When we reassembled, we were asked to hear an announcement. Owen stood there, his jaw clenched tightly, as one of the other participants explained that, because the play was "too difficult" for the group to present well, the group should quickly assemble another play about AIDS or the war in the north.

We were due to present our play in twenty minutes.

Silence. "It would be easier to develop a new play about AIDS or the war in the north than to present the play we developed this morning?" I asked. Oh yes, we were assured. It would take only "some minutes" to create such a play. More silence followed. Then Owen's spokesperson said in an undertone, "The play is too frank." Too close, too uncomfortable, too fraught. Never mind that Okello would have firmly supported their expression of indignation. The stakes of artistic representation of their personal experiences during a time of war is not only large, they're mammoth. Ehn hastened to explain that the performance itself was not important; we could simply use the time to get better acquainted. This suggestion was brushed aside, and Owen dictated a speech that he would read in lieu of our performance, a generic tale of how he came to Hope North, how grateful he was, and how wonderful it was that international visitors come to see its success.

The experience was undoubtedly rich. We, the visitors, learned that *we* were the problem and many of us took this lesson to heart. I participated in heated conversations afterwards about how we might have altered our approach. I have begun to conceive of theatre activism as a kind of ethnographic encounter that cultivates a more nuanced and complex way of understanding the world, rather than a way of changing it.[17] Kuftinec calls attention to this overlap, noting that, "[l]ike critical ethnography...ethical activism needs to wrestle with the politics of when to do less and listen more."[18] I would push this further: activism should yield to ethnography in an acknowledgement that it can be more useful as a means of generating new forms of knowledge than bringing about social change.

To state that the experience was rich begs a crucial qualification: it was rich for *me*. Even as my romanticism was punctured, I was already envisioning how I would write about it. So what are the implications of using theatre activism as a source of knowledge? An emphasis on how these encounters serve as a source of knowledge skims over the implications to these students and thus could be interpreted as a violation of this imperative, itself a tenet of universal human rights.[19] But can such knowledge pave the way for a praxis of anti-colonial compassion? Though I am distrustful of theatre activism as it is often practiced by U.S. nationals, I am not despairing. Levinas's concept of radical passivity offers a starting point for the practice of anti-colonial theatre activism and a critique of vanguard fantasy.

Radical passivity

In order to elaborate upon the idea of radical passivity as a more ethical alternative to what we practiced at Hope North, I turn to the experiences in Rwanda that *preceded* Hope North. During the last two weeks of July 2007, the "More Life" group visited genocide memorial sites, listened to survivor testimony, and attended a series of presentations by state officials on reconstruction. Although theatre workshops and a public performance were part of the agenda, the focus was on witnessing rather than artistic activity. Our mission was predicated on a concept of theatre activism that exceeds conventional understandings of activism as interventionist. In a 2007 *American Theatre* article about the CalArts/Rwanda exchange, Ehn articulates this vision:

> The essential action of the artist, the audience, is to see, to experience, to witness (and deriving from witness – to give testimony), to trust. [...] Seeing can be a moral act: We consent to take in, we draw out attention to focus, we turn our heads and open our eyes – we change our own place to put ourselves squarely in the presence of a unique event.[20]

He adds, "In seeing in this way, by deliberately committing to a new perspective, we allow ourselves to be shaped by the event – to be created by it."[21] It is telling that these passages make up almost the entirety of a section subtitled, "Arts = Activism." Rather than seeking to promote healing and reconciliation through theatre, the mission of "More Life" is to carve out a site of witnessing for the transformation of ourselves. And this, Ehn suggests, is a version of activism.

What is the point of sending U.S. theatre artists halfway across the world, if only to put the focus on their own journeys of self-transformation? But, in the context of conflict and post-conflict zones in East Africa, it marks a strategic point of departure, particularly given the limitations of our group. The majority of the U.S. participants barely spoke French, let alone Kinyarwanda or Swahili, and thus depended primarily upon the Rwandan interpreters in the group in their interactions with survivors. Also, much of their knowledge of the genocide was drawn from trade books by U.S. authors such as Philip Gourevitch's *We Wish to Inform You that Tomorrow We Will Be Killed with Our Families* and the chapter devoted to the genocide in Samantha Powers's *"A Problem from Hell": America in the Age of Genocide.*[22] Given this ignorance, the desire to "do something" needed to be thoroughly interrogated if not forestalled.

Witnessing and passivity contain landmines of their own, as one could easily become a voyeur who, in Ehn's words, "feels sexy because they've had an encounter with death and haven't died."[23] Ehn is acutely aware of the dangers of "witnessing by proxy,"[24] a phrase he uses to describe outsiders, particularly Westerners, who seek to learn and understand about the Rwandan genocide. In their attempts to develop an ethics of artistic response that evades the pitfalls of appropriation and titillation, he and the other leaders of "More Life" articulated a version of witnessing that embraced complexity, vulnerability, and precariousness. Ehn urged us to stay present, warning that "to be overwhelmed with emotion is a way of protecting ourselves."[25] Excessive emotion could easily rush into the stillness, allowing us to distance ourselves from the other for whom we are a witness. Staying present was a challenging task, as it unsettled our activist, compassionate bent to *do* something and instead asked us simply to dwell in discomfort. When one participant shared the testimony of a survivor whom she encountered on an excursion of her own, Ehn spoke with uncharacteristic sharpness that "a testimony is like a secret."[26] When another participant spoke admiringly of the courage and bravery of the survivors in sharing their testimonies, Chantal Kalisa, a Rwandan scholar of Francophone literature and an advisory memory of the IGSC, reminded us that "this doesn't mean they'll be able to get out of bed in the morning."[27] We must not only dwell in the discomfort of the tale but also in our awareness of the cost of the telling.

Emmanuel Levinas's concept of passivity helps to clarify activism as inaction, suggesting a concept of the avant-garde that is more in tune with art for art's sake, John Cage's silences and chance operations, or Yoko Ono's material ironies than the conventional vanguard fantasy. In a theory of selfhood that systemically undermines the agency and sovereignty of the subject, Levinas positions the self as *radically passive* in the encounter with the other.[28] This invokes a primal, precognitive ethical relationship in which the self is *inseparable* from an infinite responsibility for the other. To speak of responsibility in the Levinasian sense refuses the usual dichotomy of self-as-benefactor and other-as-victim. Instead, one defines the self *as* its responsibility for the other and, thus, infinite responsibility is intertwined with infinite vulnerability. His insistence on the vulnerability of the subject is often conveyed through terms such as "hostage" and "victim" to describe subjecthood.[29] "Subjectivity is being hostage," Levinas states flatly.[30] More expansively, he also writes, "The oneself cannot form itself; it is already formed with an absolute passivity. In this sense, it is the victim of a persecution that paralyses any assumption that could awaken in it, so that it would posit itself *for* itself."[31] This infinite responsibility cannot uphold the self's desire for superiority but instead erodes the singularity of the ego.

The Levinasian stakes are raised when the U.S.-theatre-activist-self encounters the Rwandan-survivor-other. Thomas Carl Wall's reading of Levinas suggests that an encounter with those who have exceeded "localizable contexts" and have become "radically dis-placed" is filled with potential to script new kinds of relations between self and other: "When this happens, all proper relations to the other are suspended and there is, before anything else, a fascination."[32] He goes on to argue that this fascination is not one that sensationalizes but one that *paralyzes*, "that to which there is no proper response."[33] He writes:

> The call of the Other will never cease to place an incoherent demand in the soul of the subject to which no response is adequate. [...] Every response to the other, every restoration to the general, will betray the demand. But at the same time, each betrayal will be a new relation with the other and thus ethics will mime or "conform" to mimesis, to the improper "itself." There will be no reaching ethics, no teaching it, no instituting it. There will be instead the slow emptying out of any determinate relation whatsoever, and this emptying out will articulate by exhaustion and exclusion the singular "itself."[34]

The singular "itself" is the abyss and perhaps in attempting to understand genocide, we should seek a glimpse of the abyss. Only then –
perhaps – would it be appropriate to act on our desire to *do*, if we still
feel ourselves equal to the task. The avant-garde's task in such a situation would be to produce the conditions that enable radical passivity.
The avant-garde acts to deny its own capacity to act. Radical passivity
could avoid the neocolonialist and imperialist connotations of cross-
cultural exchange and clear a space for the articulation of the counter-
agendas of those to whom we are a witness. Radical passivity is a means
of overturning the hierarchy that permeates human rights discourse
and providing a space for what Slavoj Žižek calls "the solidarity of the
vulnerable."[35]

Did we catch glimpses of the abyss through the practicing of radical passivity? Did we excavate the potential of vulnerability? Perhaps.
Whereas vanguardist activism tends to yield cause-to-effect linear narratives (as in the case of our Ugandan experience), the approach of radical passivity refutes such clarity. Instead of a straightforward narrative,
I offer a few of my more vivid memories of Rwanda, moments in which
we confronted the impossible.

Towards the end of the first week, we visited Murambi Technical
School, a notorious site where 45–50,000 Tutsis were slaughtered after
being lured by the promise of safety. A few hundred of the bodies were
never buried but are displayed on wooden pallets in a series of small
classrooms; the remains are regularly dusted with preservative chemi-
cals. The bodies are achingly vulnerable; it is easy to find yourself alone
with them in one of the many rooms. Local children who were playing
along the edges of the memorial site sought to make us laugh with their
antics. I came out of one classroom and encountered a smiling young
boy who held out his hands and asked for *faranga* (francs). I have no
idea what my emotional state was at that moment, but it was abruptly
broken as I confronted the world of a child who plays alongside bodies
permanently stiffened "in the postures of annihilation."[36] How humor-
ous the sobbing *bazungu*[37] must have appeared.

At the convent in Sovu where the Maria Kizito of Ehn's play helped to
orchestrate the killing of 7,000 Rwandan Tutsi, we gathered on the well-
manicured lawn complete with a volleyball net and gazebos – the very
place where the slaughter occurred while the nuns watched from the
terrace and served tea to the militias during breaks.[38] Before we could
feel "sexy" about this experience of death, a young man began scream-
ing at us through the gates. He screamed in Swahili about the murders,
the children who were killed, and the names of people involved. The

thread of Ehn's narrative about Sovu was lost as we were forced to grapple with the living legacy of the massacres.

When we traveled to the village of Gahanga in the outskirts of Kigali to listen to survivor testimony and visit the memorial site, children surrounded us as we made our way through the school grounds where thousands of the local population took refuge. As the children jockeyed for our attention, we listened to a survivor's testimony: here was where they began to kill the women and children, here was where we tried to fight them off with sticks and stones, here was the room where we hid with the livestock, and here is the garbage pit that we transformed into a mass grave because it was already paved with cement. Meanwhile, we could overhear a raucous soccer match, and we had to step around the millet that was drying in front of the mass grave. The survivor then took us to the local Catholic church where the bodies were kept until the stacks reached the ceiling. We sat in this church, which continues to serve as a house of worship, and dwelled in our discomfort. There was nothing else to do. The surreality confounded comprehension. At the end of our visit to Gahanga, we gathered for a group discussion in the open-air shelter that served as the local *gacaca* building.[39] Itamar Stern, a CalArts student who has participated in all three years of the CalArts/Rwanda exchange, spoke passionately about relinquishing the need "to connect the dots" and allow the soccer game, the church, the millet, and the testimony to exist simultaneously, to allow the labor of everyday life in Rwanda to exist alongside markers of carnage and fear.

The gaps and interruptions that characterized our days in Rwanda disallowed our attempts to reconcile contradiction, explain away paradoxes, comprehend mass death. Only rarely were we able to "lose" ourselves in a specific experience and sink into the luxury of emotion uninterrupted by present-day realities. We lived in a complexity and murk that held us hostage to the experience; it disallowed any attempt to comprehend and thus master it. Žižek might concur: "The first ethical gesture is thus to abandon the position of absolute self-positing subjectivity and to acknowledge one's exposure/thrownness, being overwhelmed by Other(ness)."[40] We were held hostage to the abyss.

Our vanguard fantasies did not take well to this approach. Many of the participants expressed a desire to "do something" – to conduct workshops in Theatre of the Oppressed (TO)[41] and meditation techniques for local groups, give money to survivors, do volunteer work for women's organizations in Kigali. It is hardly my aim to condemn these activities or to patronize the Rwandan participants, who were quite capable of rejecting, accepting, and/or transforming these offers of assistance as they deemed appropriate. I also do not doubt that, in certain cases, the workshops offered were thoughtfully and carefully shaped and eagerly welcomed, as when Brent Blair, a noted TO practitioner and participant in "More Life," offered a workshop at the National University of Rwanda. But why us and why not a Rwandan theatre artist? Certainly, TO techniques have a long history at the Center of the Arts at the university.[42] Why was I asked to give workshops at the rehabilitation center in Gulu instead of one of the members of Gulu Theatre Artists, a local theatre collective? The path of radical passivity provides a blueprint for theatre activism in such situations, describing the less sexy but perhaps more meaningful shape of coalition-building with fellow theatre artists.

I conceive of radical passivity as a *sustained* point of departure that allows for other kinds of engagement. In a summary of the 2007 trip, Ehn writes:

> The trip to Rwanda/Uganda wants to be contemplative at core, with space for listening, and ethical guidance around issues of accepting testimony and entering into colloquy with trauma. The trip is at its best when there is internal and external quiet, when we take time; the dancing and singing come out of a sweeter place when they are responsive to their counterparts.[43]

In other words, radical passivity serves as a starting point from which one might shift into "dancing and singing" and other forms of collaborative praxis.

Precarious hospitality

A theme of hospitality runs throughout Ehn's rhetoric. In his opening remarks for the 2007 Arts in the One World conference, he offered an understanding of hospitality as a kind of common ground:

> I believe the theater of the future will not be framed by style or technique, but by ethics... specifically, the theater of hospitality. Hospitality may be defined as a mitigation of estrangement. This is the world's next great phase, lest, as we communicate more swiftly, we go at each other more than grow with. Remaining strange (local), but not estranged. The lion is still a lion, the lamb a lamb, but they lay down together.[44]

Ehn's modest definition of hospitality as "a mitigation of estrangement" gives way to a utopian vision in which differences between the lion and the lamb are erased.

Elsewhere, however, Ehn provides a conception of hospitality that underscores the precariousness of the artist's position and suggests one of the ways that we might rethink the role of the avant-garde. Artists are *seekers* of hospitality rather than its providers:

> Artists who celebrate the ecological concept of hospitality run the risk of thinking they're inside the house welcoming the others into it, "Welcome the stranger, come into my house of art," when they have to understand that in their own weakness, in their own strangeness, artists make a gift of their need and serve by being welcomed.[45]

By taking the risk of hospitality, we also assume the risk of rejection. Ehn adds, "It's what I fail to bring to a community, in a way, that is my gift to the community, where my emptiness in the face of the community, my dependence on the community is what I can bring as an artist."[46] As if in direct opposition to colonialist notions of activism that inscribe the Western outsider as "the active, determining subject of judgment" (to return to Badiou) – in other words the avant-garde as conventionally conceived – Ehn sees the artist as the one in need, a suppliant rather than benefactor.

Jacques Derrida notes that hospitality usually operates within limits and affirms sovereignty (in Immanuel Kant's sense[47]). He alludes to the "rigorous delimitation of thresholds or frontiers" upon which reflections on hospitality typically depend: "between the familial and the non-familial, between the foreign and non-foreign, the citizen and the non-citizen."[48] A gesture of hospitality, of welcoming a foreigner across the threshold, works to affirm these delimitations because the host is the one who "choos[es], elect[s], filter[s], select[s] their invitees, visitors, or guests, those to whom they decide to grant asylum, the right of visiting, or hospitality."[49] In contrast, unconditional (and thus impossible) hospitality is without limits: "Let us say yes *to who or what turns up*, before any determination, before any anticipation, before any *identification*, whether or not it has to do with a foreigner, an immigrant, an invited guest, or an unexpected visitor, whether or not the new arrival is the citizen of another country, a human, animal, or divine creature, a living or dead thing, male or female."[50] Ehn's emphasis on the vulnerability and dependency of the artist upon the host dovetails with Derrida's conditional hospitality, in which the sovereignty of the hosts is affirmed and thus does not aspire to the expansive potential of Derrida's "impossible" version.

Our own brush with conditional hospitality in Rwanda clarified our vulnerability and the fragility of our relationship with our hosts. For the 2007 program, Ehn and Karegeye planned to include two public performances by the participants themselves. One performance was to consist of various interpretations of violence (not necessarily related to Rwanda) presented by individual participants during our visit to the National University of Rwanda in Butare. The second performance was designed as a collective interpretation of our Rwandan experiences, to be presented in Kigali at the end of our visit. In preparation for the Butare performance, several participants rehearsed poems, dramatic readings, and songs. This first performance could be understood as a well-intentioned attempt to share our concept of artistic creation with a Rwandan audience, to serve as the spectacle, to perform for their gaze.

The reality was that our weakness and our strangeness exploded in our faces. At the National University of Rwanda,[51] we served up a smorgasbord of performance pieces. Offerings included an improvisational dance piece by Kathy Carbone, a dance instructor and the performing arts librarian at CalArts, hip hop by Los Angeles-based Native American artist Sista Hailstorm (assisted by Vanessa Penaloza, an LA-based Chicana community activist and poet), a monologue written by the U.S. playwright and "More Life" participant Lynn Nottage and performed by Asiimwe (the Ugandan playwright who facilitated our workshop at Hope North), a Swahili popular song about poverty by the Tanzanian participant Robert Ajwang', and an abstract puppetry piece by CalArts students John Kern and Catherine Strecker. Aside from the crowd's enthusiastic response to the hip hop and the Swahili music, the reaction from the Rwandan audience was either inappropriate (to us) amusement, catcalls to the younger female performers, or ostentatious boredom. A sizable number of the spectators simply left. We made a gift of our need, and it was soundly rejected. Rest assured, none of us felt sexy.

Plans for the second performance in Kigali were abruptly discarded. But it was during this performance that our feelings of discomfort, our vulnerability, were the most acute. To return to an earlier point, the risk of rejection is one that we must embrace given the distinct possibility that our presence is not wanted. We can waltz into East Africa filled with Levinasian/Derridean notions of how the intercultural encounter can pave the way for a dismantling of thresholds and frontiers, but we must also recognize that we could be sent packing. "Is not hospitality an interruption of the self?"[52] Derrida asks. I would also ask, does not the *denial* of hospitality also produce an interruption of the (Western) self and an interruption of the avant-garde fantasy? Could the hospitality visiting U.S. theatre artists often enjoy be compulsory, or at least obligatory, in the sense that the colonial subject is often obliged to extend hospitality to the occupying power?

I am not suggesting that public humiliation is a stepping-stone towards an ethics of vulnerability. Nevertheless, I do think that methods of *de*-hegemonizing should be actively sought as a means of shedding the messianic vestiges of vanguardist activism. Such moments constitute a radical intervention into conventional frameworks of activism that reinscribe the other as victim. What Žižek calls a solidarity of the vulnerable was not achieved by us; still, this position of vulnerability served as a stepping-stone leading to the abyss. The multiple intra- and intercultural tensions, anxieties, and discomforts that we experienced were points of departure for learning to understand that the abyss does not simply exist within the other but pervades and occupies our selves.

Add fidelity and stir...

As compelling as I find the notion of radical passivity and vulnerability to be, it is hardly an anti-colonial panacea. Theatre activism that seeks to maintain a passive position in respect to the other begins to smack of masochism.[53] Given the "epistemic murk"[54] that pervades post-genocide Rwanda, such a stance could suppress critical awareness of the political stakes that surround witness testimony and explanations of the genocide.

Badiou refuses the Levinasian emphasis upon the other and instead asserts that ethical subjectivity is formed through fidelity to an *event*. As Simon Critchley puts it, "The subject commits itself ethically in terms of a demand that is received from the situation."[55] Critchley's use of the phrase "a demand that is received from the situation" places the subject in a passive position *to* the situation and thus resonates with the Levinasian approach. Once the demand is received, however, the ethical subject cannot evade it and must commit itself to the process of truth. Truth is an immanent break that "tak[es] the *sustained* form of a *faithful* process."[56] One must "persevere in the interruption"[57] of continual, ceaseless activism.

Ehn writes, "One persists through this line of inquiry, this application of art to the task of witnessing to genocide, questioning continually."[58] Certainly Ehn's commitment to Rwanda, sparked by writing a play about the 1994 genocide called *Maria Kizito*,[59] could be interpreted as Badiouian fidelity. *Maria Kizito* was the event that expanded into a sustained, multifaceted engagement with post-genocide Rwanda. His collaboration with Karegeye not only generated the annual visit to Rwanda each summer but also the annual "Arts in the One World" conferences at CalArts devoted to the intersection of arts and genocide. Their efforts culminated in the Interdisciplinary Genocide Studies Center in Kigali, a non-governmental organization that studies genocide in an effort "to understand various mechanisms and structures of violence, with the goal of preventing genocide and mass violence."[60] Through his long-term collaboration with Karegeye, Ehn has demonstrated fidelity in his rigorous examination of what it means to be human in a genocidal world.

But what kinds of truths are being understood? After his Badiouian statement about "persist[ing] through this line of inquiry," Ehn then offers "two practical pieces of advice": to travel and be *with* (his emphasis).[61] When does radical passivity and "being with" begin to interfere with critical awareness? How do you ensure that you are *with* a variety of witnesses? During those weeks in Rwanda, I noticed that our experience of witnessing and learning about the genocide was aligned closely with the current official Rwandan narrative. Ehn and Karegeye call the events that occurred in 1994 "the Tutsi genocide" instead of "the Rwandan genocide of 1994." This semantic shift erases thousands of "Hutu moderates" who were slaughtered alongside Tutsi.[62] It also sidesteps the controversy surrounding the thousands of Hutu civilians who were killed in the former Zaire and in Rwanda at the hands of the Rwandan Patriotic Army, the Tutsi-led force from Uganda that overthrew the supremacist Hutu regime and has remained securely in power since then.[63] Nothing that we heard or saw diverted from the dominant understanding of President Paul Kagame and the Rwandan Patriotic Front as the bulwarks of democracy and reconciliation.[64] In *Remnants of Auschwitz*, Giorgio Agamben writes, "At a certain point, it became clear that testimony contained at its core an essential lacuna; in other words, the survivors bore witness to something it is impossible to bear witness to."[65] A lacuna also operated in "More Life," a lacuna that facilitated a Manichean understanding of the genocide instead of delving into the epistemic murk. I am aware that what I am suggesting might be – to borrow again from Agamben – "impossible," due to the forces of genocide denial that seek to minimize the supremacist ideology of the Hutu government and the mass destruction of the Tutsi. It is easy for me, as an outsider, to take a cue from Badiou and suggest that truth should not be confused with ideology. But I am reminded of Owen at Hope North, who could not speak his truth because of his fear of the consequences. The stakes are too high at this historical moment in post-genocide Rwanda for the lacuna to be exposed, interrogated, filled. Others would disagree.[66]

My own fidelity is to continue to think through the implications of my experiences in Uganda and Rwanda, to continue to explore the ethics of cross-cultural theatre exchange, to monitor the vanguard fantasy, to try "to listen to what is unsaid."[67] Despite my reservations about aspects of the CalArts/Rwanda program, I cannot explain away my belief that it marks an *event*, a radical intervention into conventional understandings of activism. This intervention has generated the following ethical roadmap for me: (1) to commit to a stance of radical passivity; (2) if a demand emerges from that particular situation, to respond to that demand with faithfulness and fidelity; and (3) acknowledge that failure will permeate the process of truth. "Failure is inevitable," Critchley warns, "for we can never hope to fulfill the radicality of the ethical demand."[68] In this sense, then, *all* activists are failed activists, and we should embrace the potential of those failures, misunderstandings, and even betrayals as we lurch towards a mutually vulnerable world.

Notes

1. Matei Calinescu, *Five Faces of Modernity: Modernism, Avant-Garde, Decadence, Kitsch, Postmodernism* (Durham: Duke University Press, 1987), 96, 100–103.
2. Ibid., 102.
3. Renato Poggioli, *The Theory of the Avant-Garde*, trans. Gerald Fitzgerald (Cambridge, MA: Harvard University Press, 1968), 27.
4. Ibid.
5. My thanks to Mike Sell, who used the phrase "vanguard fantasy" in an e-mail exchange on March 21, 2009.
6. "More Life" is an umbrella term referring to a host of initiatives related to Rwanda that is based at CalArts; however, I am using it to refer to the cultural exchange in Rwanda and Uganda as I experienced it in July and August in 2007. See Ehn's reflections on the 2007 program, "More Life: Reflections on Rwanda, Uganda, and Bosnia," posted on http://www.themagdalenaproject.org/phpBB2/viewtopic.php?p=739 (accessed Sept. 4, 2008).
7. See Christopher Innes, *Avant-Garde Theatre, 1892–1992* (London: Routledge, 1993), 6–18, for an overview of what he calls the "cult of the primitive" (9) in avant-garde theatre. See also James Harding, "From Cutting Edge to Rough Edges: On the Transnational Foundations of Avant-Garde Performance," in *Not the Other Avant-Garde: Transnational Foundations of Avant-Garde Performance*, ed. James Harding and John Rouse (Ann Arbor: University of Michigan Press, 2006), 18–40.

8. Harding, "From Cutting Edge to Rough Edges," 24.
9. Ibid.
10. Jennifer Hyndman, *Managing Displacement: Refugees and the Politics of Humanitarianism* (Minneapolis: University of Minnesota Press, 1994), 44.
11. Alain Badiou, *Ethics: An Essay on the Understanding of Evil*, trans. Peter Hallward (London: Verso, 2001), 9.
12. James Thompson and Richard Schechner, "Why 'Social Theatre'?" *TDR* 48.3 (Fall 2004): 13.
13. Sonja Arsham Kuftinec, *Theatre, Facilitation, and Nation Formation in the Balkans and Middle East* (New York: Palgrave Macmillan), xiv.
14. Ibid., 2.
15. See also Julie Salverson, "Performing Emergency: Witnessing, Popular Theatre, and the Lie of the Literal," *Theatre Topics* 6.2 (1996): 181–191; and "Change on Whose Terms? Testimony and an Erotics of Injury," *Theater* 31.3 (2001): 119–125.
16. Jacqueline Lo and Helen Gilbert, "Toward a Topography of Cross-Cultural Theatre Praxis," *TDR* 46.3 (2002): 39. See also Rustom Bharucha, *The Politics of Cultural Practice: Thinking Through Theatre in an Age of Globalization* (Hanover, NH: University Press of New England, 2000).
17. Of course, ethnography cannot be so easily separated from activism, as Nancy Scheper-Hughes notes in "The Primacy of the Ethical," *Current Anthropology* 36.3 (1995): 409–420.
18. Kuftinec, *Theatre, Facilitation, and Nation Formation*, 4.
19. See Seyla Benhabib et al., *Another Cosmopolitanism: Hospitality, Sovereignty, and Democratic Iterations*, ed. Robert Post (Oxford: Oxford University Press, 2006), for a discussion of Kant's categorical imperative as it intersects with human rights.
20. Erik Ehn, "A Space for Truth: Meditations on Theatre – and the Rwandan Genocide," *American Theatre* 24.3 (March 2007): 36.
21. Ibid.
22. Philip Gourevitch, *We Wish to Inform you that Tomorrow We Will be Killed with Our Families: Stories from Rwanda* (New York: Farrar, Straus & Giroux, 1998); Samantha Power, *A Problem from Hell: America and the Age of Genocide* (New York: Harper, 2003).
23. These remarks were made on July 16 at the Kigali Memorial Center.
24. Ehn, "A Space for Truth," 72. Ehn's concept of "witness by proxy" differs from Primo Levi's use of the term for survivors of the Shoah. In *The Drowned and the Saved*, trans. Raymond Rosenthal (New York: Summit Books, 1986), Levi insists that the only "true" witness is a dead witness (83), and even survivors such as himself "speak in their stead, by proxy" because, by virtue of their survival, they did not experience the extent of the horror (84).
25. July 18, 2007.
26. These remarks were made during a morning gathering at Hotel Tech in Kigali on July 27.
27. Kalisa made these remarks at the end of our visit to Gahanga on July 17.
28. The phrase "radical passivity" does not come directly from Levinas's works; he uses terms and phrases such as "passivity…more passive than every passivity" ("Four Talmudic Readings," 49), "an extreme passivity" (109), a "deathlike passivity" (124), a "hyperbolic passivity" (49). My use of the

phrase is influenced by Thomas Wall's *Radical Passivity: Levinas, Blanchot, and Agamben* (Albany: SUNY Press, 1999).

29. Peter Benson and Kevin Lewis O'Neill. "Facing Risk: Levinas, Ethnography, and Ethics," *Anthropology of Consciousness* 18.2 (2007), 33–34.
30. Emmanuel Levinas, *Otherwise Than Being or Beyond Essence*, trans. Alphonso Lingis (The Hague: Martinus Nijhoff Publishers, 1981), 127.
31. Ibid., 104.
32. Wall, *Radical Passivity*, 53.
33. Ibid., 54.
34. Ibid., 56
35. Slavoj Žižek, "Neighbors and Other Monsters: A Plea for Ethical Violence," in *The Neighbor: Three Inquiries in Political Theology*, ed. Žižek et al. (Chicago: University of Chicago Press, 2005), 139.
36. Ehn, "A Space for Truth," 72.
37. Kinyarwandan word for "foreigner," usually with connotations of being European or European-American.
38. July 21.
39. *Gacaca* is the local justice system for genocide suspects. *Gacaca* trials have been held once a week throughout the country for the past few years.
40. Žižek, "Neighbors and Other Monsters," 138.
41. Theatre of the Opppressed can be loosely defined as a highly participatory methodology of theatre practice that aims to liberate marginalized and oppressed people through a series of embodied, interactive exercises that seek to analyze and deconstruct structures of power. See Augusto Boal, *Theatre of the Oppressed*, trans. Charles A. and Maria-Odilia Leal McBride (New York: Theatre Communications Group, 1985), for an introduction to the field.
42. See Chantal Kalisa, "Theatre and the Rwandan Genocide," *Peace Review* 18.4 (2006): 515–521, for a discussion of how Koulsy Lamko from Chad introduced TO techniques to the university's Center of the Arts (517–518).
43. Ehn, "More Life."
44. Ehn offered these comments at the California Institute of the Arts in Valencia (Jan. 24, 2008). See http://2wiki.theatercalarts.com/index.php?title=Arts_in_the_One_World#Key_ideas (accessed Sept. 25, 2007).
45. "Peace by Artful Means," Australian Broadcast Corporation, broadcast on Sept. 17, 2006. Transcript available at http://www.abc.net.au/rn/encounter/stories/2006/1739042.htm (accessed Sept. 25, 2007).
46. Ibid.
47. Immanuel Kant, *To Perpetual Peace: A Philosophical Sketch*, trans. Ted Humphrey (Indianapolis: Hackett Publishing, 2003).
48. Jacques Derrida and Anne Dufourmantelle, *Of Hospitality: Ann Dufourmantelle Invites Jacques Derrida to Respond* (Stanford: Stanford University Press, 2000), 49.
49. Ibid., 55.
50. Ibid., 77.
51. July 20.
52. Jacques Derrida, *Adieu to Emmanuel Levinas*, trans. Pascale-Anne Brault and Michael Naas (Stanford: Stanford University Press, 1999), 51.

53. Simon Critchley alludes to the masochistic potential of Levinas's demand. See *Infinitely Demanding: Ethics of Commitment, Politics of Resistance* (London: Verso, 2007), 11.
54. I borrow this phrase from Michael Taussig's *Shamanism, Colonialism, and the Wild Man: A Study in Terror and Healing* (Chicago: University of Chicago Press, 1986), 121ff.
55. Critchley, *Infinitely Demanding*, 42.
56. Badiou, *Ethics*, 45.
57. Ibid., 47.
58. Ehn, "A Space for Truth," 73.
59. Ehn, *Maria Kizito*, in *The Theatre of Genocide: Four Plays about Mass Murder in Rwanda, Bosnia, Cambodia, and Armenia*, ed. Robert Skloot (Madison: University of Wisconsin Press, 2007).
60. IGSC website at http://www.igscrwanda.net/en/index.php/ (accessed Sept. 10, 2008).
61. Ehn, "A Space for Truth," 73.
62. See Nigel Eltringham's *Accounting for Horror: Post-Genocide Debates in Rwanda* (London: Pluto Press, 2004), 69–79, for the controversy surrounding the terms "Hutu moderates" and "the Tutsi genocide."
63. See "The Rwandan Patriotic Front," in Alison Liebhafsky and Alison Des Forges, *Leave None to Tell the Story: Genocide in Rwanda*. Human Rights Watch, 1999. Available online at http://www.hrw.org/reports/1999/ rwanda/. See also "Ten Years Later," which was added to the report in April 2004, available through the same link (accessed Sept. 10, 2008). Nigel Eltringham refers to numerous human rights reports in his own discussion of RPA abuses: *Accounting for Horror*, 101–110. A sense of the controversy can be gleaned from Didier Goyvaerts's review of *L'Afrique des Grands Lacs: Annuaire 1996–97*, ed. Stefaan Marysse and Filip Reyntjens, *African Affairs* 97 (Oct. 1998): 577–578; and Reyntjens's response, "A Dubious Discourse on Rwanda," *African Affairs* 98 (Jan. 1999): 119–122.
64. Amnesty International and Human Rights Watch have published several reports in recent years that document repressive tendencies of Kagame's government. For a summary, see the report on Rwanda in *Amnesty International Report 2008: The State of the World's Human Rights*, available online at http://thereport.amnesty.org/eng/regions/africa/rwanda (accessed Sept. 10, 2008). See also Filip Reyntjens, "Rwanda, Ten Years On: From Genocide to Dictatorship," *African Affairs* 103 (2004): 177–210; and Helen Hintjens, "Post-Genocide Identity Politics in Rwanda," *Ethnicities* 8.5 (2008): 5–41.
65. Giorgio Agamben, *Remnants of Auschwitz: The Witness and the Archive*, trans. Daniel Heller-Roazen (New York: Zone Books, 2002), 13.
66. See Helen Hintjens, "Post-Genocide Identity Politics in Rwanda," *Ethnicities* 8.1 (March 2008): 5–41.
67. Agamben, *Remnants of Auschwitz*, 14.
68. Critchley, *Infinitely Demanding*, 55.

4

The Living Theatre's Arrested Development in Brazil: an Intersection of Activist Performances

Cindy Rosenthal

> Liberating tendencies
> Playing out physical possibilities that lead
> To hopefulness
> to inventiveness
> to certain states of mind
> that will lead to
> revolutionary
> consciousness
> We set a vector in which
> A direction is established that leads inevitably
> To certain choices later on.
>
> – Judith Malina[1]

> In the Festival de Ouro Preto, our only scene was our exit.
>
> – Judith Malina[2]

I

The Living Theatre's creative process and praxis were radically trans-formed in 1970, when co-directors Judith Malina and Julian Beck "set a vector" with "The Living Theatre Action Declaration" and journeyed to Brazil, where they finally answered their own question: "How do you get out of the trap?"[3] Breaking free of the constraints of "bourgeois" theatre practice at last, in Brazil the Living Theatre revised its troupe structure and collective creation process to include collaboration with poor and working-class people and moved their performances outside traditional theatres and into the streets.

No performance collective is more emblematic of "The Movement" and the revolutionary fervor of the 1960s than the Living Theatre. After a highly publicized New York City trial for tax evasion and impeding the duties of a federal officer in late 1963, the Living Theatre began a four-year self-imposed exile in Europe. The troupe was constantly on the move. The Living Theatre developed *Mysteries and Smaller Pieces*, *Frankenstein, Antigone,* and *Paradise Now* while touring from European city to European city. The unruly tribe of performers and their mates, friends, and family (forty adults plus nine children) often lived hand to mouth, but managed to survive by maintaining a tightly packed touring schedule, which included performing at commercial theatres and arts festivals, all carefully arranged by co-director Beck. *Paradise Now,* touted as the LT's first truly collective creation, premiered in France amidst the tumult of student and worker uprisings in May 1968. The Living Theatre declared (and many in their audiences concurred) that this piece marked a major break with all theatre work/experiences that had come before.

Although *Paradise* was organized via a chart or "map," the piece was meant to be an "open" text. The chart, which was included in the program and in the published text of *Paradise Now,* is an ornately detailed line drawing of two human figures, which map the "rungs" on the voyage for actors and spectators towards the Beautiful Non-Violent Activist Revolution. Nonetheless, when the LT returned to the U.S. with their four-part repertory (September 1968–March 1969), performing in cities and on college campuses, *Paradise Now* seemed totally out of touch with the U.S. political scene (activists in New Haven, Chicago, Berkeley, and elsewhere decried the LT's pacifism as naivety and passivity).[4] At Yale, early in the tour, co-director Malina posed a key question: "If the audience is already radicalized...how can you serve the revolution?"[5] Yet, Beck and Malina were unable or unwilling to re-vision their text as "guerrilla" theatre, highly visible, attention-getting, activist performance in public places, despite their anarchist rhetoric. The LT co-directors stated that they were limited by their "heaviness," their "history," their "being a big establishment." They felt they lacked the flexibility and mobility to fundamentally, significantly change.[6] They were trapped.

Fissures within the company deepened in the aftermath of the tumultuous, dispiriting, and financially disastrous U.S. tour. For the first time in the twenty years since the Living Theatre began, the company split apart. In the summer of 1969, discussions that began in Morocco culminated in a historic meeting on the boat that took the group to Italy for the final tour of its four-part repertory. Living Theatre members agreed that the company had begun to resemble the very institutions they were fighting against. In January, Beck distributed a new manifesto, "The Living Theatre Action Declaration":

> The Living Theatre doesn't want to be an institution anymore...all institutions are rigid and support the Establishment....Abandon the theatres. Create other circumstances for the man in the street. (The theatre buildings belong to those who can afford to get in: all buildings are property held by the Establishment by force of arms. Inside they speak in a code of things which are neither interesting to the man on the street nor in his interest.) Create circumstances that will lead to Action, which is the highest form of theatre we know.[7]

Part of creating such circumstances was the founding of a new, twelve-member performance activist group that Malina and Beck called the "action cell." The cell sought to create performances with "the man on the street"; specifically, impoverished, low-wage working-class communities in the Third World – a first for the company. The "Action Declaration" set out a plan to "serve the revolution" in new ways: "The Living Theatre doesn't want to perform for the privileged elite anymore because all privilege is violence to the underprivileged."[8] Following this tenet, the LT would no longer charge admission to its performances. The troupe would not perform in theatre buildings. This was the company's first published response to many of the accusations flung at the group during and after performances of *Paradise Now* and *Mysteries* on the U.S. and European tours. The company divided into four cells, although the plans and programs of the other three cells are not as clear in the "Action Declaration." The document briefly states that one group will stay in Berlin to pursue environmental theatre work, another will travel to London to continue to perform *Paradise*, or a version of it, and another cell would journey to India, where "their purpose was spiritual."[9] In sum, the LT radically changed the way it moved.

Malina and Beck and their core group first went to Paris where they met with Ze Celso, the director of Brazil's Teatro Oficina, who had fled troubles with his company at home to find solace with like-minded political artists in Europe. Celso had never seen a Living Theatre production, but was impressed with Malina and Beck's reputation and rhetoric and recognized them as potential comrades in political theatre work.

In conversations with Celso, Beck and Malina became convinced that Brazil was the proving ground they were seeking. Celso and members of Teatro Oficina shared an interest with the LT in Bertolt Brecht's plays and theories. Celso's work was also influenced by Grotowski's ideas. However, the political theatre Celso and his company engaged in did not involve crossing class lines and working with the poor, as was the Living Theatre's intent with their new work. Ultimately, Celso's invitation to the Living Theatre to come to Brazil did not result in creative collaboration between the two companies, and the support that Celso implied with his invitation did not materialize when the LT arrived in Brazil.[10]

Since 1964, Brazil had been under a military dictatorship; virulent attacks on those suspected of subversion and the surveillance of artists, students, and leftist intellectuals escalated in 1968 and through the 1970s. Theatre practitioners, university professors, and poets "disappeared."[11] Beck and Malina had been warned of the terrors and tortures of the oppressive Brazilian military regime, but they immediately made plans to launch their "Campaign" (referred to in their notebooks, journals and scripts as "CAMP"). The action cell members learned Portuguese (with varying degrees of success), purchased plane tickets to Brazil, and read Frantz Fanon and Gilberto Freyre. In the late 1960s and early 1970s, Fanon's work was widely read by members of the revolutionary Left in the U.S. and Europe, particularly by Black Power militants. Although Beck and Malina were against the violence espoused by Fanon, their interest in *The Wretched of the Earth* stemmed from their desire to learn more about the poor people in the *favelas*, the shantytowns of Brazil, where they hoped to co-create community performances. Malina and Beck shared Fanon's belief in the inner transformation that comes about through the struggle of the oppressed against their oppressors. In Freyre's *Casa Grande e Senzala*, they learned of the complex dynamic between masters and slaves in Brazil, a powerful image that became central in the construction of their *Legacy of Cain* plays, beginning with their favela performances (as we shall see).

The possibility of performing in a national Brazilian festival was the motivating factor for settling the company in Ouro Preto in early spring 1971. The Winter Festival, scheduled to open on July 1, was an annual gathering of leftist students and radical artists. Ouro Preto was an old mining town with impressive baroque architecture in the center of the country. Through their connections with Teatro Oficina and Brazilian actress/producer Ruth Escobar, the LT hoped to raise funds and support for their new work in Brazil. However, the kind of political theatre described in the Action Declaration – street performance focusing on community-based work in the favelas – was not like anything Celso and the Teatro Oficina actors had witnessed or participated in before. Celso had recently garnered critical attention with his production of Brecht's *Jungle of Cities*; performing leftist theatre in theatre buildings for middle- and upper-class audiences was the extent to which most of his company members were willing to go.[12] For that matter, the LT's research for their campaign, which involved interviewing residents of the shantytowns and engaging with them actively in street performances, was an entirely new practice for the Living Theatre as well.

Though Malina and Beck were interested in establishing more sub-stantive ties with artists in the Third World and actively recruited members of Oficina to join them in their work, this kind of community process and "flamboyant" presentation of brightly clad, free-spirited performers in public spaces was deemed too risky by Oficina actors, some of whom had witnessed or experienced the brutality of Brazil's military regime first-hand.[13] Creative collaboration between Teatro Oficina and the Living Theatre did not come to pass, but Celso set up a series of meetings between members of his company, the LT, and Los Lobos, a company Celso had invited from Buenos Aires, Argentina. However, Los Lobos's work had very little in common with the goals and practice of the Living Theatre, Malina and company members Ilion Troya and Tom Walker told me. "[Los Lobos] were not at all political," declared Troya, a Brazilian university student who joined the Living Theatre after one of their first street performances in Rio Claro, outside of São Paulo. "They were interested in doing physical exercises for the exercises' sake, which Judith and Julian had no patience for."[14] The failure to collaborate didn't happen due to a lack of effort. The meet-ings went on for weeks, and the talk went on for hours each night. Celso and his company proclaimed that they were also interested in "raising consciousness" and, in opposition to the anarchist-pacifist views of the Living Theatre, Celso underlined the potential of armed struggle, echoing Fanon, as a means of liberating the oppressed classes, "the poorest of the poor," who were the Living Theatre's sought-after co-collaborators. On the other hand, Freyre's classic text, *Casa Grande e Senzala*, had an enormous impact on the Living Theatre and specifi-cally on their campaign research in Ouro Preto. In constructing the first of their favela projects, Beck and Malina wrote, "The theme of *The Legacy of Cain* is the condition of slavery in which all men find them-selves. ... The purpose of the spectacle is to suggest liberating attitudes and actions."[15]

Undaunted by Celso's lack of support and follow-through, but with the loan of a van from Ruth Escobar, the Living Theatre struck out on their own with their campaign work. The troupe created a new research-team structure, which consisted of pairs of performers – a Brazilian Portuguese speaker (Troya or Ivan Araujo, the latter a young, working-class intellectual from the northeast region of Brazil) who was partnered with a European or U.S. member of the Living. The pairs moved throughout the shantytown every afternoon, taking extensive notes and tape recording their discussions with the working poor and with peasants. At night, the company came together and collectively created performances based on their research. "ACTION 4: The Favela Speaks" is a section of the Favela Project #1 script in which the tape-recorded voices of members of the community fill the air from a central location, answering questions such as, "What is Life?" "What is the favela?" "What do the people want?" At the same time, performers took on the Master/Slave pose, where the Slave kneels before the Master and the Master stands over the Slave, the Master's foot on the Slave's back. Next, according to the script, "the performers slowly move out of their Master/Slave poses and face each other. Slowly they remove their blindfolds."[16]

Fulfilling one of the "Action Declaration's" tenets, the LT performed exclusively outside theatre buildings. Beck and Malina detail the radical re-visioning of their troupe's use of performance space in the narrative written into the opening section of the Favela Project script, "Christmas Cake for the Hot Hole and the Cold Hole":

> There are plays being done in the schools, the churches, the hospitals, parks, construction sites, stores, amusement parks, cemeteries, transportation terminals, docks, mines, railroad tracks, and wherever else the geography of the city allows for theatrical expression. Outside of the towns and cities, plays are planned for agricultural workers and migrants to be performed where the work is done and where they live.[17]

Creating street theatre that was based on movement, gesture, and ritual – and less on text – seemed like the right idea in Brazil at the time. At the very least, it allowed the LT to move without gathering unnecessary attention. Non-verbal work was the LT's strategy for avoiding the watchful eyes of the military regime. A written or spoken script that communicated a radical perspective invited police response, while fleeting images and stage pictures that moved quickly remained open to interpretation and were seemingly less dangerous and incriminating. Like Teatro Oficina, the LT knew better than to perform political texts or present work that was overtly consciousness-raising, as seen in this excerpt from the last section of the favela play:

ACTION 11: THE RITE OF LIBERATION:

The rite is performed by the inhabitants of the community where the play is being performed. As the inhabitants of the community untie the performers the performers begin a chordal sound of joy and liberation. They invite their liberators to join them in making this sound.

ACTION 12: THE CAKE:

The treasure box is opened. It reveals a large rectangular layer cake, one meter wide by two meters long. The cake is decorated with icing so that it looks like the face of a 10,000 *cruzeiro* bill [the equivalent of one dollar in the U.S.]. The cake is cut and eaten while the performers and the people talk together.

ACTION 13: RETURN:

Within a week following the performance, the performers return to the favela to talk with the people again.[18]

Emphasizing community participation in the rituals and including simple movements and gestures rather than overtly political texts seemed to be the safer choice.

The goal was escaping the censors.

But on July 1, the day of the opening of the Winter Festival, the Living Theatre was busted, their house in Ouro Preto ransacked, and the company hauled off to jail.

II

The imprisonment of members of the Living Theatre by Brazilian authorities sparked an international outcry, raising global awareness about the repressive Brazilian regime and building a sense of community and outrage among the international radical avant-garde. This was spurred by a petition and public relations campaign begun by company members Pierre Biner in Paris and Stephen Ben Israel in New York, with help from U.S. poet/activist Allen Ginsberg, a long-time friend of Beck and Malina's. Hundreds of petitions circulated among artists and intellectuals across the U.S. and Europe, signed by, among others, John Lennon, Yoko Ono, Jean Genet, John Lindsay, Bob Dylan, James Baldwin, Mick Jagger, Jane Fonda, Jean-Paul Sartre, Edward Albee, Samuel Beckett, and Arthur Miller. According to Tom Walker, a significant portion of the signatures were forged initially, because of Ben Israel's rush to gather an impressive group of names and send them out quickly. Purportedly, Ben Israel was granted permission by the celebrities (Fonda, Lindsay, Jagger, and a few others) to use their "signatures" after the fact.

In Minas Gerais, the Brazilian state in which Living Theatre members were imprisoned, a media frenzy was underway. Beck, Malina, and their company had become instant celebrities. Beck and Malina's photos were on Brazilian television and in the newspapers daily, as were photos of Beck's eighty-year-old mother, Mabel, and Malina and Beck's three-year-old daughter, Isha – Mabel having flown to Brazil to visit her son and rescue her granddaughter. Theatre had an impact. The company's release from jail after seventy-one days behind bars and their expulsion from Brazil by President Emilio Garastazu Medici were the result of growing embarrassment for Brazilian authorities, as letters and telegrams on the LT's behalf poured in from top government officials, human rights organizations, and artistic and intellectual leaders from around the world.

Malina and Beck's status as U.S. citizens vociferously supported by a stellar cast of international friends and fans around the world underlined their privileged status and ultimately saved them. This was not the case for Malina and Beck's young Brazilian cellmates in the Department of Political and Social Order (DOPS) prison, which was notorious for torturing its prisoners. Their cellmates were student radicals who, unlike Malina and Beck, had no voice in the media or limelight to illuminate their cause. "Our passports protected us," Malina declared, referring to the jailed American and European Living Theatre members in the Brazilian prisons. A troupe of anarchist artists that not long before had railed against the authority of the state in the company's loud declaration in *Paradise Now*, "I'm not allowed to travel without a passport," was suddenly staking its well-being and survival on the power of their American passports and on the powerful voices of the international elite – artists/activists who came to their defense, whose high-priced, inside-the-theatre work the Living Theatre had loudly rejected. Ivan Araujo, the youngest member of the troupe *was* tortured, however. He was taken by guards into a back room the first night the company spent in the DOPS prison and asked questions about the company's marijuana use and if any Living Theatre members had guns. Electrodes were placed on his fingertips and genitals. Even under torture, he refused to reveal any information about the company. Troya and Walker both mentioned that not only race but class may have been an issue in Araujo's case. "There was a difference in status – Ivan was lower working class," Troya told me. Unlike Troya (also Brazilian), Araujo was dark-skinned (and "the prettiest," according to Tom Walker, a white American, who joined the company in Brazil after seeing their work in the U.S.[19]).

The Living Theatre's experiences in Brazil provide an interesting framework for analysis of the intersection of race, nationality, and power, especially when comparing Araujo's encounters on the streets and in the jail with African American Living Theatre member James Anderson's experiences in and out of jail in Brazil. Troya spoke of Freyre's notion of "racial diversity" – Brazil had a largely mixed-race population because, throughout its history, white "masters" had bred with and then often married their black slaves. However, in Troya's view, "racial issues were suppressed in the period that the Living Theatre was in Brazil":

> Racism in Brazil is very much like racism throughout Latin America. There are many shades of tan. But in Brazil, money made more of a difference. Class issues were more important. Ivan was of a lower class. Now, Jimmy Anderson felt that Brazil was a paradise for him. American blacks loved Brazil – they were not discriminated against; they were in a privileged class position, had status, because of their American passports.[20]

In Troya's view, the Living Theatre's breach of class boundaries in Ouro Preto played a role in their arrest. He told me, "Our dinner table was open to the poorest of the poor every night."[21] This nightly "exchange situation" between the Living Theatre and the low-wage workers and peasants in Ouro Preto threatened the stability of existing class hierarchies. The Living Theatre, behaving as true "vectors of the radical," raised the possibility of a fundamental change in societal structure, which local authorities would not tolerate.

III

The title of this essay, "The Living Theatre's Arrested Development in Brazil," refers to the unfulfilled promise of the Living Theatre's *Legacy of Cain* project, which was launched and then almost immediately curtailed with the company's arrest. Inspired by the writings of Sacher-Masoch on sado-masochism and parallel themes in Gilberto Freyre's work on masters and slaves, Beck and Malina's goal with *The Legacy of Cain* was to collectively create 100 or more plays with low-wage and impoverished communities. These plays would explore the relationships between oppression and freedom, domination and submission, by focusing on what they perceived to be the masochism of the oppressed classes bowing to the sadistic pressures and pleasures of their all-powerful leaders. The Mother's Day play, *Six Dreams about Mother*, premiered on May 12, 1971, comprised of texts created by the people of the favelas. The performance was presented in a community gathering place that was not a theatre, and, for the first time in the history of the LT, the entire work was performed by an ensemble of community members combined with LT actors. *Six Dreams about Mother* was actually the second of the *Legacy of Cain* plays, but it was a true departure from prior collective creations and an important step for the company. The central performers, in this case, were schoolchildren, their mothers (the wives of miners and foundry workers in the nearby community of Saramenha), and the teachers at the school, who had first suggested the Mother's Day play.

The play tells the dream-stories of six children and their progression from being cared for and controlled by their parents to the dramatic climax, the point at which their ties to their mothers are broken, represented by the tearing of crepe paper streamers that had attached them to their mothers. Dozens of other children lay on the floor, with Living Theatre actors among them, representing the "sea of dreams." They cried "Fly, fly, fly!" and, in the spirit of *Paradise Now*, the child-dreamer would then "fly" by leaping out onto the sea and be received and carried by those below, whose arms and legs were waving and would support them.

According to Malina and Walker, this is where the problems began. Among the spectators at rehearsals and the performance were emissaries from the local parish priests who strongly disapproved of the scene that required little girls to lie on the floor and wave their legs in the air. Despite the great success of the play among the children, their families, and teachers (Troya told me that all the children wanted to fly, and, as a result, the play went on for hours[22]), Malina believes this section of the play provoked the censors and caused the *denuncio* against the Living Theatre, which resulted in their arrest. But legs waving in the air were not the only concern; an enthusiastic mother reported to a teacher and a parish priest (in statements that were later used against the Living Theatre) that, after working with the Living Theatre, her child was never the same again. Most importantly for the purpose of this essay, with the

Mother's Day play, the Living Theatre was not "high-brow" preaching to the already converted. The LT had finally created the community-based performance they had been dreaming about for years. But the bust, Troya explained, aborted the process: "We were finally beginning to have a relationship with the miners and factory workers – we were at last getting to know the poor people and the working class."

What finally motivated the arrest remains unresolved – though all evidence points to the issue of movement. Was it because they broke class boundaries in their day-to-day encounters with the poor people of Ouro Preto? Was it the "questionable" movements of the "impressionable" schoolchildren, the libratory, anti-authoritarian spirit and aesthetic of the Mother's Day play? Or was it the overall lifestyle of the Living Theatre compared with the lifestyle of the conservative inhabitants of the small Brazilian town? As Troya put it, the LT company was a group of long-haired men living in one house with a group of colorful, good-natured women – signifying sexual liberation and political freedom. In his view and Walker's, it was the LT's lifestyle that scared away many of the Oficina performers as well. Troya notes that the timing cannot be overlooked, either. It was the opening day of the Winter Festival. By making an example of the radical foreigners, the government broadcast a clear warning to any activists/artists who might have political upheaval in mind.[23] But again, who knows? The LT's house was open to everyone. Members of the Living Theatre attest that the two kilos of marijuana in blue plastic bags that were brought to the police station had been planted under their house – most likely by the police themselves. From the time of their arrival in Brazil, the company had assiduously left no trace of their marijuana use anywhere. Malina told me with a sly smile, "The cops never found our own stuff – we were very careful. But in the toes of our sneakers, some marijuana made it out of the country and was smoked back in New York."[24] But one thing is without doubt: the Living Theatre had become too active, too mobile a minority in the community. Members of the company believed they had adequately covered their "vanguard traces," but authorities – the church, the military – were deeply concerned about reverberations in the foundation of the power structure. The Living Theatre had to be stopped and quickly. Planting two kilos of marijuana on their premises would do it.

IV

Judith Malina is, and always has been, an obsessive self-documentarian. At age eighty-two, she still painstakingly notes each day for posterity where she was, whom she saw, and what she did, minutely scrawling one line a day, allowing one page of lines per month. These pages of months are arranged in order year by year and then collected in one of two large loose-leaf binders on a shelf in Malina's apartment. Each day, Malina also records her feelings and endeavors in a more conventional, detailed diary. The two kinds of documents are meant to relate to and reflect each other. Often they do not. The "Action Declaration" may have radically changed the rules for members of the LT for how, where, why, and with whom the company created performances, but Malina's ritual act of documenting each day did not change – until the bust.

Malina's explanation for why she documents her life as she does, day to day, alludes to her sense that "all the world's [her] stage": "The numbering of the days is a way of understanding the significance of our life ... after all, *we're offstage right away* ... It has a ritual value."[25] One of the characteristics of ritual, as Barbara Meyerhoff defines it, is that "the subject ... is acting with awareness. He has taken the activity out of the ordinary flow of habit and routine, and performed the gesture to arouse in himself a particular attitude, demonstrating that his actions mean more than they seem."[26]

There are only a few times in Living Theatre history that both of Malina's chronicles cease altogether. One instance occurred when Malina and Beck did jail time in January 1964, charged with impeding the duties of a federal officer and tax evasion at the Living Theatre's 14th Street Theatre. The second was in July 1971, when Malina, Beck, and members of the Living Theatre were jailed in Brazil. When she resumed her writing in jail, however, the writing changed. As she told me, "This is the one time I wrote a diary that was not true."[27] While in jail, Malina carefully crafted a strategic performance of self. This was a complicated strategy, as she was forced to employ self-censorship in the form of necessary, frequent omissions, which she claims never to have had to do in her diaries before.

This self-censorship was a political tactic; her construction of a surrogate in the diary was perfectly in keeping with the iconic "Antigone attitude" she subscribes to, taking huge risks in standing up against the state. Malina translated, adapted, and directed the LT production of Sophocles's *Antigone* and performed the title role from 1967 onwards. Thomas Postlewait describes this kind of self-denial as common practice in the autobiographies of women in theatre, drawing on Patricia Meyer Spacks's delineations, which include a "subordination or loss of self in the cause for something larger than yourself."[28] Malina made the decision, at the suggestion of Brazilian journalist Paulo Narcisio (who courageously put his own career and safety on the line by assisting her), to perform "herstory" on the pages of *Estado de Minas*, a conservative Brazilian newspaper, knowing her diaries would have a wide, even an international audience.

By necessity, there were omissions throughout Malina's published journal accounts. Any mention, for instance, of the horrific sanitary conditions in the jail or the ongoing torture of her Brazilian cellmates was impossible; government censors would have clamped down and there would have been immediate, perhaps even lethal, repercussions. But Malina was fulfilling a higher purpose here, which Spacks identifies as a common feature of women's autobiographical writings.[29] Her goal was to avoid the censors and to reach the empathic hearts and minds of her readers/audience in the hope of saving the lives or lightening the sentences of her fellow prisoners in the Brazilian jails.

Malina knew her readers/audience expected drama – indeed, melodrama – and she was ready to take on or create the necessary roles and scenarios in her journal performances. Malina's accounts wax poetic about the youth, beauty, and love-lives of her cellmates and delved deep into her own pain and guilt at being separated from her young daughter. Thus, it is no surprise that there are very tangible traces of theatre and the theatrical in Malina's published diary accounts of the days she spent in the Brazilian jail. Herbert Blau writes, "There is nothing more illusory in performance than the illusion of the unmediated...and it is theatre, the truth of illusion, which haunts all performance."[30] Malina knew this; autobiography, as performance, is no different. "Social context," Postlewait tells us,

> always shapes the writer's discourse. It also shapes the audience's response. We need to consider, therefore, not only the writer's idea of the audience's expectations...but also the reader's ideas of the actor and the theatre that contribute to the ways the work was read...what was the rhetorical contract between the writer's report of personal information and the reader's trust, between calculated self-revelation and reader sympathy?[31]

In an elaborately coded way, Malina attempted to "talk back" to the Brazilian authorities and to the oppressive violence of the militaristic state. Malina carefully constructed her "double" – the diary persona – with the intention of illuminating in an apparently "unmediated" way prison life for her Brazilian reading audience. The cause célèbre was the plight of her young cellmates. Circulating among her reading audience,

Malina's powerful "herstories" had an impact on societal attitudes and, as a result, in small, yet significant ways, prison conditions (food, sanitation, hygiene) improved, at least temporarily.

As part of her prison journals' theatricality, Malina cast two of her fellow prisoners in the roles of Romeo and Juliet. The "Juliet" was Malina's twenty-year-old cellmate, a student radical named Maria Dalcia. In the sections of her diary published by the newspaper, Malina describes the young woman's loveliness, her hopes and dreams, and, especially, her stolen kisses in the prison corridor with another young prisoner, whom Malina called her "Romeo." What Malina did not describe in her diaries was what happened on Thursdays in jail, when Dalcia would return from being tortured upstairs. "I never wrote about that in the diary," Malina said. "I never wrote that my cellmate Dalcia's finger nails were torn out and that I bandaged them for her again and again."[32] On July 27, 1971, Malina wrote that Dalcia returned from "upstairs" and had to immediately pack her few possessions. "Dalcia said she had to leave and kept repeating, over and over, 'Horrible, horrible.' I gave her a little silver keepsake of mine. I cried." Malina said she was the last person to see Dalcia alive.[33] That information, too, was omitted from the diary. The Living Theatre never staged the details of Dalcia's torture in any of their work, but they did depict the scene and the mechanisms of Ivan's torture in *Seven Meditations*, another play in the *Legacy of Cain* cycle.

Self-censorship became an increasingly common – but never any less difficult – practice for the LT. Because of the torture scene, the Living Theatre was censored and arrested when they performed *Seven Meditations* in Italy years later. As time went on, the company (and especially Malina and Beck, as they grew older) often had to make decisions to avoid arrest, which involved changing the staging or language in their works – softening or cutting sections – in order to satisfy local authorities. "It's always an interesting choice when you have to say no," Malina told me, referring to her self-censorship in the diary and also to the company's self-censorship in performances. She recalled one instance when the group made the decision to cut the overtly sexual movements in the Bacchus Dance in *Antigone*. She told me:

> We sat around for four hours, talking about whether, if we can't do the action, should we do the play. So the question is – do we want the audience to see the play without that minor action? Or, do we want to take a stand on censorship? Maybe we can even get it in the papers if we roar loud enough. Do we want to lose the money, because we

won't be paid if we don't do the play? There are many economic, political, artistic, and ethical questions.[34]

The question of efficacy and audience response with regard to Malina's diary performances in Brazil was especially loaded. Malina made a specific, calculated choice that she believed best served her pacifist political agenda – for one, she followed the instructions of Dalcia's lawyers in her careful construction of her story in the published diary, hoping to help her cellmate's case by generating awareness of and interest in her fate. "People read Judith's diary in the paper like a real-time soap opera," Troya told me. After her release from jail, Malina learned that Dalcia had been transferred to another prison and murdered.

Yet, in Troya's mind at least, a profound shift had occurred in Brazil's "culture of silence."[35] Brazilians in Minas Gerais, if not yet in the global network of sympathizers, had become aware of the tragic lives of young people behind bars. "Judith got the word out," Troya declared. In 1971, even the conservative newspapers in Brazil were censored, so the media leapt at the chance to use the Living Theatre's unique situation to "showcase" the wide-ranging abuses and brutal oppression in Brazil. "Finally people in and outside of Brazil could talk about it," he told me. "The Living Theatre's imprisonment was a hugely important thing."[36]

V

In the long life of the Living Theatre, how does the Brazil period fit? What impact did the work in the favelas have on the re-configured troupe, The Living Theatre Collective? (This was the name of the group, circa 1971, when the company returned to the U.S.) Assessing the Brazil work prior to the company's imprisonment, Malina wrote a glowing account in a letter to one-time LT member, actor-director Joe Chaikin: "Here there has been glory and suffering. Much has happened. Changes. And the best work of our lives ..."[37] When the Living Theatre was released after two and a half months in jail, the company returned to the U.S. and relaunched its intensive campaign for the *Legacy of Cain*. In 1972, with the support of a $5000 National Endowment for the Arts grant, the company settled in Brooklyn, New York, and worked on three community-based performances including pieces about vegetarianism and eating locally produced food. With the award of a $22,500 Mellon Foundation Grant, the company moved to Pittsburgh, Pennsylvania, where they continued to collectively create *Legacy of Cain* street performances for two more years (1974–75), including "The Money Tower," which the company erected and broke down outside the gates of the steel mills, as workers left their shifts.

When asked to reflect on the company's experience in Brazil in November 2009, Malina immediately responded, "It was a glorious success. I don't know exactly what we did for them, but I know what they did for us. Brazil inspired us. Inspired the work. Being part of the struggle there changed us. Living with our beautiful revolutionary cell mates...this changed us a lot."[38] Actively moving (and moving quickly) across the intersections of race, class, and power in Brazil, staging the complex dynamic between masters and slaves in collaboration with peasants, children, and low-wage workers and activists, the Living Theatre learned valuable life and work lessons. The urgency and vitality of these vanguard exchanges carried the Living through the next five years – until funding ran out and financial woes pressured the Living Theatre to make choices that thrust them back onto the touring circuit, playing to the radical middle and upper classes in European theatres and at festivals once again. Though this period was brief, it carries with it valuable lessons of the challenges, possibilities, and ultimate limits of the Living Theatre as a vector of the radical.

Notes

1. Random Brazilian Notes: Ouro Preto (JM's notebook): Folder 4, box 49, The Living Theatre Record, Lincoln Center, NYC.
2. Jail Diary, July 10, 1971: Folder 2, box 50, The Living Theatre Record, Lincoln Center, NYC.
3. "The Living Theatre Action Declaration," *The Living Book of the Living Theatre* (Greenwich, CT: Graphic Society, 1971), n.p.
4. See *Yale/Theatre* 2.1 (Spring 1969); Renfreu Neff, *Living Theatre: USA* (Indianapolis and New York: Bobbs Merrill, 1970); and Cindy Rosenthal, "Living the Contradiction: The Living Theatre's Revision of Sophocles' *Antigone* through Brecht and Artaud" (Dissertation: New York University, 1997).
5. Malina, quoted in *Yale/Theatre* 2.1 (Spring 1969): 32.
6. Beck and Malina, quoted in Aldo Rostagno, *We, The Living Theatre* (New York: Ballantine, 1970), 46.
7. "The Living Theatre Action Declaration," n.p.
8. Ibid.
9. Ibid.
10. Based on author's interviews with Ilion Troya (June 22, 2009, June 29, 2009, Aug. 23, 2009), Thomas Walker (Aug. 24, 2009), and Judith Malina (Nov. 4, 2009 and June 8, 2009).
11. See Fernando Peixoto, "Brazilian Theatre and National Identity," *TDR* 34.1 (Spring 1990): 66, for a discussion of the brutal treatment of Brazilian artists during this period. In an interview, Ilion Troya told me of the torture of

artists and intellectuals, including university professors he knew (Aug. 23, 2009).

12. From author's interviews with Troya (Aug. 23, 2009) and Walker (Aug. 24, 2009).
13. Living Theatre performers Troya and Walker spoke to me about Brazilian theatre artists' accounts of torture. Peixoto's "Brazilian Theatre and National Identity" mentions Celso's imprisonment in 1971 (66). In a recent documentary film on Teatro Oficina, Celso speaks of being tortured as well ("Cantando o Corpo Eletrico," video.google.com [accessed November 10, 2009]).
14. Author's interviews with Troya (June 22 and 29, 2009).
15. Folder 2, box 49, Living Theatre Record, Lincoln Center Library for the Performing Arts, NYC.
16. Ibid.
17. Ibid.
18. Ibid.
19. From author's interviews with Troya (Aug. 23, 2009) and Walker (Aug. 24, 2009).
20. Interview with Troya (Aug. 23, 2009).
21. Author's interviews with Troya (June 22 and 29, 2009).
22. Author's interview with Troya (June 22, 2009).
23. Ibid.
24. Interview with Malina (June 8, 2009).
25. Phone interview with Malina (Aug. 5, 1995), emphasis mine.
26. Barbara Meyerhoff, *Remembered Lives* (Ann Arbor: University of Michigan Press, 1992), 130.
27. Interview with Malina (Nov. 4, 2008).
28. Thomas Postlewait, "Autobiography and Theatre History," in *Interpreting the Theatrical Past*, ed. Thomas Postlewait and Bruce McConachie (Iowa City: University of Iowa Press, 1989), 264.
29. Ibid.
30. Herbert Blau, "Universals of Performance," *Sub-stance* 37–38 (1983), 143.
31. In Postlewait, "Autobiography and Theatre History," 258.
32. Interview with Malina (June 8, 2009).
33. Interview with Malina (Nov. 4, 2008).
34. Interview with Malina (June 8, 2009).
35. Interview with Troya (Aug. 23, 2009).
36. Author's interviews with Troya (June 22 and 29, 2009).
37. Malina's letter to Joe Chaikin, Folder 8, box 49, Living Theatre Record, Lincoln Center Library for the Performing Arts, NYC.
38. Interview with Malina (Nov. 5, 2009).

Part II
Translations

5
Introduction

Jean Graham-Jones

Perhaps no other radical performance theorist-practitioner embodied the mobility of radical cultural exchange more than the recently deceased Augusto Boal. The founder of a movement whose participants today reside in over forty countries, this theatrical "Johnny Appleseed"[1] led a life he himself acknowledged as marked by a cyclical nomadism.[2] Born in Rio de Janeiro, Brazil, to Portuguese immigrant parents, Boal wrote and directed his first play in New York while studying chemical engineering at Columbia University. Upon returning to Brazil, he forfeited a career as chemist to work in the theatre and spent the next fifteen years primarily at São Paulo's Teatro de Arena (1956–1971), (co-)authoring and directing plays, leading writers' and actors' workshops, staging agit-prop theatre in the countryside, touring abroad, and taking the initial steps towards what became known as the "Theatre of the Oppressed" (TO). Kidnapped during dictatorship by the military, tortured, and released after three months, Boal went into exile to neighboring Argentina, where he continued to develop his practice with local actors while traveling to other parts of Latin America. Argentina's own 1976 military coup forced Boal to continue his exile elsewhere: first relocating to Lisbon, Portugal, before settling in Paris, where he was appointed to a post at the Sorbonne in 1978. In Paris, Boal established a Theatre of the Oppressed Center, and, from 1981 to 1985, the organization ran international Theatre of the Oppressed festivals. Even after his return to redemocratized Brazil in 1986, until his death, Boal continued his highly peripatetic lifestyle, traveling around the world speaking to audiences and leading workshops (often at TO centers and other collectives with whom he maintained long-term relationships), as he continued to base himself in Rio, where he directed theatre and opera, served a three-year term as one of that city's elected city council members (employing a performance technique he called "legislative theatre" to enlist audience-citizens in helping to create municipal laws[3]), and ran the local TO Center.

Boal's writings have circulated even more fluidly and broadly than their author. Autobiographical anecdotes are repeated and revised in different books.[4] Exercises are reworked and redefined in different translations and editions, proper nouns are varyingly spelled,[5] and even translations in the same language exhibit great variety.[6] Boal's first book, *Theatre of the Oppressed*, now translated into at least twenty-five languages, saw its original publication (in Buenos Aires) in a Spanish translation of the original Portuguese manuscript (itself a compilation of various essays written in the 1960s and early 1970s). The 1992 English-language *Games for Actors and Non-Actors* constitutes, in translator Adrian Jackson's own words, "a conflation of two books" published in France – *Stop! C'est magique* (1980) and *Jeux pour acteurs et non-acteurs* (1989) – with "liberal additions and alterations as Boal has added examples of his latest ever-developing practice."[7] Indeed, one might argue that it would be impossible to approximate a full picture of Boal's work without reading his writings in at least two or three languages and multiple editions.

What we know today as Theatre of the Oppressed stands as but one example of transformative performance phenomena that move across, problematize, and sometimes blur linguistic, media, and ideological boundaries. Boal's life itself poses a complicated example of precisely the "mobile materialities" this compilation of essays seeks to document and examine in the avant-garde. As the three essays contained in this section on "Translation" demonstrate, translation has never been the simple "carrying across" from one language to another as the word's etymology might suggest, nor do the standard categories of translation, adaptation, and version accurately account for translation practices' inherent complexities. These are rendered perhaps even more complex in the transnational avant-garde, to which Boal most certainly belonged, as do the artists discussed in these three essays.

A troubling of our conventional understanding of translation – as inter-linguistic transformation based on a word-for-word substitutive correspondence – underpins Siyuan Liu's essay, " 'Powerful Disseminator of Radical Thought': Anarchism and the Introduction of Modern Western Theatre to China." Liu traces the remarkable and intricate translation paths of an early twentieth-century revolutionary Western dramatic text (Polish playwright Leopold Kampf's *On the Eve*) that went on to become a "harbinger of theatrical and political revolution" in China. Through multiple translations and translocations, a relatively unknown radical Western play was transformed into a canonical text of the modern Chinese theatre. Liu's essay clearly evinces how central a more ample concept of translation is to our understanding of the vectors of the transnational avant-garde.

This is a vectoring far more complicated than suggested in traditional translation theory's principle of *adequatio* (equivalence and fidelity to the original). Indeed, any such assumed translational commonality and equality is undermined from the start by linguistic and cultural difference. Theatrical translation in performance, in which the presence of two or more texts is often sensed, exemplifies what many theorists, going back to at least Walter Benjamin's 1923 essay,[8] consider a translation's (and a translator's) unavoidable relationality. Translation's relationality contributes to our reflections on one of the enduring features of the theatrical avant-garde: its insistence on the performance potential inherent in seemingly all mediums.

In "Translation, Typography, and the Avant-Garde's Impossible Text," Sarah Bay-Cheng encourages us to rethink our understanding of translation by considering how a published text performs. She does so by taking a closely relational look at Tristan Tzara's now-classic Dadaist play *Le Coeur à Gaz* through its 1946 published edition's illustration of tumbling letters performing the "DANCE of the gentleman who falls from a funnel in the ceiling onto the table." Her detailed examination of Tzara's image and its relationship to both the dramatic text and its potential in performance suggests an elision of textual and performance bodies and serves as yet another example of translation's twists and turns. Bay-Cheng's essay explicitly demonstrates that the process of translation transcends simple considerations of language, culture, and medium.

Such a complex process understandably carries an ethical and political burden. As Sandra Bermann notes, "If we must translate in order to emancipate and preserve cultural pasts and to build linguistic bridges for present understanding and future thought, we must do so while attempting to respond ethically to each language's contexts, intertexts, and intrinsic alterity."[9] Certainly, many scholars appear to have disregarded the mobile materiality of Boal's performance praxis in their search for a "Boal method." Rarely meriting analysis (or even mention) have been Boal's stagings of classical and contemporary plays and operas, and his strong commitment to and modification of Stanislavskian directing principles have typically been glossed over in yet another comparison of Boal and Brecht (or debate over Boal's "revolutionary" ideology). Boal and his translators possibly encouraged such solidifying systematization by, for example, subtitling 1995's *The Rainbow of Desire* as "the Boal method of theatre and therapy." Yet, over the years, Boal recycled and modified terms, leading more than one scholar to confuse the early Arena and Theatre of the Oppressed theatrical form known as the "joker system" with the TO workshop joker-difficultator.

Even those who trouble the idea of a Boal "method" tend to reinforce simplistic Northern/Southern hemispheric and First/Third World divisions. David S. George, in his drastic (and informative) revision of Boal's history with Teatro de Arena, suggests that much of the Theatre of the Oppressed's techniques have their roots not in Latin American populist theatrical experimentation, but in the experimental U.S. theatre of the 1930s and 1960s. George asserts, "Theatre of the Oppressed... is mostly a first-world phenomenon that now has little connection with Brazil."[10] Mady Schutzman, in an attempt to reinterpret Boal's work in its "changing context," cautions the reader against transposing "a 'third-world' aesthetic of resistance to a 'first-world' aesthetic of self-help... North America represents the oppressors, the privileged colonialists, and Latin America represents the disempowered oppressed."[11] Both George and Schutzman present evidence of Boal's "ongoing cultural exchange,"[12] but it is a process far more fraught than suggested in the simplistic North/South homogenizing one sees in their essays. It is high time that a study of Boal and the Theatre of the Oppressed fully acknowledged TO's multiple and continuous translocations and translations.

I recognize a similar concern for the politics of revolutionary translation in the section's final essay. In "Maoist Performativities: Milton Acorn and the Canadian Liberation Movement" Alan Filewod provides a cautionary reconsideration of the Canadian New Left's two best-known Maoist organizations and their translations of Chinese Red Guard performance styles. The essay suggests how fluid and distortional seemingly fundamental tenets of radical politics can be when moving from one culture to another. The conflation and confusion of class, ethnic identity, historicity, and national allegiance on the part of the CLM constitute a strikingly negative example.

If, as the editor of this essay collection argues, the avant-garde is neither a movement nor a tendency but rather a "vector of the radical," then translation-as-material-exchange plays a critical role in such vectoring. Translation in performance, precisely because of its complexity and fluidity of engagement, carries the potential for countering, or at the very least complicating, the limitations of unidirectionality or, worse still, the absence of movement. Thus the inclusion of a section dedicated to translation in a collection of essays on the theatrical avant-garde is not only welcome but, I believe, obligatory.

It is telling that all three essays included in this section demonstrate the protagonic role played by publication in the translational movements of the avant-garde. All three further support editor Mike Sell's call to understanding the avant-garde not as a singular movement or unitary tendency but rather as multiple critical, radical perspectives. Key to a critical vanguard is translation, and key to translation is an understanding and recognition of its ever-shifting, productive relationality.

Notes

1. See Bruce Weber, "Augusto Boal, Stage Director Who Gave a Voice to Audiences, Is Dead at 78," *New York Times*, May 9, 2009 (accessed May 22, 2009).

2. In his autobiography, *Hamlet and the Baker's Son*, Boal notes, "Much of my life divides into fifteen-year periods: fifteen years with Arena, fifteen in exile, fifteen back in Brazil." See Boal, *Hamlet and the Baker's Son: My Life in Theatre and Politics* (London and New York: Routledge, 2001), 140.

3. For an account of Boal's activities as *vereador*, see his *Legislative Theatre: Using Performance to Make Politics*, trans. Adrian Jackson (London and New York: Routledge, 1998).

4. One of the most provocative examples is one of Theatre of the Oppressed's most legendary: Arena's early 1960s trip to northeastern Brazil, where Virgílio, a peasant farmer inspired by the cast's "revolutionary" performance, invited Boal and company to join the farmers' armed struggle against a local "colonel" and where Boal learned of liberation theology from a Catholic priest, Father Batalha. Most commentators of this frequently recounted experience emphasize the former's invitation to the near exclusion of the latter's commitment, which – judging from the extended dialogues reported by Boal in his autobiography – made an equal if not greater impression. As Boal notes: "Virgílio and Father Batalha changed my conception of art. At least, my way of seeing theatre and its usefulness." See Boal, *Hamlet*, 193–200 (200).

5. A particularly egregious misspelling is Adrian Jackson and Candida Baker's consistent misidentification of Chiclayo, Peru as Chacalayo in the Routledge English-language edition of *Hamlet*. Readers will recall that Chiclayo was the site of one of Boal's first experiments with "Forum Theatre." See Boal, *Hamlet*, 200–7.

6. Consider, as illustration, the Spanish-language editions of Boal's *Theatre of the Oppressed*. The 1980 Mexico City edition (*Teatro del oprimido 1: Teoría y práctica, Nueva Imagen*) begins with the 1974 Buenos Aires edition's final chapter and ends with a 1977 interview between Boal and Emile Copfermann. Subsequent Mexico City editions of other earlier Boal books also incorporate material from Boal's European experiences. See Gerardo Luzuriaga, "Augusto Boal: Transferir al pueblo los medios de producción teatral," in *Introducción a las teorías latinoamericanas del teatro* (Puebla, Mexico: Universidad Autónoma de Puebla, 1990), 147–197.

7. Adrian Jackson, "Translator's Introduction," *Games for Actors and Non-Actors* (London and New York: Routledge, 1992), xix.

8. Walter Benjamin, "The Task of the Translator," in *Illuminations*, ed. Hannah Arendt, trans. Harry Zohn (New York: Schocken Books, 1968).

9. Sandra Bermann, "Introduction," in *Nation, Language, and the Ethics of Translation*, ed. Sandra Bermann and Michael Wood (Princeton: Princeton University Press, 2006), 7.

10. David S. George, "Theatre of the Oppressed and Teatro de Arena: In and Out of Context," *Latin American Theatre Review* 28.2 (Spring 1995): 49. Campbell Britton's reassessment of TO's development within the 1954–79 Brazilian theatre context provides a more productive view of Boal's relationship to Brazilian theatre. See Britton, "Politics and Performance(s) of Identity: 25 Years of Brazilian Theatre (1954–79)," in *A Boal Companion: Dialogues on Theatre and Cultural Politics*, ed. Jan Cohen-Cruz and Mady Schutzman (New York and London: Routledge, 2006), 10–20.

11. Mady Schutzman, "Brechtian Shamanism: The Political Therapy of Augusto Boal," in *Playing Boal: Theatre, Therapy, Activism*, ed. Mady Schutzman and Jan Cohen-Cruz (London and New York: Routledge, 1994), 139.

12. Ibid., 153.

6
"Powerful Disseminator of Radical Thought": Anarchism and the Introduction of Modern Western Theatre to China

Siyuan Liu

> An adequate appreciation of the tremendous spread of the modern, conscious social unrest cannot be gained from merely propagandistic literature. Rather must we become conversant with the larger phases of human expression manifest in art, literature, and, above all, the modern drama – the strongest and most far-reaching interpreter of our deep-felt dissatisfaction.
>
> – Emma Goldman[1]

The connection between avant-garde theatre and anarchism has long been part of the narrative of avant-garde studies, Matei Calinescu claiming, "Bakunin's anarchist maxim, 'To destroy is to create,' is actually applicable to most of the activities of the twentieth-century avant-garde,"[2] Christopher Innes declaring, "The identifying signature of avant-garde art, all the way back to Bakunin and his anarchist journal *L'Avant-Garde* in 1878, has been an unremitting hostility to contemporary civilization."[3] Yet, for the most part, avant-garde scholars have let this connection stay at the theoretical level without further probing the connection between anarchistic beliefs and theatrical activities.

One way to connect the dots is offered by Mike Sell in what he calls "Critical Vanguard Studies" – "an approach that understands the avant-garde less as a substantive entity in history than as a critical perspective from which to examine sites, moments, creations, and critical methods that are 'political' in some fashion, that challenge in some way the structures and flows of power."[4] This desire to go beyond a concept of the avant-garde as "a substantive entity in history" is underscored by James Harding and John Rouse's call for avant-garde studies "to move from a Eurocentric to a transnational conception of the avant-garde – one which recognizes that the sites of artistic innovation associated with the avant-garde tend to be sites of unacknowledged cultural hybridity and negotiation."[5] In particular, Harding has challenged avant-garde theatre scholars to consider distinct theoretical areas as rough edges: "contested edges, simultaneous articulation, and apostate adaptations."[6]

A perfect example of challenging both the political and theatrical "structures and flows of power" is one of the first Western plays directly translated into Chinese, which also happened to be a political blast in celebration of the Russian revolutionaries of 1905. Written by the Polish playwright Leopold Kampf (born 1881, date of death unknown), *On the Eve* is about Russian revolutionaries bombing a governor in 1905. It eventually gained "great popularity among radical audiences of that time" because of its message of sacrifice for the violent resistance to tyrannical government.[7] Banned in Germany, prohibited in Russia, snubbed in the United States, it eventually shocked Paris in 1907 and, from there, was introduced to China by one of the first Chinese anarchists just three years before the 1911 Revolution. Once in China, it became a vanguard text in both political and theatrical spheres, a carrier of new ideological and dramatic systems. It injected a drastically different approach into the fledgling modern Western-style theatre movement as well as being an inspiration to a generation of Chinese youngsters in their pursuit of political and cultural revolution. The purpose of this essay is to explore the dynamics behind the play's transformation from a conventional theatrical piece with radical ideas in the West to a harbinger of theatrical and political revolution in China.

On the Eve in the United States and France

A three-act play, *On the Eve* concerns anti-government activists in a big city – presumably Moscow – in Russia in 1905. The first act takes place in the home of Anton and Sofia, where they and a girl named Marsha secretly print an anti-government newspaper. They host an older revolutionary named Tantale, who has just escaped from prison in St. Petersburg. A young man named Vasili enters, bringing a fake passport and much-needed lead types for the press. We then see the heroine of the play, Anna, a young woman who serves as a messenger. Tantale, excitedly waving a pistol, gives a long speech about torture and heroics in the prison and then, exhausted, goes to another room to rest. His radical rhetoric is picked up by Vasili and then Anna, who call for the "bell of blood" to toll throughout Russia. Eventually, unable to suppress his obvious love for Anna, Vasili runs out of the apartment, followed by Anna. Soon afterwards, the press is discovered by the police, who arrest Anton, Sofia, and Marsha, while Tantale commits suicide. Terror reigns in the following act, which starts with a group of revolutionaries, including Vasili, discussing their captured comrades, prompting Vasili to volunteer to assassinate the governor. After his wish is granted, Anna enters, and the couple express their love for each other, only to be interrupted by gunshots outside against a strike procession. The act ends with the two in anguished, exhausted embrace. The final act takes place in Anna's aunt's house, located close to the opera house. Anna has taken refuge here, since her uncle is an important government official and staunch anti-revolutionary. After he and another woman leave for the opera given by the governor for his mistress, Vasili emerges to tell Anna that he will be one of the bombers. He asks Anna to bring a light to the window, if the governor comes his way, as a signal to ignite the bomb. After much anguish, he breaks free from Anna and runs away. At the opera's end, we see the aunt standing in front of the window talking about the governor coming their way. Anna at first hesitates, but eventually lights a candlestick and holds it to the window. We hear a loud explosion, which brings Anna to the floor. In the final tableau, she shakily stands up:

> Anna: (*Opens her eyes wide; as if waking suddenly out of a deep slumber – looks round and frees herself from Varvara's arms. Slowly.*) Yes, Aunt – right you are. (*Drying her eyes; quickly.*) Tears are foolish. – (*Bitterly.*) Tears are foolish. – (*Harshly.*) Tears are foolish. – (*Shouts.*) The bells must ring – Onward, brothers! – (*With pain.*) The bell of blood ... (*Shouts in transport.*) Onward – Onward – (*The curtain falls quickly. Still audible.*) Onward – Onward ... [8]

Reactions to the play and its productions in Europe and the United States were decidedly mixed, from outright ban to enthusiastic embrace, from denunciation of it as bombastic propaganda to praise for it as high tragedy. All these reactions are related to the socio-political and theatrical conditions in different countries. Originally written in German in 1906 as *Am Vorabend*, the play proved too inflammatory for German authorities, who banned its productions in Berlin and Hamburg. Judging from the author's self-selected review excerpts from German newspapers that accompany the English version of the play, it seems to have garnered enthusiastic response from the audience and critics. For example, Berlin's *Vossische Zeitung* wrote that the play "seizes, clutches, captivates, lashes the nerves. ... It is of uncommonly powerful effect."[9] The *Berliner Börsen-Courier* reports that the audience received it "with great enthusiasm" and "were visibly held under the spell of the tragedy, from which a special charm, a powerful effect, emanated."[10]

With no prospect of future production in Germany, Kampf took it to New York where its first mention in the *New York Times* was a March 2, 1907 advertisement using its English title *On the Eve* and marketing it as a "drama of the Russian Revolution" "prohibited throughout Europe."[11] A week later, the paper carried a brief report, "Women Hear Kampf's 'On the Eve.'" The event was held in the Hotel Astor where the play was read by the actress and playwright Edith Ellis Baker, with Kampf as "the only man present."[12] Apparently, Kampf had held similar events before, since a copy of the English version held at the Kent State University Library has the author's autograph to Martha S. Bensley and is dated "New York, 22, II, 07." Despite such efforts, Kampf was unable to find a producer for the English version and had to settle for a limited audience when it was staged by the German Company at the Irving Place Theatre. It took place on December 20 and 21, 1907 as a benefit for the Relief Society for Russian Revolution Victims.

Kampf later attributed the lukewarm reaction to American fear of the play's subversive spirit,[13] which is certainly possible. On the other hand, a couple of reviews of the script published before the German Theatre production also suggest distaste for what reviewers considered its propagandist slant. This criticism was expressed in Emma Goldman's anarchist magazine *Mother Earth*, which called the script "disconnected, incoherent, and, worse than all, bombastic," despite the reviewer's wish "that we could speak only in praise of this work, because of its purpose."[14] The reviewer was particularly offended by the play's rhetoric and Anna's repeated usage of "the bell of blood," which "shock[s] all our sense of the fitness of metaphors" and "spoils even the last really heart-rending scene where the maddened girl repeats in her raving..."[15] If we consider that Goldman was herself an advocate of modern drama as the expression of deeply held discontent, that her partner and frequent contributor Alexander Berkman had just served a fourteen-year imprisonment for the attempted murder of Henry Clay Frick, and the magazine's regular features on modern dramatists from Ibsen to Hauptmann, the criticism carries an aura of political and dramatic authority. Of course, we should remember that, as radical as Goldman's group was, the general situation in the United States in 1907 was far different from Tsarist Russia or even from pre-First World War continental Europe, which was politically far more volatile. This might explain the heavy-handedness of the German censors and the much more receptive Parisian audience and critics.

While the play's political intent was obvious on stage, its emotionally powerful scenes often were overwhelming, as evidenced by the *New York Times* review of the German Theatre production of December 20 and 21. Like the script reviews, it starts with faulting the piece for containing "the usual shortcomings of plays written with a purpose": "Were there less feeling, and were the dramatist more detached from actual sympathy with the cause his play is designed to aid, there would probably be more of active drama, less of propaganda."[16] The reviewer proceeds to laud a number of scenes, especially the climax, calling it the "most intense moment in the piece – and a dramatic situation combined with excellent acting serves to make it highly effective."[17] In what amounts to the highest dramaturgic compliment of the time, the reviewer writes that "Dr. Kampf has developed this struggle with skill in a gripping, [Victorien] Sardou-like situation."[18]

A contributing factor to the production's success was the German actress Hegwig Reicher, who, on leave from the Municipal Theatre of Frankfurt, played Anna "with a magnificent suggestion of genuine enthusiasm."[19] Reicher's father, Emanuel Reicher, had introduced Ibsen to German theatre and she had appeared in *Hedda Gabler*, *A Doll's House*, and *Rosmersholm*.[20] Obviously, this training in modern performance was an asset for her portrayal of Anna. In return, Anna became a launching pad for Reicher's acting career in the United States, as she was invited two years later to reprise the role for a Broadway production of Martha Morton's unfortunately melodramatic adaptation. Still, a *New York Times* review hailed both Reicher and the play's "revolutionary spirit" as a "triumph." She moved "impressively, eloquently, sincerely" through the play's emotional ups and downs, despite the fact that its "tremendously moving and appealing scenes" and its "sense of clear purpose" were made a "massacre" in the adaptation.[21]

If Kampf's American sojourn was not entirely satisfactory, it catapulted him back to Europe where a sensational run in Paris established the play's stature as a preeminent work of revolutionary heroism and, more germane to this essay, launched the path to the play's immeasurable influence in China. Its Paris version opened in the Théâtre des Arts on December 23, 1907, with a translation by Robert d'Humières and direction by Armand Bour. Titled *Le Grand Soir*, the production received immediate rave reviews and ran for over a hundred performances. Critics hailed it as an inspired tragedy that perfectly blended classical narrative with the message of sacrifice, one even comparing the heroes to Christian martyrs.

The exact route for its movement from New York to Paris remains ambiguous. A 1908 article that accompanied the play's French translation notes that the production at New York's German Theatre was seen by the director of Paris's Théâtre des Arts, who happened to be passing through New York[22] while the *New York Times* review of the 1909 Broadway production credited the idea of bringing the play to Paris, to "Gertrude Andrews, an American woman resident in Paris," also inspired by the German Theatre production.[23] Regardless of who brought it to Paris, a bigger problem lies in the opening date of the German Theatre production – December 20, 1907 – only three days before its Paris debut. Given the length of translation and rehearsal, the link between these two productions is tenuous at best.

The Paris Group and the Chinese translation

Regardless of how it happened, the play struck a profound chord with a group of Chinese anarchists in Paris who were in deep mourning for two Chinese revolutionaries executed by the Qing government. The assassin was Xu Xilin (1873–1907), who killed the governor of Anhui province En Ming in July 1907. Soon afterwards, one of his comrades, Qiu Jin (1875–1907), the female president of their training base, the Datong School, was arrested and executed. Their heroism inspired the young Chinese anarchists in Paris to advertise and report the Théâtre des Arts production and subsequently translate the play into Chinese. Xu and Qiu became instant folk heroes not only for their rebellious actions but also for their legendary bravery in the face of death. In July 1907, they had planned joint uprisings in the southern provinces of Anhui, where Xu was the superintendent of the police school in Anqing city, and Zhejiang, where Qiu was principal of the Datong School in Shaoxing city, which Xu had founded in 1905 for the sole purpose of training anti-Qing soldiers. Their original plan was to kill provincial officials during the police school's commencement. However, the government learned about the preparation and moved the ceremony up to July 6. Xu and his followers still managed to assassinate Governor En Ming and waged a four-hour battle in Anqing until Xu's capture and hasty execution the following morning. According to legend, Xu laughed at the threat of having his heart cut out – which was presumably carried out after his execution – and insisted on being photographed before his execution so as to leave a smiling image to posterity. Meanwhile, Xu's brother betrayed

Qiu Jin. Government soldiers surrounded the Datong School on the fourteenth and captured her. She was executed the following morning and left only a line of poem after her interrogation: "The autumn wind and autumn rain agonize one to death" (*Qiufeng qiuyu chou sha ren*). Its patriotic and anguished sentiment for a severely weakened nation reverberated among revolutionaries in and outside China. The line also underscored her fame as "the Female-Knight of Mirror Lake" (*Jianhu nüxia*), reinforced by a well-known picture of her as a beauty holding a dagger. Their execution and heroism struck a deep chord not only throughout China, but in Chinese communities around the world, including Paris, where a number of Chinese anarchists had started a weekly anarchist magazine, *The New Century* (*Xin shiji*) on June 22, 1907. The news of their executions was published on August 24 and received overwhelming coverage, prompting a sustained focus on assassination as one of the most feasible means to effect change in government.

Immersed in the anarchist teachings of Mikhail Bakunin, Peter Kropotkin, Pierre-Joseph Proudhon, and others, which they translated into Chinese, the Chinese anarchists are known historically as the Paris Group, one of the two – together with the Tokyo Group – pioneering groups of Chinese anarchists.[24] The best-known members of the group include Li Shizeng (1881–1973), Wu Zhihui (1865–1953), and Zhang Jingjiang (1877–1950). Li was the son of a prominent Qing official and nephew of Prime Minister Li Hongzhang. Zhang was the son of one of Shanghai's wealthiest merchants, the owner of the famous Zhang Garden. In 1902, both of them left China as attachés to China's new ambassador to France. There, Zhang started a trading business between Europe and China and used his fortune to finance the revolutionary Sun Yat-sen. Li studied agriculture for three years at the École Practique d'Agriculture du Chesnoy in Montargis (Loiret) and then, in 1906, continued research on soybeans at the Institut Pasteur. It was there that Li read the writings of Jean Baptiste Emile Vidal and Kropotkin and befriended prominent anarchists Paul Reclus and Jean Grave, publisher of the French anarchist magazine *Temps Nouveaux*, which inspired the Chinese anarchists to publish their own magazine of the same title, although they preferred to use the Esperanto – the anarchist lingua franca – *La Novaj Tempoj* as their Western language title. It started publishing in June 1907 with financial backing from Zhang and featured articles and translations from Li and Wu, who had been in exile in London since 1903.

As mentioned, one of the hot issues for the magazine's readers was the role of political assassination, which anarchists in general supported as

an alternative to militant nationalism. In his July 27 answer to a letter by a reader with the pen-name Military Soul (*Junhun*), Li Shizeng
elaborated his belief that all military forces are oppressive and therefore
evil and that the goal of anarchism was to eliminate such forces and
authorities. Therefore, he continues, the basis for the anarchist opposition to militarism is not based on its use of force, but rather its usage by
the powerful throughout the world to protect their own interests. Since
the elimination of the powerful through assassination is for the common good, there is no reason to oppose it simply because of its radical
use of force.[25]

After the news of Xu and Qiu's executions arrived in Paris, the magazine devoted several issues to their memorial services, biographies,
writings, speeches, and commemorative essays. It also added regular
features touting international assassinations. It was in one of these
articles, published on December 21, 1907, that Li Shizeng wrote about
the Russian revolutionary Sophia Perovskaya and her role in the assassination of Alexander II. Identifying her as an anarchist, Li notes that
she was born into a high-ranking official's family, but became a fer-
vent opponent of the government. Furthermore, she played exactly
the same role as Anna in the assassination plot: "It was Sophia who
gave the signal for bombing Alexander II's train by lifting her veil."[26]
Calling Russian assassinations "the greatest tragedy of the new century," Li devotes the rest of the piece to introducing the Théâtre des
Arts production occurring that weekend. Without seeing the play but
apparently having read about the similarities between it and the assassination of Alexander II, Li calls the play "the greatest achievement of
revolutionary drama."[27] He then discusses its censorship in Germany
and similar efforts by the French Interior Ministry at script examination, rejected by the theatre on the grounds of legal authority. Yet Li
still worries that the government could follow the German precedent,
which only shows that "there is no good or evil between governments,
as they are all obstacles to freedom."[28]

Li concludes by contrasting the efficacy of modern Western drama to
what was commonly believed in intellectual circles to be the weakness
of Chinese theatre:

> Theatre is in fact a measurement of ideology and zeitgeist, which is
> also why it can be a trend-setter. With China's despotic system and
> superstitious population, its stages are usually filled with loyalty or
> superstition, causing what happened to the Boxers. As revolutionary
> unrest is growing in Europe nowadays, revolutionary plays are also

being staged. This proves that it is indeed true that theatre represents the level of development among peoples of the world.[29]

Here, Li is referring to the common idea that part of the blame for the Boxers' 1900 defeat by Western powers should go to their superstitious belief in their own power, overreliance on such theatrical conventions as costumes and spectacle for motivation, as well as outdated modes of combat using pre-modern weaponry. This sense of theatre being a reflection and trendsetter of a nation's evolution was reinforced by belief in the efficacy of Western realistic theatre in both staging contemporary events and advocating modernity.

Li's advertisement for *On the Eve* paid off. About a month later, *The New Century* published, over three issues, a reader's detailed report and enthusiastic reaction to the performance, thus providing insight into what the radical Chinese perceived in the play and a first-rate production of it. We know that the writer was a regular reader of *The New Century*, had seen dozens of plays in Europe, and saw *On the Eve* because of Li's advertisement, especially his assertion of the play's allusion to Sophia Perovskaya, which the writer calls into question. Nevertheless, he was so moved by the production's power that, as he wrote, "I never left my seat as the applauses [*sic*] almost deafened my ears and the tragic sorrow almost desiccated my tears. ... Among the dozens of plays I have seen since coming to Europe, I have never witnessed such a wonderful and moving play."[30] One of the most noticeable features of the review is the extent to which the writer was moved by the passion of the revolutionaries and the connections he made with their Chinese counterparts, particularly Xu and Qiu. One such example is Tantale's scene in Act One. Anxious and frail, he coughs constantly and gives a long account of his prison escape and the mental torture he had suffered by doubting and then affirming his comrade's truthfulness and bravery. Reenacting the comrade facing the guillotine, he screams "Long live social revolutions!" When asked about his passport, he brandishes a pistol and yells, "This is the best passport." From his entrance, Tantale's actions were met with reactions so enthusiastic that, the writer reports, "The applause was so loud it hurt my ears. It was most wonderful to see hundreds upon thousands of fair hands moving vehemently, which I have never seen in other theatres."[31] However, this rare reception may have had more to do with his stardom than that character's lines, an insider's knowledge the Chinese writer did not seem to possess. The minor role was played by a famous actor, Armand Bour, also the director of the production. What the writer responded to were the affinities between the Russian and Chinese revolutionaries. Indeed, the line between East and West and between stage and reality often seems blurred at times for the writer, as in the second act when the brutal suppression of the strikers' march reminded the writer of the massacre at Qiu Jin's Datong School. Then, in Act Three, when the heroine Anna and her aunt and other female sympathizers tearfully read about the torture of the revolutionaries, the writer is reminded of his own feelings reading about how Qiu's friend Wu Ziying collected Qiu's corpse for a proper burial.[32] This feeling of affinity was almost certainly one of the biggest reasons for Li's decision to translate the play into Chinese and its subsequent popularity in China. It also explains the writer's embrace of the final scene, echoing the praise of the Paris critics while contrasting the *Mother Earth* criticism. He reports that the same ending received "wild applauses and 'bravo, bravo' from everywhere in the house."[33]

There is no doubt that both Parisian empathy for the fate of Russian revolutionaries and a first-rate production contributed to the play's success, which in turn greatly influenced the young Chinese anarchists and convinced Li of its political and theatrical potential for translation. It also helped that Li knew the actress who played Anna's aunt, since she was a good friend of the anarchist geographer Élisée Reclus, one of Li's anarchist heroes whose family maintained close ties with Li and the Chinese anarchist movement for many years. It was through her that Li came to know the director of the Théâtre des Arts, who lent Li stage shots of the production for the Chinese volume, as well as Leopold Kampf, who wrote a preface for Li's translation.[34] In it, he entreats his Chinese readers to learn from the Russian revolutionaries and shed their blood for the sake of freedom:

I am very happy that my new play *On the Eve* has been translated into Chinese so that my Chinese friends will see my intentions. Nowadays, the world is as dark as midnight. It is not limited to Russia. The mission for our generation is to fight for changing this world. However, there is no freedom on earth that does not come with a price. To obtain it, we must pay a heavy price. The price of freedom is daunting for it demands no less than immeasurable blood. And this is the blood of the best among us. My Chinese friends, have you also fervently sought it? Have you also wiped your tears for their memory? My work only documents a very short period of history. The spirit of the Russian people's struggle over the past decades is beyond the reach of words. My Chinese comrades, do you grieve for them? And is your sorrow felt in solidarity with them?[35]

On the Eve in China

Kampf's call for his Chinese readers and viewers to join the Russian revolutionaries in the fight against oppression eventually found wide resonance in China both on stage and through pamphlets of Li's translation, which spread mainly through anarchist organizations. However, as a sign of its true vanguard status in both theatrical and political spheres, the impact of the play did not become obvious until a decade later. Theatrically, the decade after the play's translation was dominated by classical Chinese theatre and a hybrid form of new spoken drama known as *wenmingxi* (civilized drama) that was known for its melodramatic plot, use of scenarios and improvisation, and employment of remnants of Chinese theatrical conventions – singing and musical accompaniment, female personification, and role categories, among others. The most popular mode of staging Western plays was through adaptation instead of literary translation. The most popular European playwrights were romantic and melodramatic playwrights like Victor Hugo and Victorien Sardou.[36] *On the Eve* was not produced on the professional stage until after 1918,[37] when European realistic drama represented by Ibsen grabbed the imagination of Chinese intellectuals as the epitome of what Emma Goldman called "the strongest and most far-reaching interpreter of our deep-felt dissatisfaction."[38]

This quote comes from Goldman's "The Modern Drama: A Powerful Disseminator of Radical Thought," published in 1919 in the most influential magazine of the era, *The New Youth* (*Xin Qingnian*). Its Chinese version was translated by another anarchist, Yuan Zhenying, a senior professor at Beijing University who also wrote a biography of Ibsen and translated Goldman's "Marriage and Love" for the magazine. *The New Youth* holds a special place in modern Chinese theatre as the most potent advocate for a complete break from classical theatre and for the establishment of a modern Western-style Chinese theatre, owing primarily to its two special issues in 1918, one on Ibsen and the other on theatrical reform, as well as other writings and translations, including Goldman's essay, in which she argues that "the modern drama, operating through the double channel of dramatist and interpreter, affecting as it does both mind and heart, is the strongest force in developing social discontent, swelling the powerful tide of unrest that sweeps onward and over the dam of ignorance, prejudice, and superstition."[39] It was exactly this idea of theatre as the most powerful weapon against oppression and ignorance that best describes what reform-minded Chinese intellectuals advocated, exerting tremendous influence on generations of youth to come.

The late 1910s straddled the decline of *wenmingxi* and the rise of the more formalized *huaju* (spoken drama), the Western-theatre form as it is known today, which started in the early 1920s when Chinese students with professional theatre training returned from the United States and Europe. Disillusioned by *wenmingxi's* commercialism and lack of intellectual and ideological rigor, many young theatrical and political activists advocated the Amateur Theatre (*aimeiju*) movement, which had been part and parcel of the new Western-style theatre long before it became a movement.

The 1910s also happened to be the decade in which anarchism gained great momentum inside China and became the dominant radical ideology among intellectuals and youth, thanks in great measure to such groups as The New Century. It was under such circumstances that *On the Eve* thrived in China as both a political document and a play script whose production by amateur youth groups became a potent symbol of rebellion against an oppressive society. Such sentiment is best illustrated by the play's second translator, Ba Jin (1904–2005, originally Li Yaotang), who, in part thanks to the play, also became an ardent anarchist. His prolific writings about the suffering and rebellion of his generation earned him one of the highest places in the pantheon of modern Chinese literature.

Perhaps the most concrete evidence of the play's effect comes from Ba Jin's 1930 account of its life-changing effect on him:

> It was probably ten years ago when a fifteen-year-old boy found a little book. At that time, he had just embraced the ideal of loving mankind and the world. He had the childish illusion that a new society in which everybody is happy would rise with tomorrow's sun and that all evil would instantly disappear. Reading that little book with this state of mind, he was indescribably touched. That book opened a new world to him, unfolding in front of him the grand tragedy of a generation of youths in another country fighting for the freedom and happiness of the people. It was through that book that this fifteen-year-old boy had, for the first time, found the heroes of his dream and the cause of his life. He then introduced that book as a treasure to his friends. They even copied the book word for word. Since it was a play, they also performed it several times. That boy was I and that book was the Chinese version of *On the Eve*.[40]

Thus begins the preface to his 1930 Chinese version of *On the Eve*. (The translation was done two years earlier in Paris, but was lost when he mailed it to China.) Already an ardent anarchist in part because of his exposure to *On the Eve* and Peter Kropotkin's *An Appeal to the Young*, Ba's anti-authoritarian angst was rekindled after his arrival in Paris in February 1927 by the worldwide protest against the execution of the Italian-American anarchists Ferdinando Nicola Sacco and Bartolomeo Vanzetti. He wrote letters to Sacco before the execution and received a thankful and encouraging reply. He also wrote to Goldman and was immensely encouraged by her letters. He later referred to her as his "spiritual mother...the only person who understood my agony."[41] In fact, this renewed anarchist zeal served as the launching pad for his prolific writing career, starting from his choice of the pen-name Ba Jin, taken directly from Russian anarchists *Ba*kunin and Kropot*kin*. Many of his early characters are based on anarchist ideals and personalities. Another powerful influence was *On the Eve*, apparent in the semi-autobiographical "Torrent" (Jiliu) trilogy.

Often considered modern classics, *The Family* (*Jia*, 1933), *Spring* (*Chun*, 1938), and *Autumn* (*Qiu*, 1940) center around the awakening of a young generation in an extended autocratic family named Gao in the southeast inland Sichuan province, largely based on Ba Jin's own family. One of the crucial steps that facilitate their awakening was their own staging of *On the Eve*. Ba Jin features *On the Eve* most prominently in the second novel, *Spring*, in which several chapters are focused on a youth group's rehearsal and staging of the play, its enthusiastic reaction from the audience, and eventual banning by the police. In particular, the play has a central role in steeling the resolve of the main characters against their repressive family, one of them participating in the production and the other watching and reacting to it in a strikingly similar manner as the reader in the 1908 letter in *The New Century*.

That character is Gao Shuying, a seventeen-year-old girl who is being forced to marry a playboy simply because the young couple's parents are colleagues in the same law firm. She is a good friend of the three brothers from her eldest uncle's line, Juexin, Juemin, and Juehui. Juehui, based on Ba Jin himself, was the protagonist of the first novel, *The Family*, and has now escaped to Shanghai. The two rebels in *Spring* are Juemin, the second brother, and his girlfriend Qin, who is also a good friend of Shuying. Through the two of them, Shuying learns about their secret group and has a chance to watch their production of *On the Eve*, which becomes a turning point for her. In the end, with the help of Juemin, Qin, and Juexin, she escapes to Shanghai to join Juehui.

The episode involving *On the Eve* starts with Chapter Twenty-One, in which a group of young people form a group by the name The Egalitarian Society (Jun She) and decide to stage *On the Eve*, sent to them by Juehui from Shanghai with other anarchist pamphlets. Juemin agrees to play a minor role, but becomes hesitant on his way home, convinced that he is not ready for the discipline and sacrifice required by the secret society or the "ridicule and reprimand" from his uncles and aunts once they see him on stage. He decides to remain "a sympathizer" without participation in the Society or the play and will tell his friends the following day. But his plan is disrupted immediately after he sets foot inside his extended family compound. Trying to save a maid from humiliation by a couple of his younger cousins, he finds himself tricked by their mother, who, after hitting her own son in the face, accuses Juemin of brutality in front of his stepmother and Juexin. With Juemin insisting on his innocence, Juexin is reprimanded in front of their eldest uncle, now the de facto head of the family. By the end of the chapter, Juemin once again reverts: "He felt he was going to seek revenge not against one person but a regime. He thought proudly: 'I will join the Egalitarian Society; I will participate in *On the Eve*; and I will do everything they don't want me to do. Who cares what they will do to me?'"[42]

Later, in Chapter Twenty-Six, Shuying lies to her mother in order to watch the play with Qin. She is surprised to see many female students in the audience and excitedly asks about the actors, including the man playing Anna (women not being allowed on stage). Unlike the audience reaction in the Paris production that started with Tantale's entrance and Armand Bour's star power, here the reaction starts after his exit, when Vasili introduces "the bell of blood" which "should be struck louder and louder until our complete victory": "Immediately, applause arose from the pit. Shocked and with her heart pounding, Shuying turned to Qin, who was watching the performance with great excitement."[43] Next, Anna delivers the long and impassioned speech criticized in *Mother Earth* which ends again with the plea that the "bell of blood" must be heard everywhere since it is the only way to guarantee peace and happiness for future generations. In Ba's fictional world of backwater China, the excitement was palpable:

> "Can you hear it? Can you hear it? The sound of the 'bell of blood'?" Sofia suddenly asked with a serious expression.
>
> Immediately, the whole theatre turned quiet. Everyone was listening, trying to hear the sound of the "bell of blood."
>
> "Tomorrow," Anna suddenly yelled ecstatically onstage, sending a great shock to the audience.
>
> "Tomorrow the slavery system will be over," Marsha raised her head and spoke dreamily.
>
> Several people in the pit applauded.[44]

For the provincial Chinese audience of the late 1910s and early 1920s, the dramatic power of the piece was undeniable. It is possible Ba had experienced it himself since, as he explains in the preface to his translation of *On the Eve*, he had been involved in its production. Another possibility, which is not necessarily exclusive of the first, is inspiration from *The New Century* report, which in all likelihood he had seen. Furthermore, Ba was obviously privy to the French accolades of the Théâtre des Arts production since he quotes them extensively in a short biography of Kampf printed together with his Chinese translation.[45] It is also worth noting that his opinion was most likely not influenced by the *Mother Earth* review since he could not obtain the magazine from Goldman.[46] Therefore, it is no coincidence that the audience in Ba's fictional world closely resembles their French and Chinese counterparts two decades earlier in Paris, including the wild applause at the end of the first act when the police seize the printing shop and the three revolutionaries; the fear and anger during the bloody suppression of the strike procession; the shock, disbelief, and urge to find out more at the end of the second act with Anna and Vasili's tender love before destruction; and, finally, the ecstatic reaction to the climactic heroism, the explosion, and Anna's call for action.

On the Eve became part of the regular modern theatre repertoire in amateur and professional theatres starting from the late 1910s. It had another incarnation in 1938, right after the Japanese invasion, when it was transformed into an anti-Japanese play set in Beijing, *Soul of Freedom* (*Ziyou hun*). Again, it ends with a similar plea of continued struggle by the heroine who had just lost her lover:

> Shi: (*Widely opens her eye as if just awakened from a dream. She takes a look around and frees herself from Liu's arms*) No, I can't cry! Can't cry! (*Wipes her tears*) I can't cry over this. (*Bitterly*) Tears, tears can't bring him back. (*Shouts*) I want to step on his blood and march forward! Chinese citizens, arise, arise! (*Shouts as if in a trance*) Drive out our enemies! Long Live Republic of China! (*Curtain quickly falls, yet she keeps shouting*).[47]

Conclusion

As Arif Dirlik has argued in *Anarchism in the Chinese Revolution*, in early twentieth-century China, anarchism was at the center of revolutionary thought, not only because "the revolutionary situation created by China's confrontation with the modern world gave birth to a radical culture that provided fecund grounds for anarchism, but also that anarchists played an important part in the fashioning of this radical culture."[48] In addition, the significance of anarchism went beyond the first two decades when it was the most popular form of radicalism, as it interjected into the revolutionary discourse "concerns that would leave a lasting imprint on the Chinese revolution, reaching beyond the relatively small group of anarchists into the ideologies of other revolutionaries."[49] In a way, what I have explored in these pages offers a concrete example of the paths through which a radical Western play was interjected into the Chinese revolution and Chinese modernization as well as the play's transformation from a representative of a radical theatrical form to its absorption as a canonical dramatic piece and common frame of reference for modern Chinese theatre.

The unique factor about *On the Eve*'s path in China is its function as a vanguard of radicalism in both the political and theatrical spheres. This is certainly different from its reception in the United States and Europe where, regardless of the critical response of its artistic merit, it was viewed as a radical theatrical piece with a mission well within the bounds of the Western theatrical tradition. To its Chinese viewers, readers, and performers, though, it became a powerful provocation of sacrifice for a worthy cause against an oppressive regime, ideology, or foreign invaders by employing an equally radical and efficacious weapon – the modern Western spoken drama. It is this combination of political and theatrical vanguardism that makes the play a worthy subject of our study.

Notes

1. Emma Goldman, *Anarchism and Other Essays*, 2nd revised edn (New York: Mother Earth Publishing Association, 1911), 247.
2. Matei Calinescu, *Five Faces of Modernity: Modernism, Avant-Garde, Decadence, Kitsch, Postmodernism* (Durham: Duke University Press, 1987), 117.
3. Christopher Innes, *Avant Garde Theatre, 1892–1992* (New York: Routledge, 1993), 6.
4. From the introduction to Mike Sell's *The Avant-Garde: Race Religion War* (Kolkata, India: Seagull Books).
5. James M. Harding and John Rouse, Introduction, *Not the Other Avant-Garde: The Transnational Foundations of Avant-Garde Performance*, ed. James M. Harding and John Rouse (Ann Arbor: University of Michigan Press, 2006), 2.
6. James M. Harding, "From Cutting Edge to Rough Edge: On the Transnational Foundations of Avant-Garde Performance," in *Not the Other Avant-Garde*, ed. Harding and Rouse, 24.
7. Robert D'Attilio, "La Salute É in Voi: The Anarchist Dimension," *The Daily Bleed*, http://recollectionbooks.com/bleed/Encyclopedia/SaccoVanzetti/essayrd.html (accessed Oct 8, 2008).

8. Leopold Kampf, *On the Eve* (New York: International Library Publishing Co., 1907), 100.
9. Ibid., 102.
10. Ibid.
11. "*On the Eve* Advertisement," *The New York Times*, Mar. 2, 1907.
12. "Women Hear Kampf's 'On the Eve'," *The New York Times*, Mar. 10, 1907.
13. Gaston Sorbet, "*Le Grand Soir* au Théâtre Des Arts," in *L'illustration Théatrale* 81 (1908), inside front cover.
14. "*On the Eve* (Review)," *Mother Earth* 2.3 (1907): 168.
15. Ibid., 169.
16. "German Company to Act an Interdicted Play," *The New York Times*, Dec. 1, 1907.
17. Ibid.
18. Ibid.
19. Ibid.
20. "Hedwig Reicher," *The New York Times*, Nov. 21, 1915.
21. "'On the Eve' Triumph for Hedwig Reicher," *The New York Times*, Oct. 5, 1909.
22. Gaston Sorbet, "*Le Grand Soir* au Théâtre des Arts," *L'Illustration Théâtrale* 81 (1908), inside front cover.
23. "'On the Eve' Triumph for Hedwig Reicher," *The New York Times*, Oct. 5, 1909.
24. For detailed accounts of the Paris Group and their connections to international anarchism, see, among others, R. Scalapino and G. T. Yu, *A History of the Chinese Anarchist Movement* (Berkeley: Center for Chinese Studies, 1961), 2–21; Peter Gue Zarrow, *Anarchism and Chinese Political Culture* (New York: Columbia University Press, 1990), 59–81; and Arif Dirlik, *Anarchism in the Chinese Revolution* (Berkeley: University of California Press, 1991), 81–100.
25. Junhun and Zhen, "Laishu fu da" [Letter and Reply], *Xin shiji* [*The New Century*] 6 (1907): 1.
26. Li Shizeng, "Sufeiya" [Sophia Pénovskaia], *Xin shiji* [*The New Century*] 27 (1907): 2.
27. Ibid., 3.
28. Ibid.
29. Ibid.
30. Anonymous, "Meishuyuan guanjuji" [Watching a Play at Théâtre des Arts (1)], *Xin shiji* [*The New Century*] 30 (1908): 3.
31. Ibid.
32. Ibid., 2.
33. Ibid., 3.
34. Li Shizeng, "Chongyin *Yeweiyang* juben xuwen" [Preface to the reprint of the Chinese Translation of *On the Eve*], *Juxue yuekan* [*Theatre Studies Monthly*] 1.2 (1932): 3.
35. Leopold Kampf, "*Yeweiyang* xuyan" [Preface to *On the Eve*], in *Wanqing Wenxue Congchao* [*Compendium of Late Qing Literature*], Vol. *Xiaoshuo xiqu yanjiu juan* [*Fiction and Drama Studies*], ed. A Ying (Beijing: Zhonghua shuju, 1960), 306.
36. For details about *wenmingxi*'s adaptation and staging of Hugo and Sardou, see Siyuan Liu, "Adaptation as Appropriation: Staging Western Drama in the First Western-Style Theatres in Japan and China," *Theatre Journal* 59.3 (Oct. 2007): 411–429.

37. The evidence for this production comes from a 1919 collection of *wenmingxi* play synopses titled *Xinju baichu gaozheng* [*One Hundred New Drama Plays*], edited by Zheng Zhengqiu. The synopsis of *On the Eve*, which keeps Li's translated title *Yeweiyang* and holds the original outline and characters, is subtitled "a Yaofeng Society script, compiled by Zhengqiu" (Zhengqiu Zheng (ed.), *Xinju Kaozheng Baichu* (Shanghai: Zhonghua tushu jicheng gongsi 1919), 54). Since the Yaofeng Society was formed by Zheng Zhengqiu – pen-named Yaofeng – in 1918, it seems safe to conclude that the play was produced between 1918 and 1919.

38. Goldman, *Anarchism and Other Essays*, 247.

39. Ibid., 277.

40. Ba Jin, "*Yeweiyang Xu*" [Preface to *On the Eve*], in *Yeweiyang* [*On the Eve*] (Shanghai: Wenhua shenghuo chubanshe, 1944), 1.

41. Ba Jin, "Gei E.G." [To E.G.], in *Sheng shi chanhui* [*Confessions of Living*] (Shanghai: Shangwu yingshuguan, 1936), 63.

42. Jin Ba, *Chun* [*Spring*] (Beijing: Renmin wenxue chubanshe, 1985), 372.

43. Ibid., 411.

44. Ibid.

45. The French version by Robert d'Humières was published in 1908 in issue 81 of *L'Illustration Théâtrale*, which also includes a summary of the production process and critical praise of the play. Ba's biography of Kampf is based exclusively on this article.

46. In what is most likely Goldman's first letter to Ba, she wrote to him that she could not grant his request for a set of the magazine since "I haven't even a set of *Mother Earth* myself," because of the police raid of her office in 1917 and her subsequent exile – she wrote the letter in Toronto. See Candace Falk et al. (eds), *The Emma Goldman Papers: A Microfilm Edition* (Alexandria, VA: Chadwyck-Healey, 1990), "Letter to Ba Jin," May 26, 1927.

47. Zhao Huishen, *Ziyou Hun* (Guangzhou: Shanghai za zhi gong si, 1938), 96.

48. Arif Dirlik, *Anarchism in the Chinese Revolution* (Berkeley: University of California Press, 1991), 1–2.

49. Ibid., 2.

7

Translation, Typography, and the Avant-Garde's Impossible Text

Sarah Bay-Cheng

Tristan Tzara's typographical dance

Contained within Tristan Tzara's Dada drama *Le Coeur à Gaz* (*The Gas-Heart*, 1923) is an odd illustration, without explanation or apparent function. In the middle of Act Three, at the conclusion of a soliloquy by Mouth, Tzara demarcates a section of the text with the title "DANSE" and describes it: "(*du monsieur qui tombe de l'entonnoir du plafond sur la table*)" (DANCE of the gentleman who falls from a funnel in the ceiling onto the table).[1] Following this, Tzara places a series of letters that recreate the dance described in the stage direction. The dance appears as the letters "Y," "V," and an italicized "*r*" scattering down the page (Figure 1). The reader confronting the image may be unclear as to how the letters correspond to the stage direction. At the top of the illustration, one sees four small capital Ys positioned on top of a larger capital Y; at the bottom, a series of Ys descend both in position and in size into a capital V. At first glance, the static image appears to contradict the previous stage direction. If the letters are meant to echo the objects described – the funnel, the gentleman, the table – then the large Y at the top of the illustration appears to correspond to the table. There is no funnel present, however, unless the reader of the text rotates the page, such that the V appears inverted at the top of the page.

Read upside-down from top to bottom, the now-inverted V becomes the funnel in the ceiling, and the Ys suggest a figure falling out, growing larger as he moves closer to the viewer or more fully into the textual frame of the action. In the center of the illustration, the letter appears to move across the page randomly, changing size and shape into an italicized *r*. This letter *r* resembles the small Y, suggesting the same letter now embellished. The close approximation of size between the *r* and

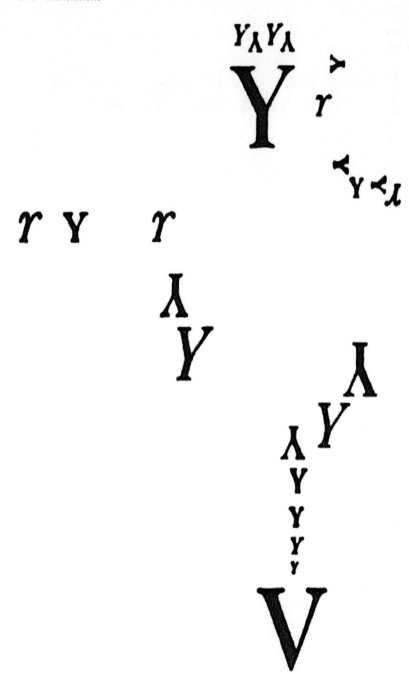

Figure 1   Image from the text of *Le Coeur à Gaz*

Y suggests an affinity between them, if they do not represent the same character changing as he moves through his falling dance. To complete the dance, the reader must rotate the image to propel the dancing figure (Y) from the open center of the page to the top of the largest Y. It is no coincidence that the largest V and Y are the same size. Both serve as static set pieces to frame the smaller, active letters in motion. Once the rotation is complete, the little Y appears to flip over twice on top of the larger Y, as if concluding the fall with the dance on the table described above. Both the composition of the illustration and the movement of the page by the reader/viewer create the "dance" of the lettered gentleman as he falls from the funnel onto the table.

The physical engagement required of the viewer in *Le Coeur à Gaz* both animates and stalls the visually unruly text. Following the gentleman's dance to its conclusion only brings the reader back to the beginning. Rather than turn past the page of the image, the reader must follow the dance in a seemingly endless loop. As long as the reader obeys the text, the play cannot progress. Ironically, the reader's animation of the text suspends dramatic time by locking the reader/audience into an endlessly repeating, rotating moment. In this printed performance, Tzara's iconographic text not only divorces language from its linguistic meaning, but violates its dramatic progression. His rebellious text interrupts and suspends the time-based, embodied enactment of the play.

Tzara's revisions to the diagram in subsequent versions of the play are evidence of its importance to the text. Significantly, his most extreme revision appeared only after the play's first performance in 1923 at the infamous *Soirée du Coeur à barbe* (Evening of the Bearded Heart).[2] This revision transformed a block of letters apparently chosen at random into a dynamic illustration of a typological character dancing across the page. Although largely ignored by scholars, this illustration anticipates an intriguing issue for modernist and avant-garde drama studies; namely, the mutual dependence and antagonism between text and performance in the dramatic text itself.

Tzara's typographical experiment in *Le Coeur à Gaz* and its resistance to translation to the theatrical stage as embodied action challenge the relation between the written text and the spoken word and, as such, articulates a dimension of Tzara's vision of the avant-garde as not only anti-textual, but also anti-body. To better understand this, I first consider the opposition between text and performance and the complications Tzara's image raises within this dichotomy. In particular, I consider his dramatic text as a form of perverse translation (via Walter Benjamin's view of translation as an unending process), one that both presumes a semantic equivalence between the written text and the embodied action and preempts any physical equivalence between the writing and its embodiment. I then analyze Tzara's typography as an autonomous performance within the dramatic text. Tzara's unique mode of dramatic writing raises as well as subverts the translation of textual bodies of the page to the stage's performing bodies and fundamentally breaks down the division between reader and performer, text and performance, paper and theatre. This breakdown suggests that Tzara's avant-garde style may not only have been anti-textual, but also anti-corporeal – a direct attack on the performing body within the milieu of the theatre itself.

Among the shifting dynamics of text, drama, theatre, and performance, it may be useful to define a few terms. I define "text" as the printed material on the page, including all visual impressions on paper, including the ready identifiers of drama – dialogue and stage directions – and what W. B. Worthen calls the "accessories of drama," including typography. Michael Vanden Heuvel's distinction between text and performance in his *Performing Drama/Dramatizing Performance* reflects much of what has been written regarding the relation between text and performance. Drama, according to Vanden Heuvel, is "that form of theatrical expression that is constituted primarily as a literary artifact, according to particular 'dramatic' conventions, and empowered as text."[3]

Conversely, "performance refers first to a theatrical medium that has traditionally acted to translate the dramatic text, but which in recent years has been ordained as an autonomous art form, as an alternative to 'literary' drama."[4] Although one could argue that Tzara anticipates this late twentieth-century conception of performance – an alternative to text-based drama – his *Coeur à Gaz* is most productively read within the tradition of drama that insinuates translation into theatrical performance. Indeed, throughout the play, Tzara raises the expectation of embodiment (not coincidentally naming his characters after parts of a body) only to undermine this by inserting a seemingly playable illustration into the play. His adherence to theatrical conventions suggests that the text can be performed – words made flesh – but he simultaneously subverts this expectation in an illustration that articulates text as a performer without a body.

Text/performance in the avant-garde

Avant-garde theatre in general and Dada in particular frequently have been categorized by a rejection of authoritarian textual dictates and, as such, have remained touchstones for those seeking to reject the tyranny of the text. Julia Walker locates the source in what she calls the epistemological split between text and performance in the European avant-gardes:

> where performance has often been the avant-garde's favorite mode of resisting the status quo. Whether understood as abstract reason, the law, the law of the father, narrative logic, or conventional forms of representation, that status quo has often been figured as language – the defining limitation that performance strains against and seeks to explode.[5]

Among other considerations of the European avant-garde, critics repeatedly articulate this resistant mode as anti-textuality.[6] Many of the essays in James M. Harding's anthology *Contours of the Theatrical Avant-Garde: Performance and Textuality* make this point, Harding himself arguing that distinctions between text and performance, "though hard to maintain as clear binary oppositions, are grounded in an historical antagonism between text and performance that has been one of the avant-garde's greatest sources of vitality."[7] Such formulations follow closely the numerous works on Antonin Artaud's Theatre of Cruelty, which have led to what Harding and John Rouse refer to as "the common assumption … that the theatrical avant-garde was fundamentally at odds with text-based theater."[8]

While a contested notion, this opposition raises fundamental, yet largely unanswered questions: What is text in drama, theatre, and performance? Is it the dialogue and stage directions? Is it any ink stamped onto paper, including page numbers, printing errors, and so on? In their many experiments with print advertising, printed leaflets, collage art, and experiments in poster and book typography, the artists of the European avant-garde were opposed neither to the printed word nor to the page as a theatrical venue. In some instances, in fact, it was the printed letter or word that could become the performer. Italian Futurist prints, such as Carlo Carrà's *Graphic Rhythm with Airplane (Homage to Blériot)* (1914) and F. T. Marinetti's various "words-in-freedom" (1915–19), used typography to convey movement and embodied action. In 1923, Czech writer Vítězslav Nezval composed textual bodies in an alphabet of stylized human poses, and, in 1928, German Bauhaus artist Oskar Schlemmer articulated the human form as language in his drawing *Man in the Sphere of Ideas*. English Vorticist Wyndham Lewis's play *Enemy of the Stars* (1914) constructed a performance entirely on the printed page, in what David Graver has described as "performing print" – a literary text that becomes a performance within itself.[9] Within the dynamic formation of experimental art, performance, and theatre, artists of diverse orientations and locations experimented with the body as a kind of text and with text as entity performer.

W. B. Worthen has suggested that the material properties of print can be read as a "mise-en-page," a site of performance. He asks, "Can we consider the materiality of writing not in opposition to performance (or, much the same thing, as governing or determining performance), but as a more dynamic index to the shifting equilibrium between writing and performance in the conception of the drama?"[10] Tzara's typographical dramatic experiment offers a useful context for engaging the question of the "dynamic index" and reevaluating the perceived opposition between text and performance in avant-garde theatre. As I explore here, Tzara uses his typography as actors within a play text that otherwise appears to be written for actors. Thus, to fully understand the play, one must engage this illustration both as a text that performs autonomously and as a text that requires translation into performance.

The illustration itself is clearly not dialogue, although one could attempt to articulate sounds associated with the letters and to correlate their size and position on the page with volume and physical location onstage. The structure of the illustration, however, prevents any straightforward vocalization, since, in order to be read aloud, the image must be rotated, thereby creating a never-ending repetition of sounds from which the rest of the play cannot escape. Conversely, the dance of the gentleman clearly does not fall within the category of a stage direction. The illustration does not tell us what the performers do onstage – the letters perform it themselves. The action of the illustration is literal; there is no implied action by a performer, only the explicit movement of the text. Whereas Worthen identifies typography and layout as "the effort to render the book a distinctive platform for the play's realization," Tzara's use of typography occurs not to realize the play, but to undermine and destabilize the performance of the play as a text and to complicate the viewing position of its reader/spectator/viewer.

Translation from text to performance

Perhaps it is the metaphor of translation that provides a suitable frame for the interpretation of Tzara's play. I introduce the concept of translation here as a distinctly theatrical anticipation in which the dramatic text in print emerges onstage in the bodies of performers. Unlike Worthen's "dynamic index," translation suggests a semantic equivalent between the text on the page and the action on the stage. One must remember, however, that this is not exclusively the oft-mentioned linguistic metaphor that has been challenged since Anne Ubersfeld's influential *Lire le Théâtre* (1977).[11] The etymological roots of translation can in fact be found not in change of text, but in the movement of bodies. In its earliest English-language usage (c.1350), translation was defined as the "removal or conveyance from one person, place, or condition to another" (*OED*), and, by the mid-sixteenth century, translation meant "removal from earth to heaven, *orig.* without death, as the translation of Enoch; but in later use also said *fig.* of the death of the righteous."[12]

Tzara's illustration-as-translation requires both a literal and physical definition. The typographical dance of the falling gentleman positions itself both as a literal translation – a semantic equivalence between text and performance – and against metaphysical translation – the movement of bodies across a phenomenological divide from the page to the stage. Suspended thus between printed text and embodied performance, Tzara's text ensures its own destabilized theatrical role. To read the play, one must enact the performance of the typographical illustration; to perform the play, one must eliminate the illustration. Unlike other textual omissions that occur with embodied performance (rarely does anyone read the stage directions as printed), this illustration has no physical equivalent on the stage either in speech or movement. Character names imply which actor is speaking, stage directions suggest specific locations and movement, and punctuation guides the tempo and rhythm of theatrical speech. Tzara's illustration, arguably realized only on the page, has no physical equivalent in performance. To perform the play, it must be eliminated, with no trace of the action left behind. In this way, Tzara realizes the dramatic equivalent of his infamous 1918 manifesto: If to be against Dada is to be Dada, then to perform the play is to destroy the play. Following Benjamin's theory regarding the impossibility of translation (which I'll discuss below), Tzara's typographical Dada drama can be read as a perverse act of translation, one that suggests the equivalence between written language and performance and the movement of bodies across a phenomenological divide, even as the text subverts this effect.

Translation, as a critical concept, has not fared particularly well in theatre studies. Since the 1970s, scholarship has repeatedly rejected the metaphor of translation as an adequate reflection of the relationship between text and performance. There are two major objections. The first, appearing in semiotic studies of theatre, proposes that the characterization of theatrical performance as a translation is reductive.

To cite one prominent example, Michael Issacharoff concludes his anthology, *Performing Text*, with the assertion that "[t]he playscript is in no way 'sacred'; performance is never merely a 'translation' of it to the stage. To exist, it is contingent on performance."[13] If, as Issacharoff suggests, the text is contingent on performance, then theatrical understanding requires the analysis of performance as a distinct realization of the text in a new form, not as the governing principle for performance. The text is not simply translated – shifted between different sign systems – but conceptually reorganized. The second objection argues against translation's apparent privileging of text as such. Marvin Carlson dismisses the concept of translation because "the written text is 'translated' into theatrical terms only in a very special sense. True, words are spoken instead of read, an important phenomenological shift, but they remain the same words. The original is in one sense changed, but in another it is literally embedded in its own presumed translation."[14] Such conceptions of the relationship between text and performance inherently assume the persistence of what Vanden Heuvel has called the "presence" of text across the phenomenological divide from print into performance. "No longer can we accept a linear, Newtonian model that describes the text and its affects," he writes, "as the absolute reference for measuring theatrical work."[15] Much of the critical work of the last twenty years has attempted to redefine this relationship. According to Vanden Heuvel, theatrical performance must be seen as a fundamental reworking of text in more complex relations, rather than the translation from the linguistic to the verbal.[16]

And yet this is precisely what Tzara attempts to create. Typography as a kind of theatre necessitates the concept of translation precisely because the text demands a single, exact realization by the reader qua performer. Tzara's typography cannot remain the same words onstage, as Carlson suggests. The letters cannot be enacted, the textual dance cannot be replicated by human actors, and the sounds the letters might make as speech do not contain the presence to which Vanden Heuvel refers. Unlike most other aspects of dramatic text, the movements of the letters are not open to interpretation by either another body or another voice. The reader cannot make his or her own variation or interpretive reading or performance of the text. Simply to read the text is to be constrained by it. Of course, one can ignore it, read past it, or omit it from further reproductions. But these are all choices that require the elimination of the illustration – its non-performance – not simply a different interpretation. A reader might understand the positions of the letters differently, but there is only one possible enactment of Tzara's typography as it is written, because the actors are literally inscribed in their roles. Thus the reader/performer is left with two options: either perform the illustration by rotating the illustration ad infinitum or reject it outright and cancel the performance. Structured as a kind of *mise-en-abime*, one cannot fully read through the illustration, let alone play it onstage.

In this sense, Tzara's play appears to follow Benjamin's description of translation as a continuing process that simultaneously reproduces and destroys text: "Finally, it is self-evident how greatly fidelity in reproducing the form impedes the rendering of the sense. Thus no case for literalness can be based on a desire to retain the meaning. Meaning is served far better – and literature and language far worse – by the unrestrained license of bad translators."[17] Instead of reproducing the literal translation, Benjamin suggests that translation instead must perform the original text, perhaps indefinitely. He writes, "[A]s regards the meaning, the language of a translation can – in fact, must – let itself go, so that it gives voice to the *intentio* of the original not as reproduction but as harmony, as a supplement to the language in which it expresses itself, as its own kind of *intentio*."[18] Benjamin frames translation as an interpretive and repetitive enactment of the original, one that develops in time, much like the performance of a play.

Of course, like Tzara's play, this is an impossible performance. Carol Jacobs argues that Benjamin's "task" for the translator is ultimately one of surrender, what she terms a "monstrous loss."[19] Betsy Flèche takes this argument further when she turns the problem of translation inward from the translator to Benjamin himself. She argues that Benjamin eschews ideological criticism in favor of "performative criticism."[20] Flèche's notion of performative criticism suggests that Benjamin's text destabilizes itself as it goes, revising the meanings of words and resisting the translations of subsequent authors and critics. Significantly, Flèche's understanding of Benjamin's strategy is one that resists the authority of the original text. She states, "There is no authority for the critic to rely upon. The essay produces interpretive crises, keeps its readers deliberately off-balance."[21] In other words, the text performs dynamically, even metonymically, and thereby resists efforts by others to contain it within other translations or secondary texts. It continually redefines the relationship between the reader/translator and the text itself. Like Tzara's play, translation is an open-ended process that evades any final realization. Whereas other conceptions of translation attempt a kind of fixed or ideal lucidity, Benjamin's own writing presents the text as a perpetual activity that does not reach its conclusion. As commentators note repeatedly, one cannot adequately enact the performance of translation that Benjamin himself suggests. The text performs unendingly; the reader must either persist in the process or give up.

Typography as performance

To understand how Tzara manages both to command an exact translation and to subvert the text simultaneously, one needs to consider the role of typography in the illustration. I have thus far used the word "illustration" to describe what Tzara calls his typographical "dance," but "illustration" is perhaps a mistaken term. The image in Tzara's play is not drawn, but is created by the manipulation of printed letters, fonts, and their placements on the page. The image's ambiguous status within the text of the play makes even its definition difficult. Is it a diagram? An illustration? A textual performance? It is telling that these letters, like much of Dada's non-sense, remain unchanged in interlingual translations.[22] These images of text, turned iconographic on the page, exist outside the usual textual expectations of the play itself. To understand this textual performance, one must consider the typography as an autonomous object.

Although Tzara's play is frequently referred to in studies of Dada and the European avant-garde and has been repeatedly anthologized in English translations, his dramatic typographical experiments have been largely overlooked. This omission is surprising given that studies of Tzara often note the performativity of typography in his poetry. For example, Johanna Drucker's examination of typography in modern art and poetry argues that Tzara's textual appropriations from advertising move his language from a private, personal context into the public domain of commodities, a domain aligned with the public performance of the theatre. This shift invites a public audience to view the language as a material object as an "object, with material properties, a life, a history, and a semiotic and economic function to perform in the cultural context of linguistic operations."[23]

In her essay, "Motion, Vision, and Coherence in the Dada Poetry of Tristan Tzara," Mary Ann Caws similarly describes Tzara's poetry as "a constantly varied spectacle" in which the reader is called to participate in the action of the text.[24] Through the textual spectacle of language, the Dadaist's poetry not only asserts itself as a material social object, but further enlists the reader as a kind of spectator/participant who both witnesses and enacts the movement of language as a dynamic graphic image. Tzara's typography demands its own translation by the reader, but simultaneously destroys itself in the process. This destructive shift

from the private to the public, from the literary to the embodied, trans-
forms printed text from its standard role as the invisible bearer of linguistic meaning to a performing agent.

As previously described, the central illustration commands the reader
to physically rotate the text, thereby inhibiting the progression of the
play. Closer inspection enables an understanding of Tzara's view of the
avant-garde as anti-body. Tzara's play enacts its translation as a destruction of the mimetic human body in the theatre, much like the disintegrated face that appears in the play's other characters, Mouth, Nose,
Neck, Ear, and Eye. Avant-garde drama in this instance becomes both a
resistance to the words made flesh and to the fleshy body itself. Indeed,
like Benjamin's untranslatable "Task of the Translator," the theatrical performance of Tzara's play is predicated on a radical distortion (the elimination of the illustration) of the text as written. This textual slippage reveals
a gap between the original text and its subsequent enactment and the
destructive potential of the move from the page to the stage.

At first glance, it may appear that nearly all of Tzara's *Coeur à Gaz*
opposes embodied performance. The characters Mouth, Nose, Neck,
Ear, and Eye are only parts of a face, and their incessant and repetitive
non sequiturs eliminate any suggestion of character, motivation, or clear
action. From the start, it is difficult to see how the characters could
ever be fully embodied in the theatre. Like many of his contemporaries, Tzara denaturalizes stage language by playing with puns, obscene
suggestions, and ridiculous groupings of words. But his most radical
obstruction of performance is the stage direction and illustration that,
in their textual form, are utterly contrary to performance and translation. But the implications of Tzara's typography are more radical than
the merging of text and action, or even the destruction of text. Through
the use of typography and visual placement, Tzara creates a theatrical
moment in which textual performance of letters arranged on the page
replaces human performance. The dance of the gentleman literally leads
to his theatrical death. Tzara's textual bodies literally (and literarily)
perform the mise-en-scène, or gestural undertext, of the original and
thereby prevent their enactment by physical bodies. Tzara's dancing
illustration aptly demonstrates that the resistant textual performances
of Dada drama can be simultaneously anti-text and anti-body.

Tzara's typographic bodies

In most criticism, typography in the avant-garde serves as the primary
means for transforming language into art object. For example, Jean-
Gérard Lapacherie credits Dada in general and Tzara in particular with

moving the "typographic cacophony" from the title page or poster to the body of the text itself. Experimental typography radically destabilizes the text's role as the invisible conduit of linguistic meaning. According to Lapacherie, Dada's violation of the agreement between the appearance of the text and its original meaning "deindicalises" typography and turns language into "pure graphic signifiers."[25] Dada manipulations of the visual text create tension between the text as meaning and visual object. Typography in Dada, Lapacherie argues, does not follow any rule other than the arbitrariness of the authors, creating not new significations of typography, but rather reducing language to pure form. For his part, Timothy Benson sees the performing text in Dada as ultimately one of function. This new role serves "to establish connections and to produce new meanings" rather than to enact text within the space of the page.[26] Like Worthen's mise-en-page, this is yet another interpretation of typography as performance, of which *Le Coeur à Gaz* is a particularly relevant example.

Although these poetic and graphic considerations of avant-garde typography culminate in the text as image, we might extend avant-garde violations of typography beyond pure form to consider the ways in which typography performs within avant-garde drama and its representation in performance. Whereas Tzara's poetry may articulate motion as objects propelled in visual space, the typographical interruptions of his drama, especially *Le Coeur à Gaz*, use pieces of text to create a performance within the play. Letters divorced from unified words become free-floating bodies. Unlike Tzara's poetry, which creates the echo of everyday life and public spectacle by appropriating existing text, and his posters and manifestos, which reformulate individual letters and words as graphic images, Tzara's drama animates typography appropriated from graphic advertising into its own literal theatre.

Although most English translations of Tzara's play represent this section of the play as a simple stage direction connecting the graphic illustration to the dialogue, the version published by G. L. M. in 1946 and reprinted in *Oeuvres Complètes* (1975) visually separates the dance from the action of the play. The "DANSE" is announced in capital letters, parenthetically defined by the stage direction. In a widely anthologized translation, Michael Benedikt translates this stage direction into the past tense: the original "DANSE / *du monsieur qui tombe de l'entonnoir du plafond sur la table*" becomes "Dance of the gentleman fallen from a funnel in the ceiling onto the table."[27] But syntactically *"qui tombe"* is much more complicated than Benedikt suggests. The verb *tomber* carries numerous meanings and idioms, including the connotation of failure, the biblical fall of mankind from paradise, and falling in love. Indeed, the dialogue that follows the dance juxtaposes the active love of the Mouth ("J'aime" is repeated in each of the four sentences preceding the dance) with the language of loss immediately following the dance. As Eye confesses, "Imagine my dear friend I no longer love."[28]

Whereas the dialogue immediately following the illustration suggests loss and past events, the phrase *"qui tombe"* of the stage direction implies that the gentleman described in the play falls, or is falling. Rather than describe a dance that occurs after the gentleman has already fallen, the phrase "DANSE / *du monsieur qui tombe"* suggests that the gentleman is falling and dancing simultaneously, or perhaps dancing as he falls. Following the Mouth's declaration, "I love the young man who makes tender declarations to me,"[29] the monsieur who falls and dances may be the young man falling (in love?) from the words of the Mouth. The Mouth itself acts as a kind of speech funnel, dripping language without logic.[30]

It is significant that Tzara revised this section of the play only after its 1923 performance. Affected perhaps by the play's performance amid the volatile antics of Dada's *Soirée du Coeur à barbe*, his revision of this illustration reveals an antagonism towards both the audience and the live performer. In the first printed version of the play for *Der Sturm* in 1922, Tzara's interest in the typographic dance appears to be little more than visual. He represents the dance as a more or less random assortment of letters arranged in groups of one to three and collected in a compact block in the center of the page.[31] The impact of this mass of letters is clearly visual. The arrangement of letters resembles the 1920s craze of "word-cross" puzzles that were first introduced by the *New York World* in 1913 and popularized in Europe by Britain's version of cryptic word puzzles.[32] This configuration tempts the reader to seek out linguistic meaning among the letters, perhaps suspending dramatic progression, though hardly constituting a rebellion against the live actor.

In Tzara's 1938 revision, however, the letters threaten to replace the bodies of the actors. This displacement of the actor's body articulates the play's relentless resistance to the mimetic presence of the actor. Throughout the play, Tzara attempts to undermine the integrity of the performing body. Characters are not granted physical unity, but are fractured into anatomical parts, each representing only a piece of a larger organic whole. The costumes designed by Sonia Delaunay for the 1923 production rendered the actors immobile behind large cardboard cutouts, threatening to decapitate them. Although the title of the anthologized English translation (*The Gas-Heart*) bears the connotation of a kind of indigestion, the original French title, *Le Coeur à Gaz*, threatens to fundamentally undo the body's most central function. First translated into English by Leslie Singer in 1969 as *The Gas-Burning Heart*, the play's title produces an image both of a heart dislocated from an organic whole and transformed into a kind of machine, and simultaneously that of a heart reduced to a less solid molecular state – the heart of gas.[33]

Yet neither title nor costume can fully displace the mimesis of the actor's human body within performance. Tzara's dramatic typography sows the seeds of its own destruction. The textual bodies cannot cross into performance; they resist translation. To perform the play, one must destroy these text-based figures, replacing them with inadequate human representations. In this context of a body fractured and dismembered – the central organ of the body on life-support or evaporating – the actor's centrality is replaced by the physical presence of the dancing monsieur embodied as the letter Y.

Much in Dada and other related avant-garde movements of the early twentieth century argued against the authority of the human body and against the authority of the text, thus establishing a trend for later works. It is significant that the replacement of bodies with text began with the start of the First World War, when actual human bodies were disintegrating and decomposing in the European theatres of war. In the midst of such realities, Dadaist Hugo Ball perceived the fragmentation in art as "one more proof of how ugly and worn the human countenance has become, and of how all the objects of our environment have become repulsive to us."[34] It should come as no surprise that Ball relates this attack on the integrity of the physical representation to language as linguistic representation. In response to the "ugly" human countenance, modern art eliminated visual representations of the human form. According to Ball, "The next step is for poetry to decide to do away with language for similar reasons."[35] Ball's juxtaposition hardly surprises, given typography's long history as a parallel to the human body. As early as 1529, Geoffrey Tory's *Champ Fleury* associated the visual appearance of letters with the proportionate form of the human body: "Our Attic letters (i.e., 'roman type') are so well proportioned to nature that they agree in measure and proportion with the human body."[36] Typography unified in meaning, syntax, and appearance echoes the integrated and well-proportioned human body. Just as avant-garde performance undermined the authority of text, so also could avant-garde text rebel against the inherent realism of the human body.

By now, it has become commonplace to describe *Le Coeur à Gaz* as a parody of, or an attack on, theatrical performance. Most critical studies point to Tzara's use of lists, *non sequiturs*, and repetitions as examples of his critique of theatre's linguistic conventions. However, the use of typography and its usurping of performance as the exclusive domain of the human body advance a far more devastating critique than does his attack on language. Avant-garde dramatic typography suggests a dramatic text that is fundamentally at odds with embodied performance – an impossible theatre. In place of an autonomous human body, dramatic typography animates text; instead of human bodies performing in space and time, the repetitions of the typography interrupt and suspend the progression of the play. Most significantly, however, the typography of avant-garde drama renders the material body obsolete. In this way, Tzara echoes Edward Gordon Craig's *Übermarionettes* by suggesting a theatre composed independently of, even antagonistically towards, a live body. Like Benjamin's impossible process of translation, Tzara's play introduces an impossible theatre fundamentally opposed to the physical performing body: an anti-body theatre.

Impossible text

This anti-embodied, theatrically impossible text must become irrevocably at odds with the essential nature of performance. But this is neither the closet drama of the modernists nor the individually imagined theatre suggested by artists like Craig; rather, the anti-body theatre of Dada is an attack on the theatre as the mimetic articulation of the human body and the translation of word into body. It creates a theatre that is, by definition, incomplete and unperformable. Rejecting the theatre's ontology as a sacred space in Western civilization, Tzara seeks to undo the religious and ritualistic connotations of the live body by replacing this body with an unperformable text. Whereas most writing for the theatre outlines the presence of human bodies – where they stand, what they say, what they do – and awaits its fulfillment by the actor, dramatic typography stands for nothing but itself. Hence the perversity of Tzara's typographical translation. While live actors may attempt to enact the gestures illustrated in *Le Coeur à Gaz*, they are inadequate copies of the original textual performance. Indeed, their physical bodies can sustain neither the endless repetitions nor the simultaneous positions possible in the performing text.

The dialogue following Tzara's textual dance further points to the impossibility of physical realization in the avant-garde theatre. Shortly after the dance of the falling gentleman, Eye – that essential organ of the theatre – describes the impossible physical excess of love and the lack of connection: "My blood trembles. Your eyes are blue. Why can't you feel it, Clytemnestra, the quiet laughter of my cells awaiting you, the violence of my breath and the sweet childish possibilities in store for us?"[37] Immediately following this physical separation between Eye and the object of his affection, Neck and Nose recite a long list of adjectives describing an unidentified entity, possibly Clytemnestra, possibly Eye, who says nothing after the speech, but is described as falling (*tombe*).[38] Neck and Nose's list is contradictory (including descriptions such as "small," "short," "feeble," and simultaneously, "magnificent," "strong," and "fat"), but the visual layout of the list as a series of single word lines and the lack of additional information suggest that all the adjectives describe the same thing.[39] Tzara's lists, repetition, and *non sequiturs* foreground not meaning but rather the text of the play – the words – independent of the figures who speak. Although previous interpretations of the play attempt to find a rationale among the characters and a consistency within their speech, any of the lines of dialogue in the play could be readily assigned to any of the characters.[40] The words, not the physical actors, are the performing agents.

Like Benjamin's task for the literary translator, the fundamental task of theatrical translation in Tzara's play is to destabilize the textual body in an unending and repetitive process that can never become fully realized. Typography, then, both ensures the disruption of text and undermines the possibility of performance itself. Tzara creates an unstable theatre, a theatre that actively resists the translation of text into action, even as it appears to create a textual action within the mise-en-page. Just as experimental typography undermines language as the conduit for linguistic meaning, Tzara's dramatic typography sabotages the human actor as the conduit for meaningful action. Even in the live performance of the theatre, Tzara contains and reduces the performing body, foregrounding the performance of avant-garde text as the essence of a non-mimetic, non-ritualistic, and anti-performing theatre.

Why then did Tzara write a play? I conclude by returning to Worthen's question posed in the introduction to his *Print and the Poetics of Modern Drama*: "Can we consider the materiality of writing not in opposition to performance...but as a more dynamic index to the shifting equilibrium between writing and performance in the conception of the drama?"[41] As with most of Dada, one can imagine an emphatically negative response. Tzara's play undoubtedly pits text and performance against each other, but the implications of his text go beyond simple opposition. Like Benjamin's encounter between the translator and original text, the opposition between the text and its presumed performance in Tzara's play synthesizes into an ongoing force that is simultaneously productive and destructive. It is this tension – the impossibility and incompleteness of both text and performance within a play to be performed – that becomes the essential performance of the play. As the necessary animator for the performing text, the reader becomes embroiled in this conflict. By continuously rotating the textual image, simultaneously enabling the textual performance and thwarting the progress of the embodied play, the reader/performer unwittingly (and perhaps unwillingly) becomes trapped in the perpetual repetition of the performing text. Thus the impossible text emerges like so many Dada performances: as an assault on its audience, one that breaks down the division between the creation and the audience and inserts its art into the praxis of life – in this case, into an act of reading. What is text? For Tzara, it is an attack both on the conventional notions of print and audience (reading or viewing) and a new kind of anti-textual, anti-embodied performance. Tzara deftly conscripts the unsuspecting reader into simultaneous service as reader, performer, spectator, and Dada destroyer of text and flesh.

Notes

1. Tristan Tzara, *Le Coeur à Gaz* (Paris: G. L. M., 1946), 33. Written and first performed in 1921, *Le Coeur à Gaz* was first published in *Der Sturm* (March 1922): 33–42. Following the 1923 performance, Tzara revised the play significantly and the revised version appeared in May 1946. Unless otherwise noted, all translations of the play are mine.
2. See J. H. Matthews, *Theatre in Dada and Surrealism* (Syracuse, NY: Syracuse University Press, 1974), 36; and Georges Hugnet, *L'Aventure Dada 1916–1922* (Paris: Galerie de l'Institut, 1957), 98. For corroborating descriptions, see also Annabelle Melzer, *Dada and Surrealist Performance* (Baltimore, MD: Johns Hopkins University Press, 1994), 156–160; Hans Richter, *Dada: Art and Anti-Art* (New York: Thames & Hudson, 1997), 188–191; and Elmer Peterson, *Tristan Tzara: Dada and Surrational Theorist* (New Brunswick, NJ: Rutgers University Press, 1971), 77–79. For slightly different versions of the evening, see Michael Benedikt and George Wellwarth (eds), *Modern French Theatre: The Avant-Garde, Dada, and Surrealism* (New York: Dutton, 1964), xxii; and Michel Sanouillet, *Dada à Paris* (Paris: Jean-Jacque Pauvert, 1965), 384.
3. Michael Vanden Heuvel, *Performing Drama/Dramatizing Performance: Alternative Theater and the Dramatic Text* (Ann Arbor: University of Michigan Press, 1993), 2–3.
4. Ibid., 5–6.
5. Julia A. Walker, "Why Performance? Why Now? Textuality and the Rearticulation of Human Presence," *Yale Journal of Criticism* 16.11 (2003): 155.

120   *Translations*

6. For this reading, it is most useful, at least initially, to locate the play within a predominantly European context. I have no doubt, however, that more productive work may yet be done by locating the play in a broader global context.

7. James M. Harding, Introduction, *Contours of the Theatrical Avant-Garde: Performance and Textuality*, ed. Harding (Ann Arbor: University of Michigan Press, 2000), 3.

8. James M. Harding and John Rouse, Introduction, *Not the Other Avant-Garde: The Transnational Foundations of Avant-Garde Performance*, ed. Harding and Rouse (Ann Arbor: University of Michigan Press, 2006), 9.

9. David Graver, *The Aesthetics of Disturbance: Anti-Art in Avant-Garde Drama* (Ann Arbor: University of Michigan Press, 1995), 179.

10. W. B. Worthen, *Print and the Poetics of Modern Drama* (Cambridge: Cambridge University Press, 2006), 11.

11. See Anne Ubersfeld, *Lire le Théâtre*, 3 vols. (Paris: Éditions sociales, 1977). The English translation of volume one appears as *Reading Theatre*, trans. Frank Collins, Paul Perron, and Patrick Debbèche (Toronto: University of Toronto Press, 1999).

12. "Translation." *Oxford English Dictionary*, 1st edn, 1971.

13. Michael Issacharoff, "Postscript or Pinch of Salt: Performance as Mediation or Deconstruction," in *Performing Texts*, ed. Michael Issacharoff and Robin F. Jones (Philadelphia: University of Pennsylvania Press, 1988), 139.

14. Marvin Carlson, "Theatrical Performance: Illustration, Translation, Fulfillment, or Supplement?" *Theatre Journal* 37.1 (1985): 8.

15. Vanden Heuvel, *Performing Drama/Dramatizing Performance*, 4–6, 7.

16. See John Rouse, "Textuality and Authority in Theater and Drama: Some Contemporary Possibilities," in *Critical Theory and Performance*, ed. Janelle G. Reinelt and Joseph R. Roach (Ann Arbor: University of Michigan Press, 1992), 146–158.

17. Walter Benjamin, "The Task of the Translator," in *Illuminations*, ed. Hannah Arendt, trans. Harry Zohn (New York: Schocken Books, 1968), 78.

18. Ibid., 78–79.

19. Carol Jacobs, "The Monstrosity of Translation," *MLN* 90.6 (1975): 765.

20. Betsy Flèche, "The Art of Survival: The Translation of Walter Benjamin," *Substance* 28.2 (1999): 107.

21. Ibid., 105.

22. See Michel Benedikt's translation of the play in *Modern French Theatre: The Avant-Garde, Dada, and Surrealism: An Anthology of Plays*, ed. and trans. Michael Benedikt and George E. Wellwarth (New York: E. P. Dutton, 1964), 131–146.

23. Johanna Drucker, *The Visible Word: Experimental Typography and Modern Art, 1909–1923* (Chicago: University of Chicago Press, 1994), 206.

24. Mary Ann Caws, "Motion, Vision, and Coherence in the Dada Poetry of Tristan Tzara," *The French Review* 1 (Winter 1970): 6.

25. Jean-Gérard Lapacherie, "Typographic Characters: Tension between Text and Drawing," trans. Anna Lehmann, *Yale French Studies* 84 (1994): 71.

26. Timothy O. Benson, "Conventions and Constructions: The Performative Text in Dada," in *Dada: The Coordinates of Cultural Politics*, ed. Stephen C. Foster (London: G. K. Hall, 1996), 87.

27. Benedikt, *Modern French Theatre*, 143.
28. Tzara, *Le Coeur à Gaz*, 34.
29. Ibid.
30. Tzara's other typographical image from the play suggests this idea as well. On the last page of the play, the usual "fin" is positioned above a diagonal arrow pointing down to the final word of the play, "L'Amour," as if the entirety of the play has fallen into love.
31. See Henri Béhar's notes on earlier versions of the play in *Oeuvres Complètes*, Vol. 1, ed. Henri Béhar (Paris: Flammarion, 1975), 670.
32. See Roger Millington, *Crossword Puzzles: Their History and Their Cult* (New York: Simon & Schuster, 1975).
33. Similarly, Peterson translates the play as *"The Gas Operated Heart"* in his *Tristan Tzara*, 78.
34. Hugo Ball, *Flight Out of Time: A Dada Diary*, ed. John Elderfield, trans. Ann Raimes (1927; repr. New York: Viking Press, 1974), 55.
35. Ibid.
36. Quoted in Lapacherie, "Typographic Characters," 66.
37. Tzara, *Le Coeur à Gaz*, 34.
38. Ibid., 35.
39. Ibid., 35–38.
40. For additional criticism of the play, see Katherine Papachristos, *L'Inscription de l'Oral et de l'Écrit dans le Théâtre de Tristan Tzara* (New York: Peter Lang, 1999), 83–102; and Robert A. Varisco, "Anarchy and Resistance in Tristan Tzara's 'The Gas Heart,'" *Modern Drama* 40.1 (Spring 1997): 139–149.
41. Worthen, *Print and the Poetics of Modern Drama*, 11.

8

Maoist Performativities: Milton Acorn and the Canadian Liberation Movement

Alan Filewod

If we Canadians, following the programme advocated by many, but most clearly by the Canadian Liberation Movement, seized the foreign-owned industries in our territory – and if the principal foreign owner, the American Empire, launched military operations against us – what are the odds? Would we win? ... A people armed with a modern Marxist-Leninist ideology is invincible in a defensive war.[1]

This militant assertion of Canadian revolutionary valor may be typical of the New Left in Canada at the close of the 1960s, but it is remarkable because it is the thesis of an essay in one of the best-selling volumes of poetry in Canadian publishing history. Milton Acorn's 1972 *More Poems for People* sold 10,000 copies in a country where the average poetry volume sells less than 500. It marked the high point of Maoist sentiment in Canada, not just because Acorn was one of the most highly regarded Canadian poets, but also because his celebrity legitimized a small fringe party that called itself the Canadian Liberation Movement (and underwrote its publishing house, New Canada Press). Acorn was the iconic face of the CLM's highly romanticized Maoist ideology of national liberation in the cultural sphere. But while his celebrity projected a façade of party stability, it masked (and perhaps exacerbated) bitter internal contradictions in a movement that was described, after its collapse in 1976, in language characteristic of the sectarian Left, as "a national chauvinist, social-fascist, absolutely degenerate organization."[2]

My consideration of Acorn's role in the CLM and his theatrical reformulation of its principles in his play *The Road to Charlottesville* begins with comparison of the performative and textual strategies deployed by the CLM and its primary opponent, the Communist Party of Canada (Marxist-Leninist), as they vied to mobilize the "people" and construct a Maoist Marxism-Leninism appropriate to the cultural and historical conditions of Canada. Although the CPC-ML continues today as a registered political party with an unashamedly Stalinist party apparatus, it seems clear that the CLM's improvised, ideologically confused, and politically naïve activism was more successful in commanding public response and, by recruiting highly visible artists, some measure of support. If the CPC-ML can be seen as a *simulation* of an avant-garde party with a mass base that mimicked the structure, rhetoric, and appearance of the Communist Party of China, the CLM in contrast can be considered an *improvisation* of revolutionary unrest. Both of these terms suggest a fundamental performativity, but they encode crucial differences, too. A simulation follows a patterning script in a regulatory structure, whereas an improvisation enacts changeable, reactive structures.

In both cases, performativity refers to the relationship of political parties as signifying practices to the structures of reception they command. This relationship can be understood as spectacles of power played through texts constructed out of icons, behavioral codes (such as dress and appearance codes), and the public role of the leader. All political parties are performative, insofar as they function in a field of image production and reception. The performativity of a political party activates a complex set of legitimating relationships, both internally with the mechanisms of power and capital that sustain leadership and externally in the broader public sphere. The legitimation of a political party in this sense depends on the narrative role of a public that is larger than the party that claims to speak for it. Any party's claim to vanguard status depends on the effective deployment of its performativity and its narratives of legitimacy.

As fringe parties whose boundaries of reception rarely exceeded their cadres, the CLM and the CPC-ML both depended on a cult of leadership to fill the absence of a legitimating public. Relying on the reciprocal gaze of spectacle, leadership cults are in effect political pageants, in which the moment of reception actualizes a sense of community. As a simulation – a party that played all of the signs of a mass party in the absence of structures of popular support – the CPC-ML presented leadership as the public face of the party. In the CLM, leadership was exercised in private, exclusive dramaturgies and reinforced by iconic figures, leadership strategies for which the figure of Milton Acorn was particularly critical. In both parties, leadership was legitimized by spectacle. Leadership must be seen to lead, and to lead it must be seen.

The CLM and the CPC-ML were the most visible of the Maoist tendencies in the Canadian New Left. Both arose out of the student movement of the late 1960s, defined themselves against the politically paralyzed Soviet-client Communist Party of Canada, and flourished in the wake of the New Left's failure to establish a secure power base in a major political party. Although in style and rhetoric Canadian New Leftists seemed similar to those in the United States, they operated in a different historical context. The origins of the New Left in Canada began, as they did in the United States, with the peace campaigns of the early 1960s, principally through two organizations: the Canadian Universities Campaign for Nuclear Disarmament and the Student Union for Peace Action. The turning point, again as in the United States, was the Vietnam War, which radicalized a generation of students and rehabilitated as anti-imperialism the anti-Americanism that had been one of the formative principles of Anglo-Canadian nationalism since the émigré loyalist settlements of the American Revolution.

If the American New Left was activated by the Civil Rights Movement, the Vietnam War, and campus democracy, in Canada the major issues were postcolonial nationalism (in Anglophone Canada and Québec) and American control of the Canadian economy and cultural production. In these issues, the New Left overlapped with the left wing of the New Democratic Party, which had its origins in agrarian socialism in the 1930s and, by the 1960s, as a consequence of a structural alliance with organized labor, had become a major presence in parliamentary politics. The NDP had governed in several provinces and was a potent opposition force in most others as well as in the federal parliament. In a sense, the Canadian New Left can be defined as the loose aggregate of issue-based movements that were impatient with the NDP's gradualism. This impatience was largely generational, exacerbated by the distrust of "redneck" labor. The major accomplishment of the New Left was the pressure it applied on the NDP to adopt a left-nationalist stance.

For the Canadian Left, the U.S. was at once family (in the figurative and often in the literal senses) and imperial threat. Canadian public opinion tended against the U.S. intervention in Vietnam, and the Canadian government quietly eased the way for U.S. war resisters to cross the border. In the late 1960s, anti-war sentiment eroded the continentalist sentiments of the 1950s and began to merge with cultural nationalism. The primary sources of this nationalist sentiment came from bitterly opposed camps. On the one hand, the independence movement in Québec: most Left organizations in Canada accepted an independent Québec and recognized Québécois nationalism. (Many

Anglophones wondered, if Québec is a nation, what are we?) The countervailing source was the federal government, which, under Pierre Trudeau, advanced a program to build a Canadian national sentiment founded on bilingualism and multiculturalism. It was during the Liberal Party regimes of the 1960s and 1970s that the monarchy disappeared from Canadian life.

From the perspective of the New Left, the NDP bogged down in the soft center, and the federal government rode the tide of cultural nationalism. Attempting to move these forces to the Left, a small caucus in the NDP composed the "Manifesto for an Independent Socialist Canada" in 1969. Known as the "Waffle Manifesto" because, as one of its authors quipped, if the group waffled, it "would waffle to the Left,"[3] it was the most articulate statement of Left nationalism. From its premise that "[t]he development of socialist consciousness, on which can be built a socialist base, must be the first priority of the New Democratic Party," it made the point that "[t]he major issue of our times is not national unity but national survival, and the fundamental threat is external, not internal. ... The American empire is the central reality for Canadians. It is an empire characterized by militarism abroad and racism at home."[4] The Waffle challenge was one of the messiest chapters in the NDP's history, because it enlisted considerable support from the younger membership. The battle lasted three years, ending on the convention floor in 1972 when the Waffle caucus surrendered. Following the subsequent purge, core members of the Waffle founded the Movement for an Independent Socialist Canada, which in turn fragmented into factions, the most notable being the Independent Socialists, one of the many student Trotskyite organizations. The defeat of the Waffle marked the failure of the New Left to capture a main party in the political arena, but it marked a moment of change that, in the long run, revitalized the party and opened it to the social justice movement. From that point on, the left wing of the NDP would be the demarcation line of the "extreme" Left.

Several years later, Tina Craig, writing in *Old Mole* (the newspaper of the Trotskyite Revolutionary Marxist Group), made the insightful, if disputable, comment that

> Nineteen sixty-nine marked the real termination of the New Left. Socially, the period was characterized by the relative apathy of the domestic working class; the escalation and extensification of the Indo-Chinese war; and the development of a youth and student radicalisation. The three components of ideological determination

were (for these reasons) "culturalism", youth-vanguardism, Third Worldism. The form of Marxism that most "fitted" these conditions was Maoism, which absolutely permeated the New Left.

She was, however, less insightful in her concluding comment that "[a]fter 1969, the end of the Cultural Revolution and the right turn of the Chinese bureaucracy made Maoism less ideologically attractive."[5]

The failure to consolidate the NDP brought Maoist alternatives to greater prominence. In Toronto, a small proto-Maoist party, Progressive Worker (allied with the Progressive Labor Party in the U.S.), founded Canadians for the National Liberation Front to mobilize anti-war action, which can be seen as a precursor to the CLM. In Vancouver, Hardial Bains founded the Internationalists in 1963 and transformed it into the CPC-ML in 1968.[6] In China, the Cultural Revolution was already mired in its bloody endgame, but it was just beginning its life as a cultural export.

Not far from the seedy inner-city tavern hotel that was Milton Acorn's Toronto home, in a Chinatown divided by loyalties to Hong Kong, Taiwan, and the PRC, the Great Wall bookstore supplied Canadian youth with Mao pins, Little Red Books, and scripts, posters, and recordings of the Revolutionary Model Peking Opera troupes. For would-be Maoists, these images were the reality of revolutionary China. The increasing appeal of Maoism and importation of its texts and artifacts in the early 1970s had been boosted by Canadian diplomatic recognition of China in 1970. One of the immediate consequences of diplomatic ties was the recuperation of an authentic Canadian Maoist hero: when Canadian officials hosted Chinese diplomats, they were mystified by requests to visit the birthplace of Norman Bethune, a name that few Canadians recognized. Mao's essay on heroic internationalism, "In Praise of Dr. Norman Bethune," began to circulate, and the Communist doctor from rural Ontario who invented mobile blood transfusion units in Spain and died volunteering with the Chinese 8th Route Army became an overnight celebrity and the subject of popular stage, film, and TV biographies.

In the absence of informed accounts about the Cultural Revolution, Maoism was reduced to the iconography of the Long March, Bethune, Red Guards, and cheerful peasants. Sympathetic reportage such as Edgar Snow's *Red Star Over China* and William Hinton's *Fanshen* popularized Maoism as communism that worked, and Maoist ideology was made known primarily through *Quotations from Chairman Mao Tse-Tung*, a North American bestseller from Bantam.[7] The Chinese

Embassy in Ottawa happily provided free copies of the journal *Chinese Literature*, with its articles on Maoist cultural theory and extracts from revolutionary operas, to anyone who didn't mind having the Royal Canadian Mounted Police open their mail. This composite image of the Chinese revolution offered three solaces to radical youth: it was modern and liberatory and opposed to the bureaucratized Soviet Union; it validated youthful dissent; and, most importantly, it situated Canada as a colony of an American empire. Canada's subaltern status in North America was, for the first time, a point of pride; as the CLM would shout (in Milton Acorn's words), "Canada is the first colony of the American empire."[8]

However, the CLM and the CPC-ML diverged in their analysis of nationalism, and it is in this that their performative strategies of leadership and mobilization differed. The CPC-ML is the more familiar structure of a revolutionary party. Its organization adhered to the Stalinist template, but in its rhetoric, public campaigns, and sloganeering, the CPC-ML mimicked its Chinese sponsor, to the point of what appeared from the outside as fetishism. (Even its publications looked like pamphlets from China, with their red covers, yellow hammer and sickle, grainy photographs, lengthy slogans, and cheap paper.) This mimicry was essentially a performance of heroic revolutionary struggle devised to sustain the appearance of mass support, activated by a cult of the leader modeled after Chairman Mao.

As national leader of the party, Hardial Bains emulated the rhetoric and posturing of the Chinese and, after 1978, the Albanian parties. His party congresses featured prolonged exhortations, mass recitations of slogans, and the familiar icons of Chinese banners: Marx, Engels, Lenin, Stalin, and Mao. These simulacra defended a rigidly "internationalist" party template rather than allowing a "Canadian" style of organization and rhetoric which would allow nationalist tendencies to obscure the internationalism of the party. Whereas the CLM presented itself as an indigenous movement produced by the moment of crisis, Bains repeatedly announced that the CPC-ML was the only legitimate heir of the original Communist Party founded in Guelph, Ontario, in 1921. Positioning his party as the vanguard, he enforced a fierce Leninist conception of the party as "the general staff" of the revolution. At the "Fifth Consultative Conference" of the party in 1978, he made the stern point that "[o]nce the Party is founded, then the Marxist-Leninist party cannot be consolidated without the Party actively, in a vigorous manner, with courage, without fear and vacillation, leading the class struggle against the reactionary bourgeoisie."[9]

Echoing Mao's remark that a revolution is not a dinner party, Bains invoked a Bolshevik regime of dictatorial control "with courage, without fear and vacillation":

> A genuinely Marxist-Leninist party is not a debating society and it cannot be formed out of debates by speculating on Marxism-Leninism A genuinely Marxist-Leninist party does not permit any speculation on Marxism-Leninism and does not permit any factions within it. It does not permit "freedom of criticism" and it does not permit any loosening of its iron discipline. It builds its unity of thinking and action in battle against the class enemy and it strengthens itself by opposing revisionism and opportunism of all hues.[10]

Bains reserved his most ferocious attacks for the "class enemies" on the Left; especially, the rival Maoist groups, and, above all, the Soviet-client CPC:

> [F]or them to say that they are "Marxist-Leninists" is merely to strike a posture, a frill, like adorning their hat with plumes, but in essence, they are the same – reformists, terrorists, anarcho-syndicalists – you name it. And their social base is petty bourgeoisie and lumpen proletariat.[11]

"The revisionists" countered with the same charges, accusing their rivals of being mere performers. Following the 1974 federal parliamentary election, in which Bains received a mere sixty votes, William Kashtan, leader of the CPC, wrote that "[t]he Maoists' pseudo-revolutionary phrase-mongering serves the interests of reaction and must be thoroughly exposed in the working-class and democratic movements and in the popular movements of the people."[12]

The CPC-ML's moment of heroic crisis came with its 1978 break with China. With the statement that "Marxism-Leninism-Mao Tsetung Thought belongs not just to the proletariat of China but to the international proletariat,"[13] Bains positioned himself as a custodian of Maoism even as he took his party to a new sponsor, Enver Hoxha. Until the collapse of the Albanian Party of Labor, the CPC-ML and its affiliates were slavish in their devotion to Hoxha. Bains celebrated the new affiliation in hyperbolic rhetoric: "The PLA has Comrade Enver Hoxha at its head, the great Marxist-Leninist. The Marxist-Leninist of the calibre of Marx, Engels, Lenin, Stalin, and Mao Tsetung. He stands at the helm of the International Marxist-Leninist Communist Movement. All glory to the

PLA for such an outstanding Marxist-Leninist, Comrade Enver Hoxha, at its head!"[14] As the tide of Maoism receded following the suppression of the Cultural Revolution, the CPC-ML's overheated rhetoric appears increasingly parodic. Although Bains pointed out that Hoxha began the PLA with only 200 members, a number roughly equivalent to the undisclosed membership of the CPC-ML, the entire party congress could fill one room.[15] The vanguard was the very mass that it mobilized. Bains's organization strategy was in this sense a mass party without a mass, but it performed itself with the full panoply of power. As the Chinese and, later, the Albanian parties succumbed to "revisionism," the CPC-ML stubbornly clung to its Stalinist purity. Not surprisingly, the CPC-ML made few inroads in the broader cultural sphere. After Bains's death, the noted poet and playwright George Elliot Clarke published "Homage to Hardial Bains," in which he wrote:

But you, Bains, you were the bane
of Capital – that sadomasochism,

and damned the shit that is money,
and damned that shit called money,

impeaching Nietzsche, and clawed
off bankers' coldly horrifying masks,

for you hated medieval-vile police,
and let poems comfort you at night... [16]

But this is the only indication of cultural interest within the CPC-ML. The party's failure to attract artists went along with its rigid adherence to the textual and iconic signifiers of Stalinism. This was perhaps one of the key reasons why the CPC-ML, despite the noise and acrimony it generated on the Left and in the mainstream media, was never able to overturn its public perception as an extremist fringe. The CPC-ML endorsed the theory of national liberation, but distrusted nationalism as "national and social chauvinism."[17] Its optic was resolutely internationalist, seeing national liberation as a phase of the class struggle. This position failed to harness the nationalism that characterized Canadian cultural production in the 1970.

If the CPC-ML was a mass party without a mass, the Canadian Liberation Movement was a following without a party. Its structures were unstable, its leadership little more than revolutionary roleplay, and its ideology fundamentally incoherent – but its popular appeal was undeniable. The CLM catchphrase "Canada is a Colony" was resonant with romanticized images of heroic Third World guerrillas and inextricable from the resurgence in populist localism. This was, for the most part, a sentimental fetish of "the land" and assumed an unproblematized and unexamined "authentic" Canadianness. In this climate, the CLM prospered by turning such sentiment into material cultural production. From the outside, the CLM appeared remarkably energetic, sponsoring rallies and poetry readings, publishing a newspaper, and publishing a list of titles designed to legitimize its position as an intellectually responsible movement.

The CLM was formed in 1968 by anti-war activists who wished to transport the signifiers of national liberation struggle out of Vietnam and into the specific historical contexts of Canada.[18] A core discussion group, which included two of the leaders of the Waffle and a University of Toronto English professor, soon drifted apart, leaving the proto-organization in the hands of Gary Perly. A former student anti-war activist at the University of Toronto, systems analyst for IBM, and later head of his family's map-making firm, Perly established the group as the CLM, with himself as National Chairman. Although the CLM later imploded over a crisis of leadership cultism, it is a significant that Perly was rarely identified in the movement's literature by name, only as "The National Chairman." His anonymity was the absence that Acorn's celebrity filled.

Perly built his organization much as Bains did his, from the top down, but without the regulating script of the party apparatus that stabilized the CPC-ML. The CLM was comprised of a National Executive, local clubs (mostly in Ontario), the publishing house, and organizing drives in the labor movement. The structure appeared to be one of democratic centralism; in practice, it was non-democratic and extremely centralized. The local clubs were inexperienced, young, and unreliable, consisting mostly of students. (The surviving minutes of a branch meeting in Guelph record a contentious discussion about acceptable levels of beer consumption in the group.) The National Executive was the editorial and management board of the publishing house, which was also the certified shop of the syndicalist Canadian Workers Union, founded by the CLM, and whose principal organizer was a member of the National Executive and a major author of the publishing house.

The National Executive also comprised the Marxist-Leninist Caucus of the movement. The CLM's membership criteria were ostensibly non-sectarian, asking only that members be anti-imperialist, pro-socialist, and "not anti-Communist." The presence of the Marxist-Leninist Caucus was destabilizing, the site of fierce battles and abuse similar to those associated with religious cults. The papers of former members contain testimonies of bullying, abuse, and torture. But they also expose the inner performativity of the movement, a performativity comprised of witnessed rituals of submission and privileged revelations of unmasked leadership.[19] There is a visible strain of masochism in the many "self-criticisms" in the archive, in which members denounce themselves and identify their primary and secondary contradictions. In one case, the principal theorist of the movement wrote after a meeting with a right-wing worker at a shop he was trying to organize, "I should...be physically punished by the members of this caucus, to make sure that I understand the seriousness of my crime."

Even more abject is a forty-page document, written in various hands, including shorthand (which suggests it was dictated, again suggesting a public ritual of humiliation) and then compressed into an edited typescript by the woman who had been abused at the "Organizing School," in which she states:

> I don't like being a rotten Yankee agent. I don't want to continue in my evil deeds, manipulating, lying, covering up, creating false images and impressions, splitting and wrecking, serving myself, being sectarian, opportunistic, arrogant. I want to fight for Canadian liberation, to be a CLM member, to be an anti-imperialist, to become a Canadian, to use my abilities and skills for the Movement, to care about people, for people to care about me not because of false images but because I want to change, for my comrades to help me change.[20]

All of this suggests that the CLM was indeed "a national chauvinist, social-fascist, absolutely degenerate organization." Unlike Bains, who consolidated his leadership cult with the same self-discipline he demanded of the membership, and whose lengthy writings demonstrate a genuine erudition in the literature of Marxist-Leninism, Perly appears to have ruled by force of personality alone. It may be that the CLM's courses on Marxist-Leninist theory (complete with written exams) intensified contradictions within the group.

Milton Acorn, the movement's only real veteran of the Left, hinted at this in his valedictory remarks to the membership:

> I have a suggestion to offer to those comrades who want to declare the movement Marxist-Leninist. Don't contribute to splitting in the Marxist-Leninist Movement! Join the CPC (ML) or the

Marxist-Leninist League. Struggle there to reform their sectarianism.
The rest of us will wish you well...

Now back to the causes of sectarianism. It wasn't because Gary
Perly was a bad man. It wasn't because we over-emphasized the role
of leadership. It was Perly himself who over-emphasized his own role
and gathered a claque around him. Again, what was the cause of
this? Internal contradictions are primary, there is no escaping our
personal responsibility for what has happened to our movement.
But internal contradictions are often set off by contradictions in the
external world.[21]

The CLM struggled against "Perlyism" but could not survive Perly; when
he was expelled, the organization collapsed. He was the central actor in
what appears to be a fundamentally unplanned improvisation. We can
only guess at the damage and conflict within the group that brought it
to crisis, but on the basis of the self-criticisms, the psychological pressures within the group must have been extreme.

From the outside, however, all of this was invisible. New Canada
Press put the CLM logo in all of its books, ensuring that it would reach
thousands of readers in libraries across the country. In 1974, it made
a bid for legitimacy with the publication of Barry Lord's *The History of
Painting in Canada*.[22] Despite the widespread condemnation of the book,
it is important because, although it is the most developed expression of
the CLM's theoretical principles, its critical failure, measured against
Acorn's success, reveals the extent to which performativity rather than
ideology legitimized the movement. The CLM's intellectual and a member of the National Executive, Lord was a prominent art historian and
former editor of *artscanada* magazine who had held a number of senior
curatorial and administrative posts, including the directorship of the
Vancouver Art Gallery and Education Director at the National Gallery
of Canada. While many agreed with his thesis that Canadian art had
been marginalized by the hegemony of the "imperial" art world, his
over-the-top rhetoric ruined the effect. Writing in *Labor Challenge*, Ian
Angus summarized the book when he wrote, "It is terrible because his
entire approach is rooted in the mixture of crude Canadian nationalism and Maoism-Stalinism that passes for political thought in the
CLM."[23] *The History of Painting in Canada* reads like a party pamphlet,
a reading confirmed by the inclusion of the CLM anthem as a preface
and a full-page recruitment ad for the CLM at the end. Lord was a
serious and reputable critic, but his book was received as an aberra-
tion. In contrast, Milton Acorn, who held the same convictions, was

received as an authoritative voice whose political principles enriched his poetry. The 10,000 copies of *More Poems for People* may have done more to popularize the CLM than all of the rest of the movement's efforts together.

And so we return to Milton Acorn who, in the mid-1970s, was a familiar sight on Spadina Avenue, Toronto's equivalent to New York City's Canal Street. Acorn was one of the most famous of Canadian poets, but most people who passed him on the street would likely have dismissed him as a derelict. Then in his fifties, he lived in a shabby room above one of Toronto's seediest taverns. A communist since his youth, a Second World War army veteran, a laborer from the small maritime province of Prince Edward Island, Acorn was Canada's most celebrated working-class writer. His poetry was angry, passionate, intensely lyrical, and popular. In 1969, he was shortlisted for the Governor General's Award, Canada's highest literary prize, for his collection *I've Tasted My Blood*.[24] When he was passed over, an angry group of fellow poets who believed that Acorn had been shafted by an American-born judge invented "The Canadian Poet's Award" for him and named him "The People's Poet."

A short time later, according to various accounts, Acorn was walking by the CLM office, popped in for a quick look, and joined on the spot. His membership in the CLM was a stroke of luck for Perly, but his support was a mixed blessing. To have the People's Poet as a spokesman and bestselling author for New Canada Press reinforced the CLM's bid for cultural legitimacy, and his long history on the Left brought political experience and a touchstone to historical tradition. But Acorn was also a complex and demanding personality – he had, after all, quit every party he had joined – and he required care and tact. Perly seems to have been understandably ambivalent about the presence of an older man who, if he had the cultural capital to legitimize the movement, could by the same token destroy it. A CLM newsletter in 1972 registers this ambivalence:

Milton Acorn in Thunder Bay

In addition to getting considerable creative work done, he has found time to be a valuable temporary addition to our Club here, helping with New Canada sales and other mass work, taking principled unliberal positions in criticism/self criticism sessions, visiting with contacts and taking an active part in meetings and classes. We have found that we have much to learn from Milton's past political experience, and that, contrawise, Milton has much to unlearn ...

> Milton is not yet convinced that his CLM membership should be publicly known across Canada. Til he, in consultation with other members, makes a definite decision, this information should be kept within the organization.[25]

Acorn allowed himself to be outed in *More Poems for People* in that same year. He was an active member and participated in the Marxism-Leninism course three years later. Acorn's communism was reinforced by a knowledge of dialectics and theory, but it was built on long experience in struggle, and he was by nature an anti-authoritarian maverick. At the same time, he believed in the possibilities of the CLM and appears to have tried to mediate a solution to its final crisis. As he told the membership at the end, "Our basic line is correct. The conditions of membership are correct. What we need now is a constitution, and a preamble to that constitution, stating our aims. In time we must write and publish a Canadian Manifesto."[26] The CLM could not heed this advice nor could its fundamentally improvisational character be concretized in a manifesto. As far as it was concerned, Milton Acorn *was* their manifesto. After the movement disintegrated, Acorn helped revive New Canada Press with the nationalist critic and poet Robin Mathews as Steel Rail Publishing. He then proceeded to write his manifesto in the form of a play, "a real gunpowder play…Dry and fresh in the pan."[27]

Terry Barker calls *The Road to Charlottetown* "the clearest expression of…Canadian nationalist Marxism."[28] Acorn wrote the play in collaboration with Cedric Smith, a folk singer and actor who had been on the fringes of the CLM, and was best known as founder of the group Perth County Conspiracy (Does Not Exist), for whom he set Acorn's poetry to music. Acorn was an iconic figure for Perth County. His poetry spoke fire, his life embodied struggle, and his demeanor was a self-performance of rough working-class masculinity. This was an image that he wrote into *The Road to Charlottetown*. The title of the play encodes a double meaning, referring literally to the roads blocked by tenant farmers who rebelled against British absentee landlords in Prince Edward Island in the early nineteenth century and gesturing metaphorically to the Charlottetown Conference of 1864, which hammered out the details for the confederation of Canada three years later. Acorn's thesis was that Confederation was a betrayal of the working classes, handing the country to agents of imperialism who were no different from the land agents who had oppressed the tenant farmers of his island home. Confederation was simply a modernization of imperialism designed to improve the capitalist system, as described by a politician in the play: "In other systems, slaves are unwilling, they sabotage everything they do, only capitalism makes people into willing slaves."[29]

The Road to Charlottetown developed over two years in several different versions. Originally, Acorn wrote it as a cabaret of episodic scenes, poems, and songs. It was performed with four actors and began its first tour by playing in prisons in Ontario. It then played briefly in Toronto, where it was reviewed enthusiastically by *The Globe and Mail*, and in the summer of 1977, after revision, opened in Charlottetown (in the version published twenty years later). In 1978, a rewritten version with six actors opened at Theatre Passe Muraille, advertising itself as "a toe-tappin' Maritime musical about Landlords and Tenants," to mixed reviews. *The Globe and Mail* wrote, "This is a hell of a show. The story of the island in the 1840s crackles with a zest and fidelity as palpable as red mud on your boots. The best of the humor packs a lovely ironic wallop. And the music ranges from rambunctious rallying cries to touching, simple songs of a very special beauty."[30] This view was endorsed by the Communist Party's *Canadian Tribune*, whose theatre critic Oscar Ryan (writing as Martin Stone) was a veteran of the workers theatre movement of the 1930s. He wrote that it was "rollicking fun," a "boisterous outpouring of folksongs, sketches, satire, and farce abetted by singing actors and acting instrumentalists – all bristling with irreverent protest and popular defiance."[31] In contrast, the tabloid *Toronto Sun* dismissed it as a "sophomoric revue" filled with "mawkish folksongs and bucolic clog dances...based upon limping meters and dissonant rhymes from doggerel written by a self-proclaimed P.E.I. poet named Milton Acorn."[32] That a critic in the *Sun* would not recognize Acorn's name would surprise no one; what is of interest here is that familiarity with Acorn's poetry may have conditioned the more literate reviewers to view the show as culturally "authentic" although it was performed by a cast of Toronto actors.

The central character of the play is named either Milton Acorn or Old John Acorn, depending on the version (Old John in the published text):

I, Old John Acorn, not at first aware that was my name
And what I knew was life,
Came from an island to which I've often returned
Looking for peace and usually found strife,
'Til I came to see it was no pocket in a saint's pants
While outside trouble reigned...and after all
My favourite mode of weather's been a hurricane.[33]

However named, he is clearly the author retrofitted into history as a Falstaffian rebel determined to fight oppression with his fists and his words:

> *Mary*: So ye thin ye're saying to write a play, Milton? Let's see where
>   ye'll start it.
> *Milton*: No I didn't say I was going to write a play.
>   They play's in my head. It'll come out in time
>   but not to raise idle fancies, hopes that are too
>   far ahead, like Canada when we began.
>   It'll come out when people can dig into it
>   then dig out of it, dig something
>   Out of it.
>   It'll be a real gunpowder play,
>   Not to get mouldy. Dry and fresh in the pan
>   I'll explode with maximum force.
>   Maybe one of my great-grumpedty-granph
>   Grandchildren will write it.
> *Mary*: There's always been a Milton Acorn,
>   Long as our traditions go
>   And no doubt there'll by [sic] many more
>   Maybe another Milton Acorn'll write it
>   Let's see where you'll start it.[34]

After five years with the CLM, Acorn's turn to the stage followed logically from the performativity of his role in the movement. A bestselling poet, he could have easily published the play as a cycle of poems; it would have been received in a wider field of critical reception and it might even have made money. The choice to do a play that few people would actually see seems curious, until considered as an extension of his public role in the CLM. Even though it never mentions the CLM, *The Road to Charlottetown* theatrically rehabilitates the movement and recuperates its principles. In these terms, it is not particularly important that relatively few people actually saw it. (Records from Theatre Passe Muraille indicate 1,935 over five weeks.) By transforming the argument of the CLM into theatre, Acorn transformed political improvisation into activism in and of the public sphere, and he freed himself from the ambivalence of his iconic position. In the play, Acorn historicized himself as author and subject, announcing, "All days are those days, even the days we're living in; because history doesn't stop, not for an instant it's carving us, and we're carving it, right now."[35] The show was an avatar of Acorn, distributing his public face among a community of actors and spectators. The public figure of Milton Acorn became a collective.

Carved by history and carving history, Acorn appears to have realized that the struggle for socialism in Canada required an approach freed from its political culture. It was this culture that he sought to mythologize in *The Road to Charlottetown*, and this may offer another explanation for his decision to express himself through theatre, a platform where history speaks through the plural bodies of actors rather than the texts of political doctrine. Doctrinal texts lead to variant readings and sectarianism, but texts played through the naturalizing bodies of actors manifest consensus.[36] In his final address to the CLM, Acorn appealed for an end to sectarianism on the Left with the warning that "time lost may mean that the Canadian phase of the World Peoples struggle for Liberation and Socialism may be fatally crippled and a permanent scar left on history, having after-effects lasting for thousands of years."[37] It may be that Acorn saw the theatre as the road through sectarianism.

The conjunction of Hardial Bain's party congresses and the CLM's private rituals of power demonstrate the failure of the Maoist Left in Canada. As a simulation of a mass party, the CPC-ML in the end became little more than a reiterative performance that continued to rehearse its script of revolutionary purity; as an improvisation of a political movement, the CLM could not survive its own Red Guardism. In *The Road to Charlottetown*, Acorn attempted to resolve this contradiction by historicizing ideology, liberating politics from the authorizing scripts of the failed revolutionary past, and embodying a Marxist-Leninism rescued from iconic cults of leadership. His transformation of his own celebrity into a collective theatrical community was his most articulate critique of the Canadian Liberation Movement and its vanguardist ideology.

Notes

1. Milton Acorn, *More Poems for People* (Toronto: New Canada Press, 1972, 10).
2. Ed Pickersgill, Editorial, *Alive Magazine*, Oct. 2, 1976, 8.
3. Desmond Morton, *The New Democrats, 1961–1986* (Toronto: Copp Clark Pitman, 1986), 92.
4. The Waffle Group. "The Waffle Manifesto: For an Independent Socialist Canada," http://www.socialisthistory.ca/Docs/Waffle/WaffleManifesto.htm (accessed June 8, 2009).
5. Tina Craig, "A Brief History of the Canadian New Left," *The Old Mole* (1972), http://www.socialistaction.ca/sa-farc_om.html (accessed May 3, 2002).
6. Communist Party of Canada (Marxist-Leninist) (CPC-ML), *Documents of the Fifth Consultative Conference of the Communist Party of Canada (Marxist-Leninist),*

November 11–13, 1977 (Montreal: The Communist Party of Canada [Marxist-Leninist], 1977), 23.

7. Mao Tse-Tung, *Quotations from Chairman Mao Tse-Tung* (New York: Bantam Books, 1967).
8. Acorn, *More Poems for People*, 102.
9. CPC-ML, *Documents*, 21.
10. Ibid., 21–22.
11. Hardial Bains, *Six Years of CPC (M-L): A Great Revolutionary Movement Against Revisionism and for Proletarian Revolution* (Toronto: Norman Bethune Institute, 1976), 8.
12. William Kashtan, "The Federal Election – What Next?" in *Toward Socialism: Selected Writings* (Toronto: Progress Books, 1976), 232.
13. Bains, *Six Years*, 8.
14. CPC-ML, *Documents*, 78.
15. Ibid., 77.
16. George Elliott Clarke, "Homage for Hardial Bains (1939–1997)," *Oyster Boy Review* 12, http://www.oysterboyreview.com/12/Clarke-Homage.html (accessed May 3, 2002).
17. CPC-ML, *Documents*, 86.
18. Terry Barker, "Origins of the CLM by Terry Barker; Reconstructed from remarks by Phil Taylor, July 7, 1984," Canadian Liberation Movement Fonds, William Ready Division of Archives and Research Collections (McMaster University Library, Hamilton, Ontario), 1.
19. The self-criticism documents are all signed and dated, and are held in the Canadian Liberation Movement fonds at the McMaster University Library. I have chosen not to identify the authors.
20. Ibid.
21. Canadian Liberation Movements, Canadian Liberation Movement Fonds, William Ready Division of Archives and Research Collections (McMaster University Library, Hamilton, Ontario), 4.
22. Barry Lord, *The History of Painting in Canada: Towards a People's Art* (Toronto: New Canada Press, 1974).
23. Ian Angus, "A Stalinist and Nationalist View of Art," *Labor Challenge*, Feb. 24, 1975.
24. Milton Acorn, *I've Tasted My Blood* (Toronto: Ryerson Press, 1969).
25. Canadian Liberation Movements, *Newsletter* 1.2, Canadian Liberation Movement Fonds, William Ready Division of Archives and Research Collections (McMaster University Library, Hamilton, Ontario).
26. Anonymous [Milton Acorn], "Final Draft," 4. Canadian Liberation Movement Fonds, William Ready Division of Archives and Research Collections (McMaster University Library, Hamilton, Ontario).
27. Milton Acorn, *The Road to Charlottetown*, typescript, Theatre Passe Muraille Archives, McLaughlin Library, University of Guelph, n.d., n.p.
28. Terry Barker, *After Acorn: Meditations on the Message of Canada's People's Poet* (Hamilton, Ontario: Mekler & Deahl, 1999), 18.
29. Milton Acorn and Cedric Smith, *The Road to Charlottetown* (Hamilton, Ontario: Mekler & Deahl, 1998), 68.
30. Bryan Johnson, "Road to Charlottetown Retains Its Earthly Allure," Toronto *Globe and Mail*, Nov. 10, 1978: 15.

31. Martin Stone, "Class War in PEI," *Canadian Tribune*, Nov. 20 1978.
32. Mackenzie Porter, "Wrong Turn Taken in this Road Show," *Toronto Sun*, Nov. 13, 1978.
33. Acorn and Smith, *The Road to Charlottetown*, 13.
34. Acorn, *Road to Charlottetown*, typescript, D.1.
35. Ibid., D.3–4.
36. On the creation of consensus through actor performances, see Robert Nunn, "The Meeting of Actuality and Theatricality in *The Farm Show*," *Canadian Drama* 8.1 (1982): 43–54; and Alan Filewod, *Collective Encounters: Documentary Theatre in English Canada* (Toronto: University of Toronto Press, 1987), 24–49.
37. Anonymous [Milton Acorn], "Final Draft," 1.

Part III
Divergences

9
Introduction

Alan Filewod

I've never seen a Banksy work, but, like millions, I know him as the emblematic insurgent artist whose graffiti stencil images circulate through reproductions on the web. From his earliest forays as an anonymous graffiti imagist (imagista?) in the streets of Bristol and London, to his legitimation by arts councils and his chic installations in New York, Banksy offers a perfect example of the paradox of the radical artist negotiating the celebrity and institutionalization made possible by mass communication. In this negotiation of insurgence and institutionalization, Banksy has sustained a performance of anonymity.

Adding a further complication, as galleries and dealers clamored for his works, London Transport and the Westminster City Council were painting over his street stencils, and the Bristol City Museum was mounting a major exhibition of his works. Banksy exists simultaneously on the street and in the gallery market. While his paintings have sold for more than $500,000, his website store gives away selected images for free non-commercial use.

Like Matisse and Jeff Koons before him, Banksy operates in a loop of parody and violation. The more his work seeks to disrupt, the greater the value it commands; the more he reinforces his anonymity, the greater his celebrity; the more local his work, the more universally acclaimed it becomes. Banksy is both a postmodern trickster and a case study of the trajectory of "the avant-garde." Banksy exists in a closed loop, that system of self-referentiality that we have come to understand as "the avant-garde" and that suggests to critics such as Peter Bürger that it is dead.[1] Banksy is classically "avant-garde," but he is not, I suggest, "vanguardist" in the sense that this anthology seeks to develop.

Why "vanguard" and not "avant-garde"? The two terms denote exactly the same thing, but, in the connotative gap between them, there can be discerned a tension between a *historical formation* constituted through metropolitan art practices and a distributed, decentered *position* of artistic radicalism. It is this tension that critical vanguard studies seeks to address by delinking the operative principles of "vanguard" cultural practice from the troubled genealogical structure of "the avant-garde." I suggest that "the avant-garde" operates in two ways: as self-positioning by artists as they claim place in fields of reception, consumption, and distribution, and as a critical assignment by critics, arts marketers, and historians seeking to establish the value and genealogy of artworks.[2] While "the avant-garde" is primarily an instrument of art-historical categorization and thus opens up questions about art, markets, and reception, "vanguard" is a term concerning social and ideological positioning. Both terms imply a progressivist teleology, a directionality that postmodernism refutes. But, if the avant-garde is an archive and a domain of reception (that is, a market), the vanguard is variously a tendency, a gesture, an act, and a phenomenon.

However, substituting "vanguard" for "avant-garde" is merely a bait-and-switch unless the substitution enables us to perceive more clearly how radical art practices actually produce change. As the essays in this section indicate, one way the idea of "vanguardism" works is to refute the singularity of "the" avant-garde and its implications of transcultural, universal modernity. A discourse that emphasizes positionality (the vanguard, as opposed to the avant-garde) enables us to see the plurality of avant-gardes and thus to question their centrality. I would urge us to use "the avant-garde" then to identify the critical and canonical tradition of classification, and "vanguard" to locate the cultural and political radicalism of art practice in context.

The impulse behind the monolithic and monumentalizing genealogical obsession of "the avant-garde" can be traced through the canon of critical writings centering around Bürger's influential arguments about the institutional location of the avant-garde.[3] Such views are predicated on a silent assumption that "the avant-garde," as practice, as history, and as domain of reception, is inherently transcultural and deracinated. This assumption's sources are the uplift humanism of the Second International and in the class-differentiated internationalism of the radical Left of the early twentieth century that followed from it.[4] Perhaps the clearest expression of this position today is in the radical humanism of Alain Badiou, who argues that art is necessarily universal. In his "Fifteen Theses on Contemporary Art," Badiou writes, "Art cannot merely be the expression of a particularity (be it ethnic or personal). Art is the impersonal production of a truth that is addressed to everyone."[5]

Wrapped in contemporary critical theory, this is the canonical position that has ordered understandings of the avant-garde as an archive of diverse practices and principles and a coherent historical narrative. That coherence rests upon a universalist assumption that the essays in this section all seek to dismantle. Standing or looking outside the metropolitan Euro-American critical tradition, they tend to be aware of the fact that vanguardism is fundamentally relational, not formal or critical, and point to the artist's situated agency in systems of political and discursive power. Indeed, what emerges from these essays is the suspicion that academic discourse on the avant-garde, paradoxically, has always been more concerned with the situation of the artist – that is, his or her metropolitan position – than with the actual art practice.

Bearing in mind Pierre Bourdieu's point that systems of classification "produce the groups, the very groups which produce the principles and the groups against which they are produced,"[6] the very proposition of both the vanguard and the avant-garde is self-referential and retrocursive. It takes moments of position – of artists, scholars, and critics – as historical evidence of positionality. In effect, the subjunctive terms of cultural stakeholding enter history as positivist evidence. Rhetoric, marketing, critique, and theory all blur into a vaguely defined historical formation that produces boundary mechanisms shaping the conditions of subsequent practice. Perhaps the clearest example of this took place in the 1930s, when centralized organizations and model template troupes affiliated with the League of Workers' Theatres tried to mobilize the vast and diverse field of radical Left theatre work into an ideologically coherent "movement." Histories of the period accept the proposition of that movement on the basis of the organizational polemics it sought to create. Political strategy has become historical fact.

Some boundary mechanisms, such as curatorial valorization and market success, have become familiar tropes in avant-garde discourse. Indeed, the relation of vanguard practice and celebrity is particularly troublesome and provides one of the threads that work through the chapters in this section. The celebrity status of the artist structures bodies of work in retroactive sequences, to the point where juvenilia – think of Brecht's *Baal* – are invested as examples of emergence.

These three chapters examine very different historical problems, but they share a critique of what we might call the metro-European basis of "the avant-garde." This leads to the fundamental principle that "vanguards" must necessarily be local and relational, and that no cultural artifact, practice, or theory is inherently radical. For example, if radically innovative artworks can lose their dissident edge when relocated (from street to museum or from studio to corporate boardroom), so can canonical and conventionalized artworks acquire a radical edge when recontextualized. Historians and critics have paid very little attention to questions of audience and spectatorship – indirectly promoting the concept of the avant-garde – but a truly critical approach to the vanguard requires attention to the problem of who's looking, where, and why. Questions of form and method – the traditional concerns of "the avant-garde" – give way to questions of effect.

This principle underlies the three chapters in this section. Esther Kim Lee's examination of the South Korean state's institutionalization of the personage and legacy of Nam June Paik as an icon of national modernity, Praise Zenenga's account of the high-stakes politics of artistic innovation in Zimbabwe's war of liberation, and Graham White's microhistorical examination of the radically different political futures seeded in the Sex Pistol's 1976 inaugural concerts all provide examples of art practices that express different and indeterminate values in different contexts. In each, moments of progressive dissent are superimposed on the realities of critical, dissident, or subversive arts captured by political movements. As was the case in the 1930s – when the work of Futurists, Expressionists, and other critical art movements were exploited by the Right – these more contemporary vanguard arts exercise a disturbing appeal to mass political movements and revolutionary power.

But if any ascription of "vanguardism" is necessarily contextual, and if any art practice can be identified as "vanguard" depending on that context, how do we account for the circulation within the discourse of "the avant-garde" of artistic practices tropes that seem to be universally recognized as "avant-garde"? I would argue that it is the persistence of these practices and tropes that has constituted the historical formation of the avant-garde.

The first point to be considered is that these have remained virtually unchanged since the early twentieth century. Deconstructed narratives, machine performance, decentered bodies, collage and fragmentation, theatrical mobility, resituated venues and discomfiting patterns of signal to noise – to cite only the most prominent – have contributed to an artistic and critical-scholarly vocabulary that "speaks" modernity and innovation. The incorporation of new technologies into artwork, for example, invariably begins with creating a rupture in habituated practices of production and reception, and theory invariably identifies these ruptures as evidence of the new. Artistic dissidence expresses itself by breaking with hegemonic patterns of production and reception. Hence

Clement Greenberg's notorious (and overworked) comment on Jackson Pollock, that "all profoundly original art looks ugly at first."

The second point is that these kinds of disruption coalesce as patterned formations, meaningful practices that evidence cultural authenticity. Recurrently, we have seen such practices offered as evidence of suppressed or marginal cultures, particularly when oppositional practices become essentialized as affirmative properties. Consider, for example, the deployment of tropes of authenticity in the 1960s and 1970s. Praise Zenenga offers one such example in the history of *pungwe* performance, which he describes as an "amalgam of meetings, song, dance, political teachings [and] dramatic skits" fostered by the freedom fighters in Zimbabwe's anti-colonial liberation war. Referencing traditional performance culture, the *pungwe*'s vanguardism came from a reclaimed cultural authenticity at least in part due to its simultaneous refutation of traditional and modernist European theatrical practices. At the same time, in Western Europe and North America, feminist artists proposed an artistic mode that contrasted phallocentric linearity with gynocentric circularity (a proposition articulately expressed in Hélène Cixous's 1977 "Aller à la Mer"). Simultaneously, First Nations artists in North America, such as playwright Tomson Highway, contrasted Eurocentric linearity with indigenous circularity. And we see the same principle at work in the neofascist "Blood and Honour" punk movement of the last two decades, as Graham White shows in his essay. In each case, the refusal of the artistic methods of hegemonic power – including those powers recognized as "avant-garde" – served a strategic purpose in supporting the kind of communal authenticity that often allows vanguard identity to be constructed and deployed.

Thirdly, these chapters show three directions of divergence, three moments in which "the avant-garde" splits into separate vectors of celebrity, local effect, and distributed image. Celebrity valorizes the artist more than the art, "the avant-garde" more than the "vanguard." Nam June Paik and the Sex Pistols share this projection into the sphere of celebrity. As Esther Kim Lee demonstrates, Paik's "heroic status" as an icon of Korean modernity signifies the transnational power of the New York avant-garde and its capacity to rebrand a nation. For their part, the Sex Pistols are ultimately more important for their gutter fame than for their actual music (although their fans would disagree).

Each of these examples exerted profound local effects on their audiences, and they all, to varying degree, had influence well beyond that local situation. This dynamic relationship of the local and the universal is discussed by each of these writers. As an experimental artist, Paik was part of a movement that sought new ways to understand and deploy the human body and the video image, and this enabled both renewed forms of situated vanguardism and the strengthening of South Korea's image as a modern nation. As an archetypal punk band, the Sex Pistols unleashed an incoherent working-class rage that has found adherents around the world, despite the very different socio-economic circumstances in which they were listened to and emulated. In Zimbabwe, artists returning from exile practiced in the methods of the avant-garde theatre entered complex negotiations between Western modernity and nationalist traditionalism.

Each of these chapters explores moments in which vanguard art changes radically through distributed images of itself. And in their difficult complicities with power – state power in South Korea, military power in Zimbabwe, and the unruly masculinist power of neo-Nazi punks – they all expose the discourse of avant-garde radicalism as a failure. The discursive abstraction of "the avant-garde" collapses radical art into historical formation and formalism; a discourse of the "vanguard," on the other hand, embraces risk and all of the possible, unexpected, desired, and undesired futures risk entails. Vanguards, in other words, perform.

Notes

1. For the critique of the neo-avant-garde, see Peter Bürger, *Theory of the Avant-Garde*, trans. Michael Shaw (Minneapolis: University of Minnesota Press, 1984).
2. For discussion of the discourse of the avant-garde, see Fred Orton and Griselda Pollock, *Avant-Gardes and Partisans Reviewed* (Manchester: Manchester University Press, 1996); Paul Mann, *Theory-Death of the Avant-Garde* (Bloomington: Indiana University Press, 1991); and Mike Sell, *Avant-Garde Performance and the Limits of Criticism: The Living Theatre, Happenings/ Fluxus, and the Black Arts Movement* (Ann Arbor: University of Michigan Press, 2005).
3. Bürger, *Theory of the Avant-Garde*.
4. Alan Filewod and David Watt, *Workers' Playtime: Theatre and the Labour Movement since 1970* (Sydney: Currency Press, 2001), 28–30.
5. Alain Badiou, "Fifteen Theses on Contemporary Art," *Civic Centre: Reclaiming the Right to Performance*, Conference catalogue (London: Roehampton University, 2003), 35.
6. Pierre Bourdieu, *Distinction: A Social Critique of the Judgment of Taste*, trans. Richard Nice (Cambridge, MA: Harvard University Press, 1984), 479.

10
Avant-Garde Becomes Nationalism: Immortalizing Nam June Paik in South Korea

Esther Kim Lee

The Korean-born video art pioneer Nam June Paik died on January 29, 2006, at the age of seventy-three.[1] He died in the United States, where he lived most of his life. After his death, obituaries appeared in major newspapers around the world, paying respect and expressing admiration for the artist who, in addition to his remarkable body of work as an artist, is credited for coining the phrase "electronic superhighway" in 1974. The writers of the obituaries focused on video art installations such as his landmark piece *TV Buddha* (1974), as well as his involvement with the Fluxus movement. Also remembered was Paik's famously playful persona, both subversive and entertaining. The funeral, held at the Frank Campbell Funeral Chapel in New York City, commemorated his impressive artistic career and celebrated his life. It brought together a rare gathering of major Fluxus and video artists, all of whom were Paik's longtime collaborators and friends. Bill Viola, Christo and Jeanne-Claude, Merce Cunningham, and Yoko Ono were among the 400 attendees.[2] The funeral also featured a Fluxus-inspired performance, which was led by Paik's nephew, his oldest brother's son, Ken Paik Hakuta, who surprised the attendees by taking out a basket full of scissors and instructing everyone wearing a tie to cut it off. The performance, for those who knew Paik, was an obvious reference to Paik's 1960 Fluxus act in which he cut off John Cage's tie while the two were co-performing *Etude for Piano*. Yoko Ono was the first to perform; she cut off Hakuta's tie and placed it on Paik's body, which lay in an open coffin.

Respecting his request, Paik was buried in ten countries. His ashes were sent to locations significant to Paik's career, including Deutsche

Guggenheim Berlin and Nam June Paik Studio in New York City. But his final place of burial was South Korea, a country Paik considered home despite his U.S. citizenship and unquestionably cosmopolitan outlook. In a 2004 press conference, Paik announced, "I wish to go back to Korea and be buried there [when I die]."[3] When his ashes were brought to Korea, his life was celebrated wholeheartedly with numerous public memorial ceremonies and a massive amount of media coverage. Paik's posthumous homecoming was described as the return of "a giant artist" or "a genius artist." Such titles were often accompanied by a phrase that can best be translated as "an artist who was borne by Korea," connoting a sense of a mother country that literally gives birth to her people. Paik was someone who made the Korean people proud of his accomplishments abroad. He epitomized the modern Korean hero.

But Paik was an unlikely hero, especially in a society that still values a traditional sense of decorum and Confucian ethics. Paik's outrageous artworks such as the battering of a piano with an axe (*Henny Penny*, 1966) or creating a cello with the semi-nude body of Charlotte Moorman (*TV Bra for Living Sculpture*, 1969) would have embarrassed a typical Korean, especially at the time they were performed. In the 1960s and 1970s, experimental art was not a priority in a country that was still struggling to rebuild itself after the Korean War, which ended in 1953. Art, in general, was a luxury that only a select elite could enjoy. Moreover, Paik's family background presented a political problem. Paik's father was a prominent businessman in the textile industry during the Japanese occupation of Korea (1910–1945) and was among those who were prosecuted after 1945 for aiding the Japanese government. The label *chinil-pa* (pro-Japanese group), which was attached to the members of such families, continues to have strong persecutory connotations. In short, a descendant of *chinil-pa* is perceived as an enemy of Korea, the polar opposite of the image of a national hero.

Why and how, then, did Paik become widely and proudly embraced by Koreans? Why did Nam June Paik become a modern-day national hero in South Korea? How did he align himself with a modern sense of Korean nationalism? And what is the role of his art in the creation of such an image?

The journey of a cosmopolite: a brief summary of Nam June Paik's life and career

Born in 1932 in Seoul, Paik grew up in an unusually privileged family, surrounded by modern technology and Western culture. He read writings by Karl Marx and learned about the modernist music of Schönberg. Of the latter, he once remarked, "As for Schönberg, I am still quite proud that I was able to discover him in the information-starved Korea of 1947 when I was only fourteen-and-a-half years old."[4] When the Korean War broke out in 1950, Paik's family moved to Japan, and Paik attended the University of Tokyo, graduating in 1955 with a senior thesis on Schönberg. In 1956, Paik went to West Germany to study music, first at the University of Munich and then at the Musikhochschule in Freiberg. He met John Cage for the first time in 1958 at the Internationale Ferienkurse für neue Musik in Darmstadt where Cage gave lectures and performances. Described by Paik as a meeting that changed his life, the encounter gave Paik the confidence to integrate his non-Western background into his modernist-influenced art. As a Buddhist, Paik saw Cage's application of Zen Buddhism in his music as a form of validation.

At the time, Paik was among a relatively small number of Asian, mostly Japanese, avant-garde artists working in Europe and the U.S. With his family background and education, Paik was very much an insider with the Japanese group, which included artists such as Yoko Ono, On Kawara, Yayoi Kusama, and Shigeko Kubota (whom Paik married in 1970). Indeed, for many years, Paik did not present himself as a Korean artist but as an "Oriental" or Asian one. As Jieun Rhee argues, Paik negotiated his Asian body in the Western avant-garde world as a "cultural terrorist," "yellow peril," and a "Zen master" – but not as a Korean.[5]

While Paik developed professional and personal relationships with Japanese artists in the U.S. and Europe during the 1960s and 1970s, Korea went through a phase of government-sanctioned cultural purification that did not allow the importation of any Japanese culture, including film, music, art, and popular culture. The ban, which was partly lifted in 1998, was intended to get rid of the effects of thirty-six years of Japanese occupation.[6] Paik, on the other hand, found commonalities with Japanese artists, and he did so with Zen Buddhism. In 1961, he began to experiment with second-hand television sets by combining performance art with the new electronic medium and named many of his new works with the term "Zen." His first solo exhibition, *Exposition of Music: Electronic Television*, which opened in 1963 at Galerie Parnass in Wuppertal, included the installations *Zen Chair* and *Zen for TV* that represented his interpretation of Zen Buddhism.[7] He often called Zen philosophy "ours" with Japanese artists despite the fact that Zen Buddhism is a specifically Japanese version of Buddhism.

For instance, in a 1993 interview with Arata Isozaki, a Japanese architect, Paik said:

> You are born only once. You die only once. The most important things happen only once. A human being has an essential yearning or angst for the non-repeatable. The reason I became well-known through destructive art was also because of this non-repeatability. Once you break an expensive piano, it cannot be put back together. Once you throw water on the ground, you cannot scoop it back up. From this fear and yearning born of the fragility of life, our philosophy of the "eternal return" emerges.[8]

Isozaki responded, "Video has a mechanism in which it loses the eternal each second, yet regains the eternal in the next second.... In this sense, Mr. Paik, since you are an Asian, you may have intuitively discovered that side of video – the fragility or transitory quality of this new medium."[9] Zen Buddhism functioned in multiple ways for Paik. It led him to John Cage and the Fluxus movement and allowed him to find camaraderie with Japanese experimental artists as a fellow Asian. And it made the inclusion of television and video art philosophically and aesthetically consistent with his earlier performance art work. Throughout the 1970s, Paik continued to experiment with what he called electronic art – exemplified by *Global Groove* (1973) and *TV Buddha* (1974) – and became a seminal figure of the new form.

By the early 1980s, Paik had gained an international reputation as a core member of the Fluxus movement and the inventor of video art. It was only after such unquestioned success that Paik returned to Korea for the first time since the Korean War. In 1984, he received the invitation of a Korean broadcasting company which participated in *Good Morning, Mr. Orwell*, a live satellite program broadcasted internationally at noon on New Year's Day, 1984. *Good Morning, Mr. Orwell* was the first international satellite "installation" envisioned by Paik since at least 1973, when he created *Global Grove*, a video project that aspired to connect the world through television.[10] Before *Good Morning, Mr. Orwell*, Paik was virtually unknown in South Korea outside of a small circle of artists and art historians. Nor did Paik make an attempt to be known in Korea before then.

But Paik's increasing emphasis in his art on global culture and media technology coincided with the South Korean government's desire to make the country a global leader on the economic, cultural, and technological fronts. The military dictatorship of President Chun Du-Hwan was tyrannical domestically, but it had the ambition to make South Korea a global country. For instance, as soon as the military power reestablished itself in 1980, President Chun led the winning bid to host the 1988 Summer Olympics in Seoul, thereby justifying his leadership in the domestic public eye and announcing a new South Korea internationally. With such a politically motivated backdrop, the celebrated return of Paik in 1984 was definitely about the celebration of an artist with a global vision, not about an expatriate with a problematic family background.

After his return, Paik received almost limitless support from both the government and corporations, and he took full advantage of the opportunity. Paik was frequently commissioned to create projects for international events hosted by Korea, including the 1986 Asian Games, the Summer Olympics of 1988, and the Daejeon EXPO of 1993. For the Olympics, Paik built the installation *The More the Better* with 1,003 video monitors, all of which were made by Samsung. (During this time, Samsung was virtually unknown outside of Korea as an electronic brand.) In fact, Samsung announced that it would continuously support Paik under the condition that he only use its TV monitors. Paik began his career in video art with Sony monitors and frequently complained of the high cost. But during the 1980s, Paik no longer had to purchase TV monitors because they were abundantly provided by Samsung. Samsung and Paik had a symbiotic relationship, and both promoted a newly modernized, globalized Korea.

With the aid of government and corporations, Paik quickly gained popularity among the Korean public. Technology-driven and futuristic, his work was also accessible to everyone, from children to the elderly. But Paik's homecoming sent a shock tremor throughout the world of the arts in South Korea. While the average Korean person saw Paik as a strange genius-artist who seemed to represent Korea's future, artists were unsure about his radical, yet decidedly apolitical view of art. At least since the 1910s, Western experimental and modernist art had been imported to Korea, and a small group of avant-garde artists had formed the modernist Korean Avant-Garde Association in 1969. However, all cultural expressions throughout the 1960s, 1970s, and 1980s were heavily censored by the military regime, which did not hesitate to imprison intellectuals who offended its legitimacy.

In the 1980s, the type of art that popularly represented South Korea was named *minjung* art, which means "the people's art." Anti-dictatorship and pro-democracy, *minjung* art was leftist in ideology and emphasized socialist realism, not artistic experimentation. It depicted peasants and laborers as heroes and used traditional Korean folk culture as its primary source. And it mocked Western modern art as imperialistic and bourgeois.[11] Not surprisingly, *minjung* artists were suppressed by the government and conservatives, who accused them of supporting North Korean communist propaganda. Unlike *minjung* art, which was overtly political, Paik created what Yongwoo Lee calls "formalist video," or work in which one finds an "aesthetics of moderation that underlines, then surpasses the problems of ethics and society."[12] In all ways, Paik represented the opposite of what Korean artists were accustomed to: total artistic freedom that transcended politics. Paik's introduction to the Korean art world coincided with the decline of *minjung* art, which lost its influence when the military dictatorship began to lose its control over the nation in the mid-1980s.

According to Youngna Kim, "the polemics and the division of the art world between those for and those against *minjung* art ended suddenly around 1988, the year of the Seoul Olympics, when the Korean government adopted more open policies and deregulated foreign travel."[13] In 1993, President Kim Young Sam declared an age of globalization for Korea, and Paik was front and center in introducing Western avant-garde art to Koreans. That year alone, he was a leading figure in bringing the Whitney Biennial in Asia to Seoul and helped establish a Korean pavilion at the Venice Biennale. Also in 1993, he was vital in organizing the Seoul Fluxus Festival. Throughout the 1990s, Paik's reputation as a "genius artist" of modern and postmodern art grew in South Korea. He welcomed governmental and corporate support while presenting himself as a rebel and a charlatan. His image as a world-renowned artist freed of national politics was enhanced by his vocal criticism of protectionist tendencies in Korea. He repeatedly argued for better English education, advancement of information technology, and a cosmopolitan worldview. He was, and still is, controversial amongst Koreans, especially for those against Westernization and capitalistic globalization and for those critical of his art, but by the mid-1990s, he was an icon that represented the nation and its new identity.

The forty-ninth day memorial: participatory reenactment and the final homecoming

As mentioned at the beginning of this essay, Paik's funeral took place in New York City with guests who participated in a Fluxus-inspired performance, thereby commemorating his playfulness and spontaneity. Joseph Roach, in *Cities of the Dead*, notes that, in any funeral, "the body of the deceased performs the limits of the community called into being by the need to mark its passing."[14] Paik's deceased body, covered with truncated ties, was both passive and active participant in the performance and thus became for the community of artists and friends in New York City a "symbolic embodiment of loss and renewal," as Roach puts it. In South Korea, Paik's life was remembered in fundamentally different ways. The absence of the actual body contributed to the difference, but the main distinction derived from the local community, which was not made up of Paik's fellow artists and friends, but of the Korean population who viewed him as a national icon. In Korea, Paik's body embodied loss and renewal at the national level.

According to Buddhism, the spirit of the dead exists between life and death for forty-nine days, and the memorial held forty-nine days after death is critical in helping the spirit enter the next world. Two days before Nam June Paik's forty-ninth day memorial, Ken Paik Hakuta brought Paik's ashes to Korea and placed them at Bongeun-sa, a Buddhist temple in Seoul. Founded in the eighth century and located in the country's capital, the temple has come to symbolize the prominent role Buddhism has played in Korean history and culture. The main memorial event took place at the temple with the participation of over 1,000 people, including ordinary citizens and children. The event began with a shaman dancing on knives and cutting cloths, both of which are traditional acts featured in Buddhist memorials, with the purpose of purging the spirit's bad karma. Freed from the world and past misdeeds, Paik's spirit was blessed to be reborn in a better life. Led by Hakuta, the event then moved on to commemorative performances that included participatory reenactments of Paik's performances. He dragged a violin on a string, copying Paik's *Action With a Violin on a String* (1961), and a group of participants smashed a hundred violins simultaneously, as in *One for Violin* (1962). Everyone was then encouraged to carry lit candles and play a piano with them, covering the instrument with candle wax. After all the participants had the chance to play the piano with their candles, Hakuta and others overturned the piano and dismantled it. In the background, participants placed their candles around a cloth replica of Paik's video sculpture *The More the Better* (1988), Paik's most famous piece in Korea, located at the National Museum of Contemporary Art. The memorial event ended with the cloth replica dropping to the ground while the candles remained on the structure that surrounded it. That all of this was understood in the sense of a homecoming was signaled by the large banner that was hung on the temple, reading, "Welcome Home, Nam June Paik" in both Korean and English.

A number of smaller ceremonies and performance events occurred around the country in major cities, including Daejeon and Chonju. In Daejeon, the Korean performance artist Hwan Ryu and others presented performances that included reenactments of some of Paik's early performance pieces. In the middle of the street, Ryu, covered in blue paint, wrapped another artist's body with white cloth, bound it with black rope, and then beat a piano with a hammer, recalling Paik's *Hommage à John Cage: Music for Tape Recorder and Piano* (1959). With Starbucks, the ubiquitous symbol of Western capitalism and globalization, in the background, Ryu's performance aimed to "shed light on the deceased's artistic spirit," as Ryu himself described it.[15] Other commemorative events around the country resembled Ryu's in the ways in which they combined reenactments of Paik's famed Fluxus performances with the individual artists' performative interpretations of the meaning of Paik's life and legacy. The primary purpose of the performances, whether they were original or reenacted, was the appeasement of Paik's spirit. The reenactments were intended to let Paik's spirit know that his work was being remembered, and the original performances aimed to show his lasting influence on Korean contemporary art.

Unlike the New York funeral, which required a specific time and location as an open-casket funeral, the forty-ninth day memorials in Korea occurred around the country in multiple locations and times mostly without coordination. Such widespread multiplicity was possible because the commemoration of Paik in Korea was rooted simultaneously in the spiritual traditions of Korean shamanism and Buddhism as well as in the national sense of his final homecoming. Koreans celebrated what they saw as Paik's permanent return to Korea, as though his life had come full circle in both physical and metaphysical ways. He returned physically when his ashes were brought to Bongeun-Sa but, because his ashes were also placed in other parts of the world as requested by Paik, it was more important to emphasize his spiritual, metaphysical return.

Spiritually, Paik could return only to Korea, an interpretation described by the Korean writer Yong-do Chung in his assessment of Paik's life and career for *The Buddhist Review*. Chung writes that Paik and his family accumulated karma when they escaped the hardships of Japanese occupation and the Korean War. According to Buddhist philosophy, Chung continues, such karma can be alleviated through contribution and action: "In that sense, we can confirm the essence of an artist's conscience through Paik's wandering on world stages of art. His art strives to achieve individual freedom, a hope for a new world, and freedom from human limitations. We can therefore call him a cosmo-politan who left [Korea] for artistic navigation."[16] Such interpretation of Paik's life and career not only atones him for his and his family's politi-cal wrongdoings, it also explains why he had to leave Korea and do the "crazy" and destructive art that he made in the early part of his career, and how the contribution he made to Korea since 1983 was what was needed to balance his karma.

In less metaphysical terms, Paik's heroic status in Korea can be attrib-uted to his general philosophy of art and life. On a number of occasions, Paik stated that art is "deception" or the most profound kind of fraud. He described his art as mere "playing," as in child's play. His favorite kind of art was that in which everyone is deceived without realizing the deception. For instance, on June 9, 1998, President Kim Dae Jung visited the White House, and a number of celebrated Koreans, including Paik, were invited to the state banquet hosted by President Clinton. The invitees lined up to shake hands with the President and First Lady, Paik joining the line in his wheelchair. When the time came for Paik to greet the President, he slowly stood up, apparently to show respect. As he extended his hand, he whispered to his nephew, who was holding his arm, "I think my pants are falling down." His pants then did fall, reveal-ing Paik without underwear and exposing his penis. All, including the media, thought it was an accident; Fox News aired the incident as one of the most embarrassing moments in history. The visit took place during the height of the Monica Lewinsky scandal, which involved discussions of the president's exposed penis in the White House, so some, mostly other artists, suspected purposeful performance. A major hint was the lack of suspenders, a signature wardrobe piece for Paik. Hakuta, in his remarks at Paik's funeral in New York City, confirmed for the first time that the act was "the ultimate Fluxus event."[17]

In the Western sense of avant-garde art, the White House incident certainly deserves to be called a Fluxus event because of its shock value, humor, and deceptiveness. But it is also consistent with a traditional Korean aesthetic, which emphasizes play as a major concept in high and low art and performance. To Koreans, Paik was reminiscent of a familiar character in Korean art and folklore. He embodied the play-ful, mischievous, irreverent Buddhist monk or artist who comments on, yet transcends worldly values with fun deceptions and self-deprecating humor.[18]

At the suggestion of Hakuta, both the New York City funeral and the forty-ninth day memorial events in Korea featured acts that celebrated Paik's irreverent humor and playfulness with reenactments of his Fluxus performances. Undoubtedly, the acts at both events commemorated Paik with a light, fun tone that would have been preferred by Paik himself. But the reenactments of Fluxus performances functioned quite differently in the two locations. In New York City, the cutting of the tie reminded the attendees of who Paik was as an individual, artist, and friend. In Korea, the dragging of the violin and dismantling of pianos reminded the partici- pants that Paik's artistic philosophy was quintessentially Korean. Despite his family's problematic past, his U.S. citizenship, and his marriage to a Japanese woman, Paik was recognized as having used his Koreanness in order to succeed in the world. His daring attitude was heralded as one that every ambitious cosmopolite should possess. It was with such under- standing that Paik's spirit was widely welcomed by Koreans.

The Nam June Paik Art Center: a home for a stationary nomad

On October 8, 2008, the Nam June Paik Art Center opened to the public after seven years of planning and construction. Located in the city of Yongin in the province of Gyeonggi, about a one-hour drive outside of Seoul, its facilities include exhibition spaces and an extensive archive of Paik's work.[19] The design of the Center is based on the German architect Kirsten Schemel's *The Matrix*, which was selected out of 430 entries in an international competition in 2003. With Marian Stankovic of KSMS Schemel Stankovic Architects in Berlin, Schemel created a building shaped like a shiny grand piano with a total area of over 60,000 square feet of internal space. The Center is located on top of a sloped hill with two stories of the building underground and three stories above ground. In 2001, Paik negotiated with the Gyeonggi Cultural Foundation, a non- profit organization endowed by the Gyeonggi provincial government, to construct the Center, and the final cost of construction approached 30 million U.S. dollars. It houses sixty-seven of Paik's major installa- tions, including *TV Garden* and *TV Buddha*, as well as an archive of over 2,000 video art pieces such as *Global Groove*. It also has a room that replicates Paik's studio in New York City with the actual furniture and equipment Paik used. Its opening events included the first Nam June Paik Festival, "Now Jump!" which, according to the center's publicity materials, aimed to "not simply rely on past achievements" but also to represent "the ambition of the Nam June Paik Art Center to leap into the future."[20] Paik reportedly named the Center "home where Nam June Paik lives for a long time" and wrote the phrase in Korean on the site plan.[21]

In a 1991 interview with the Korean philosopher Pil-Ho Hwang in the performing arts magazine *Gaeksuk (Auditorium)*, Paik used the phrase "stationary nomad" to describe himself.[22] According to Paik, "stationary nomad" was a term coined by a futurologist and refers to the ways in which humans can mentally move without physical motion. By using telecommunication and other forms of technology, one can be anywhere though one is physically in only one place. Such a form of existence, according to Paik, can lead to increased communication and mutuality.

Paik's definition of the term is limited to the application of technology to human communication, but "stationary nomad" also signifies Paik's life as an itinerant without a permanent home. He is what the French scholar Jacques Attali calls a "hyper-nomad" or "voluntary nomad," an intellectual or artist who willingly lives the nomadic life for the sake of creativity and intellectual freedom.[23] Art historian Youngna Kim also describes him as a "transnational, nomadic artist" who did not settle anywhere around the world.[24] In this sense, Paik's life and career can and should be described in terms of what James M. Harding and John Rouse call the "transnational avant-garde," an idea based on Homi Bhabha's notion of cosmopolitan hybridity. But it should also be emphasized that Paik's nomadism precedes and transcends conventional concepts of nation and culture.[25] Theories of the "transnational" assume the existence of nations, and "hybridity" necessitates the formation of a cultural identity, but Paik's nomadism enacts a condition that requires neither. Paik was home both anywhere and nowhere. But this has made decisions about his official memorialization all the more difficult to settle.

Respecting Paik's desire to return to Korea, the Center intends to be his permanent spiritual home. The Center is not alone; when its opening was delayed over a year, Shigeko Kubota expressed sadness at having no home for her husband's spirit. While Paik lived a life free from national boundaries and artistic labels as a nomad, the Center, as a permanent building, is a fit but stationary form of commemoration. The finality of the building contradicts the very philosophy of Paik's art, but it is also made necessary by his death and his national and transnational significance. This contradiction was revealed and accentuated during Paik's forty-ninth day memorial, when personal tensions between Shigeko Kubota, Ken Paik Hakuta, and the Gyeonggi Cultural Foundation were made public. All three parties had some claim on Paik's immortality and distinct understandings of his place in global culture: for Kubota, the Center was Paik's spiritual home, a place he wanted to be after his death; for Hakuta, the Center was one of many sites around the world that should house Paik's works; and for the Gyeonggi Cultural Foundation, the Center was, like Paik himself, the province's and Korea's pride. Kubota and the Foundation came to the agreement that the Center would be the primary site of Paik's works. On the other hand, Hakuta reminded everyone that Paik had made it explicitly clear that Hakuta would hold the legal power and sole rights to execute his will and manage his archive.[26] However, in February of 2008, Hakuta visited the Center and expressed satisfaction with its construction. He announced that all of the disagreements had been resolved and that all parties had moved on. Hakuta even stated in interviews that he believed Paik's spirit may well be at the Center because Paik's mother's grave was in Suwon, a nearby city.[27] But he has continued to pursue exhibitions of Paik's works in internationally renowned museums elsewhere, has never described the Center as an exclusive or even central site for Paik's work, and gave a vaguely negative answer when asked about allowing the Center to house Paik's ashes, which are still kept at the Buddhist temple Bongeun-sa in Seoul.[28]

While the Center and Hakuta share the goal of publicizing and commemorating Paik and his works internationally, the core philosophies of that goal differ for each. For Hakuta, Paik's identity as a Korean is insignificant compared to his identity as an international avant-gardist. That view reflects Paik's own self-identification as a nomad, exemplified in the interview with Pil-Ho Hwang. In that interview, Hwang asked Paik whether he considered himself a Korean, an American, or a cosmopolitan. Paik replied, "I don't think about it...One just needs one's own truth." When Hwang followed up with the assertion, "It sounds like you've transcended national borders with your art," Paik joked, "But there's not much I can do because I get stared at when crossing national borders."[29] Paik's joke contains the contradictory life of a stationary nomad and illustrates the philosophical differences between Hakuta and the Foundation. Paik desired to transcend all borders, but he also knew he had to live within, outside of, and across them.

Because of Shigeta Kubota's support and Paik's verbal wish expressed towards the end of his life, the Gyeonggi Cultural Foundation understood itself to be the primary agent of Paik's immortalization. Although the building is called an art center, its primary purpose is a museum that contains and showcases Paik's career and life. Indeed, as a physical structure prominently placed at the top of the city's main hill, the Center is reminiscent of traditional Korean gravesites that were always on hills and mountains. In discussing the role of the museum and contemporary art, Peter Weibel and Andrea Buddensieg note that museums are "places that…represent changes in culture and in the demands of national imagination."[30] That national imagination includes narratives of the past, present, and the projected future. As a symbol of Paik's gravesite, the Center commemorates the specific past of one venerated man, and as a site of international art festivals, it celebrates the present and its artists.

But the primary goal of the Center, at least according to its self-description, is forward-looking. In its publicity brochures and on its website, the Gyeonggi Cultural Foundation emphasizes that the establishment of the Center "symbolizes the cultural era of the twenty-first century and expresses the artistic world of Paik Nam-June." But it also says that the Center will "enhance the position of Korean art museums to stand in the middle of the international network."[31] This latter vision is consistent with the Korean government's nationalistic goal to make Korea a leading country in the twenty-first century by making it an international cultural and economic hub. By hosting international art festivals such as "Now Jump!" the Center aims to become a place for artistic creativity and collaboration for contemporary artists around the world. In that sense, it successfully symbolizes Paik's life as a stationary nomad by attempting to have a worldwide influence while being in only one, culturally specific location. In this paradox, it is simultaneously a place for commemoration and a space for immortalization – and utterly appropriate to Paik's identity.

Nostalgia of the hero: Paik's last work, *Om-Mah* (*Mother*)

Paik was cosmopolitan in outlook and global in orientation with his ability to speak five languages and worldwide reputation as a video artist, but he also retained a specific culture shaped by his childhood Korea. In fact, throughout his life, he frequently spoke about his memories of growing up in Korea. But that nostalgia for home was aggravated by his inability to speak one of those languages well (his Korean was worse than his Japanese) and the fact that his family never returned to Korea. Paik's last work is most representative of this contradictory pull between cosmopolitanism and nostalgia. Created in his New York studio while he was barely mobile after suffering a stroke, *Om-Mah* (*Mother*) features a traditional Korean overcoat worn by women, the kind worn by Paik's mother while he was growing up. Behind the overcoat is a monitor showing a videotape of three young girls – perhaps representing his own sisters – in traditional Korean dress dancing, playing, and calling their mother. In contrast to the immobile overcoat, the girls in the monitor continuously play as the videotape repeats.

Om-Mah was shown for the first time at the forty-ninth day memorial in Seoul and confirmed for Koreans Paik's deep identification with his homeland. Indeed, it is his most personal work, but many have interpreted it as his most nationalistic work. A more accurate translation of *om-mah* is "mommy," a name used particularly by small children and with a different connotation from the word *omeo-ni*, which means "mother" in a more formal sense. The piece is about Paik's childhood memory, though it also references broader cultural memories. For example, though the coat is an antique, purchased from a New York City antique gallery (Hakuta speculates it to be of the nineteenth century[32]), it is like one of his mother's, made with the kind of colorful dye only the rich could have afforded in the 1940s. The coat is also a reminder of Paik's family textile business, the influence of which can still be seen in Korea today. The way the coat is hung, on a long bamboo bar, is also an accurate portrayal of the traditional way that such a piece of clothing was kept at home.

The work is Paik's most autobiographical installation piece and, arguably, one of his most nationalist. John Hanhardt, the Senior Curator of Film and Media Arts at the Guggenheim Museum of Art, describes the piece as "a poetic and evocative expression of hope and renewal for Korea, his homeland."[33] Affirming this notion, the image of *Om-Mah* is one of four works featured in the official Korean stamps released in early 2007 to commemorate the first anniversary of Paik's death. The other three works, *TV Buddha*, *Megatron/Matrix*, and *The More the Better* are Paik's best-known video installations, of course. It might strike us as odd that none of his earlier Fluxus performances (including those reenacted during the forty-ninth day memorial events) is featured in the collection, but the use of telecommunication technology, which represents the future and economic development is, for Koreans, Paik's signature venue of creativity. (Indeed, it was only upon Ken Paik Hakuta's insistence that the organizers of the forty-ninth day memorial included reenactments of his performance-based artworks.)

Because *Om-Mah* is his last work, Koreans tend to view Paik's life through it from a nationalistic and nostalgic perspective, which is vastly different from that of the attendees of the funeral in New York City. Abroad, Paik is commemorated as an avant-garde "cultural terrorist," but in Korea, he is a prodigal son who finally came home. Such is the narrative presented by the journalist Hee-sung Kim in her article, "In Memory of the Great Video Artist Paik Nam-June." She quotes Paik in the article as having said, "I try to hide rather than express my affection toward my homeland. My belief is that, if I do well, it will also benefit Korea."[34] According to Kim, Paik has long showed his affection for Korea, though indirectly, by including bits of Korean culture inconspicuously in his works. For example, he included verses of Korean poets and images of historical Korean figures in video installations without explaining them, thus making them recognizable only to those who knew Korea and Korean history. But he also created works such as *Geobukseon* (*Turtle Ship*), a replica of the warship that was used against Japanese invaders in the sixteenth century. Some view the installation as his most overtly nationalistic work that shows his affection for Korea in an obvious way.

Om-Mah, on the other hand, goes beyond nationalistic affection; it represents the old Korea or, perhaps, a lost Korea for Paik. It also shows what both Korea and Nam June Paik have sacrificed for success. The overcoat hanging on the bamboo pole is no longer worn by the modern Korean mother, and Korean girls wear traditional dresses only on special holidays. Instead of being "a poetic and evocative expression of hope and renewal for Korea," as John Hanhardt asserts, *Om-Mah* looks back to Paik's memory of Korea before Westernization. The simplicity and innocence of the piece provides the perfect summation of his life. It symbolizes the polyphony of influences that made Paik's life: East and West, past and present, play and work, electronic signals and machines, home and nomadic life, nostalgia and cosmopolitanism. It could very well be the expatriate's last dream before death and a reminder of what Jacques Lacan once asked of dreams: "Is not the dream essentially, one might say, an act of homage to the missed reality – the reality that can no longer produce itself except by repeating itself endlessly in some never attained awakening?"[35]

National heroes typically represent the nation's past either mythically or historically. Nam June Paik, unlikely hero that he is, also represents the future. It is his inventive, daring, cosmopolitan outlook and technological savvy that made him – and make him – the ideal icon of the twentieth century. It is the massiveness of the Nam June Paik Art Center that symbolizes Korea's ambition in the new millennium. But with *Om-Mah*, Paik seems to remind the country of what has been lost and sacrificed for the progress. To borrow Homi Bhabha's phrase, it symbolizes "the Janus-faced ambivalence" of Korean history and national identity.[36] It is looking both to the past and to the future. Most South Koreans, in the process of immortalizing Paik, are focused on the face that is looking towards the future.

Notes

1. All translations in this essay are by the author, unless noted otherwise. I use "Korea" in this essay to connote "South Korea." On the Korean peninsula, in both North and South, there is a popular desire to speak of Korea as one nation. It is therefore acceptable and common to use "Korea" and "South Korea" interchangeably. I thank Sandra Lee, my research assistant, for her help in researching for this essay.
2. Raphaele Shirley, "Homage to Nam June Paik," *Perpetual Art Machine* (Feb. 5, 2006), http://www.perpetualartmachine.com/index.php?option=com_cont ent&task=view&id=74&Itemid=40 (accessed Jan. 5, 2009).
3. Keun-min Bae, "Paik Nam-june to Be Buried in Homeland," *The Korea Times*, Jan. 31 2006, http://times.hankooki.com/lpage/200601/ kt2006013117134210230.htm (accessed Feb. 5, 2009).
4. Nam June Paik, "Pensée at 59," in *Nam June Paik: Video Time – Video Space*, ed. Toni Stoos and Thomas Kellei (New York: Harry N. Abrams, Inc., 1993), 17. Quoted in Jieun Rhee, "Performing the Other: Asian Bodies in Performance and Video Art, 1950s–1990s" (Dissertation: Boston University, 2002), 31.
5. Rhee, "Performing the Other," 47–72. For a study of Japanese women artists in the U.S., see Midori Yoshimoto, *Into Performance: Japanese Women Artists in New York* (New Brunswick: Rutgers University Press, 2005).
6. The ban on Japanese culture was the official law of the land, but various Japanese cultural products were imported during that time. For instance, children's animation shows, which were never revealed as being of Japanese origin, were immensely popular amongst Koreans, and Japanese imports were always available in the underground networks. The ban on Japanese popular culture and some films was lifted in 1998, but other forms of culture continue to be censored in Korea. See "S. Korean Minister Says It's Too Early to Lift Restrictions on Japanese Culture," *International Herald Tribune*, Sept. 14, 2006, http://www.iht.com/articles/ap/2006/09/14/arts/AS_A-E_ SKorea_Japan_Culture.php (accessed Jan. 6, 2009).
7. See Rhee, "Performing the Other," 49–50 for details about the exhibition.
8. Arata Isozaki, "A Conversation with Nam June Paik," *Nam June Paik: Video Time – Video Space*, 125.
9. Ibid., 126.
10. A clip of the video can be seen at *Media Art Net*, http://www.medienkunstnetz. de/works/global-grove (accessed Jan. 30, 2008).
11. See Youngna Kim, "Two Traditions: Monochrome Art of the 1970s and Minjung Art of the 1980s," in *20th Century Korean Art* (London: Laurence King Publishing Ltd., 2005).
12. Yongwoo Lee, "Hybridity and Anonymity," *Nam June Paik: Fluxus und Videoskulptur* (Duisburg: Stiftung Wilhelm Lehmbruck Museum, 2002), 46–47.
13. Youngna Kim, "Two Traditions," 268.
14. Joseph Roach, *Cities of the Dead: Circum-Atlantic Performance* (New York: Columbia University Press, 1996), 14.
15. "Paik Nam June 49th Day Memorial Performance in Daejeon," *Dong Ilbo*, Mar. 18, 2006.
16. Yong-do Chung, "Nam June Paik's Video Art and Buddhism," *The Buddhist Review* 26 (2006), http://www.budreview.com/article.asp?cnt_id=3629 (accessed Jan. 6, 2009).

17. For Hakuta's description, see Alexandra Anderson-Spivy, "NO REWIND," *artnet Magazine*, Mar. 3, 2006, http://www.artnet.com/magazineus/features/anderson-spivy/anderson-spivy3-23-06.asp (accessed Feb. 7, 2009).
18. Robert J. Fouser attributes Paik's sensibility to Korean modernist aesthetics and more specifically to the concept of *chaemi*, which can be translated as "fun, amusing, satisfying, and surprising." While I agree with his main premise, I think the Korean modernist movement had minimal influence on Paik. He found his artistic niche in Europe after having met John Cage and others of the Fluxus movement. Moreover, the concept of *chaemi* has a longer history than the modernist movement in Korea. See Fouser, "Looking for *Chaemi*: Nam June Paik and Korean Modernist Aesthetics," in *Perspectives on Korea*, ed. Sang-Oak Lee and Duk-Soo Park (Sydney, Australia: Wild Peony Pty Ltd., 1998), 124–136.
19. For images of the Center and details of its collection, see *Nam June Paik Art Center*, http://njp.kr/ff_eng.html (accessed Jan. 9, 2009).
20. "Overview," *Nam June Paik Art Center*, http://njp.kr/root/festival/html_eng/overview.html (accessed Jan. 6, 2009). This page includes an extensive list of artists featured in the festival.
21. Chun-il Choi, "Stationary Nomad, Paik Nam June," *Suwon Art Center Newsletter* 10 (2006), 29.
22. "The Video Artist Nam June Paik vs. the Philosopher Pil-Ho Hwang," *Gaeksuk* (Jan. 1991), 189.
23. Jacques Attali, *L'homme Nomade* (Paris: Librairie Arthème Fayard, 2003), 356.
24. Youngna Kim, "Constructing Transnational Identities: Paik Nam June and Lee Ufan," *Journal of Korean Modern and Contemporary Art History* (Jan. 2007), 217.
25. James M. Harding, "From Cutting Edge to Rough Edges: On the Transnational Foundations of Avant-Garde Performance," in *Not the Other Avant-Garde: The Transnational Foundations of Avant-Garde Performance*, ed. James M. Harding and John Rouse (Ann Arbor: University of Michigan Press, 2006), 18–40.
26. After the forty-ninth day memorial, Hakuta publicly criticized the Foundation for using the Center for political purposes and for making decisions that went against his (and, by extension, Paik's) wishes. He also felt disrespected and deceived by those at the Foundation. Kubota and the Foundation accused Hakuta of monopolizing Paik's works without justification. Hakuta's Japanese citizenship, despite being biologically Korean ("Hakuta" is the Japanese pronunciation of Paik), may have contributed to the tension. However, the city of Yongin gave Paik's widow Kubota (who is fully Japanese) honorary citizenship, but did not do the same for Hakuta, leading to the speculation that the controversy was more personal than nationalistic. The accounts of these public accusations were reported in all major Korean newspapers in March 2006. See, for example, "What Would the Cosmopolitan Paik Nam June Think? The Conflict Surrounding the Construction of the Art Center," *Dong-A Ilbo*, Mar. 18, 2006, http://www.donga.com/fbin/output?n=200603180007 (accessed Jan. 5, 2009).
27. "Hakuta: 'Paik Nam June Art Center is Excellent,'" *Yonhap News*, Feb. 22, 2008, http://news.naver.com/main/read.nhn?mode=LSD&mid=sec&sid1=103&oid=001&aid=0001971519 (accessed Jan. 5, 2009).
28. Ibid.

29. "The Video Artist Nam June Paik vs. the Philosopher Pil-Ho Hwang," 189.
30. Peter Weibel and Andrea Buddensieg, "Editorial," in *Contemporary Art and the Museum: A Global Perspective*, ed. Peter Weibel and Andrea Buddensieg (Ostfildern, Germany: Hatje Cantz, 2007), 8.
31. From the English-language version of the Gyeonggi Cultural Foundation's "Cultural Projects" page, http://english.ggcf.or.kr/channel_02/paik.html (accessed Jan. 5, 2009).
32. "Paik Nam June's 'Mother' is Made Public," *Dong-A Ilbo*, Mar. 16, 2006, http://www.donga.com/fbin/output?f=jz_&n=200603160321 (accessed Jan. 6, 2009).
33. The quote appeared on the official site for the Nam June Paik Studio (http://www.paikstudio.com) in 2006. The archived version of the site can been seen at http://web.archive.org/web/20060714093718/http://www.paikstudios.com/ (accessed Jan. 6, 2009).
34. Hee-sung Kim, "In Memory of the Great Video Artist Paik Nam-June," *Korea.net*, Jan. 28, 2007, http://www.korea.net/News/news/NewsView.asp?serial_no=20070126016&part=112&SearchDay= (accessed Jan. 6, 2009).
35. Jacques Lacan, *The Four Fundamental Concepts of Psychoanalysis*, ed. Jacques-Alain Miller, trans. Alan Sheridan (New York: W. W. Norton & Company, 1998), 58.
36. Homi K. Bhabha, Introduction, *Narration and Nation*, ed. Bhabha (London: Routledge, 1990), 3.

11
The Avant-Garde of Necessity: the Protest Theatre Movement in Zimbabwe

Praise Zenenga

This chapter not only explores the inherently avant-garde nature of Zimbabwean theatre, but also examines changing notions of avant-garde theatre in space and time. To further underscore the dynamic nature of theatre as a changeable cultural practice, Antonys Gyltzouris defines avant-garde theatre as "simply what a given society at a given time regards as such."[1] Zimbabwe has its own unique avant-garde theatre, but its avant-gardeness is dependent upon context. Thus, I would assert that what constitutes avant-garde theatre not only differs from one society to another, but also gets transformed from time to time. Joachim Fiebach argues that what is often regarded as inventions of the Western avant-garde have been "traditional" African culture for centuries.[2] This chapter explores the exchanges, adaptations, and appropriations between the Western avant-garde movements and African avant-gardes – and within the latter. As such, my discussion primarily focuses on the extent to which avant-garde theatre in Zimbabwe defies, challenges, borrows, capitalizes, and builds upon the work of its predecessors and its peer practitioners from around the globe. I argue that transformation, innovation, and sometimes experimentation are endemic to Zimbabwean theatre out of necessity, not choice.

Zimbabwean theatre has constantly and actively engaged in political struggles against both the colonial state and the autocratic nationalist regimes that assumed the reins of power after political independence in 1980. The protest theatre movement in post-independence Zimbabwe has turned out to be the most avant-garde theatre in the country's history both in terms of aesthetic innovation and in its attack on the old order. What makes this theatre the most avant-garde is its constant search not for a new form – it borrows freely from older African and European forms – but for a new mode of existence. Revolutionary and experimental theatrical practices in contemporary Zimbabwe include Hit-and-Run Theatre, Panic Theatre, Urgent Theatre, Invisible Theatre, Guerrilla Theatre, Radical Theatre, Street Theatre, Community Theatre, Agit-Prop Theatre, and many others. Unlike conventional theater, these popular theatrical forms "are tied to the specificities of their time and place and they continually reincarnate themselves to reveal the new truths of each specific time and place in which they are performed."[3] Although the avant-garde has always been a global phenomenon, every country has its own heritage, values, politics, history, and traditions that shape theatrical performances.

Hegemonic avant-garde of the colonial era (1890–1980)

Colonialism brought European performance cultures into contact with indigenous traditions in Zimbabwe. Although Ngũgĩ wa Thiong'o notes how global economic and political processes invariably give rise to cultural links and exchanges,[4] Zimbabwe's history shows that these do not always occur on an equal basis. Cultural domination, subordination, and resistance characterize Zimbabwe's relationship with the West, particularly during the colonial era (1890–1980). This relationship gave birth to a radical, anti-establishment avant-garde which resisted European conventions. During the nationalist era, it was culturally and politically incorrect to imitate or show any affinity with European performance traditions.

As part of the colonial process, local African performance traditions were repressed. The theatre of the dominant European cultures established itself as the mainstream theatre. It replicated conventional European performances, spaces, and training schools. European settlers were careful not to introduce their colonial subjects to the artistically and ideologically avant-garde theatre practices flourishing in the West at the same time; indeed, they even avoided exposing their subjects to classical or Shakespearian plays that depicted challenges to authority. To encourage subservience and respect for authority, schools and churches spread Christian morality plays among the subordinate populations.

Although the colonial theatre introduced in Zimbabwe was not avant-garde by European standards, it amounted to a sweeping rejection of indigenous aesthetic conventions and traditions and therefore translated into an avant-garde experience for the subjugated populations.

The colonized viewed European theatre as a kind of hegemonic avant-garde. Its attack on indigenous cultural values and radical criticism of the African past thus necessitated the creation of a "counter-avant-garde avant-garde," which called not only for a rejection of Western theatrical trends, but for a revival of traditional performance forms to express a revolutionary nationalist ideology and its complementary socialist aspirations.

The fight against colonialism was a fight against cultural extinction. Among nationalists, any affinities with European theatrical forms were considered not only unpatriotic but also potentially subversive of liberation efforts. Not surprisingly, the colonial regime regarded the mere act of reviving traditional African performances as a covert political statement and thus heightened censorship and regulation of black theatre and performance.[5] For many decades, these two traditions remained separate, distinct, conservative, and, to a large extent, antagonistic. This would change.

Challenging cultural conservatism in colonial Zimbabwe: boundary pushing avant-garde (1960–1980)

How does one become avant-garde in a culturally and ideologically conservative society where art, especially theatre, constitutes national identity and carries the whole cultural freight of a people? Like in many other African societies, theatre and other arts embody the Zimbabwean people's spiritual, religious, political, and social values. To transform a cultural practice like theatre implies the conversion of the whole people and ultimately the death of indigenous cultures. During the nationalist era, Zimbabweans viewed Western theatrical conventions as "not from here." For many, incorporating European traditions was understood not only as corrupting African cultures, but as part of the colonial project.

Thus, theatre artists who experimented with new forms were accused of abandoning their traditions. They were seen as "lost," as outcasts who "didn't not belong." To this day, unless one is specifically targeting an audience in the expatriate, diplomatic, or international communities, going experimental without incorporating the familiar is tantamount to committing business suicide. Thus, highly experimental companies like Over the Edge and Tumbuka Dance Theatre rely on more liberal international audiences, while traditional performance artists such as Iyasa Dance Theatre and Siyaya Theatre are popular with a more culturally conservative Zimbabwean audience.

Despite colonialism and other global cultural intersections and exchanges, African traditional aesthetics are still at the root of theatrical performance in Zimbabwe. Because the majority of Zimbabwean theatre in the twenty-first century continues to be rooted in traditional rituals, ceremonies, and other performance forms, its avant-gardeness is not to be found in the invention and application of unconventional techniques, or in a radical break from established traditions and norms, but in a painstaking process of pushing thematic and aesthetic boundaries.

The 1968 United Nations sanctions not only isolated what was then called Rhodesia from world markets but also restricted intellectual and cultural exchanges with the rest of the world.[6] These circumstances forced both traditional and boundary-pushing theatrical traditions to be more inward looking. However, at the height of the liberation struggle in the 1960s and 70s, shrinking civil and performance spaces gave birth to formal experimentation aimed primarily at evading censorship. Similarly, thematic boundary pushing evolved as more traditional theatrical and cultural performance artists became increasingly critical of the conditions of black Zimbabweans. But artists in colonial Zimbabwe did not stay in a hermetically sealed bubble for ever. Freedom fighters crossed the borders in large numbers to seek military training in Ethiopia, Mozambique, Tanzania, Zambia, China, and the Soviet Union. Upon returning to Rhodesia and embedding themselves among civilian populations, they not only brought back new military skills, but performance styles and ideological content. Freedom fighters were the true vanguards, presenting performances to mobilize, conscientize, and educate the civic population about the struggle, as we see in the *pungwe* form, the key performance strategy of the liberation era.[7]

The *pungwe*: a wartime avant-garde aesthetic (1965–1979)

The proliferation of communism, pan-Africanism, and nationalism fueled thematic boundary pushing. Traditional songs and dances were incorporated into short dramatic skits as part of *pungwe* gatherings to mobilize and educate audiences about the liberation struggle's objectives and processes. The same era also saw a radical shift from apolitical thematic concerns to a strong revolutionary political content. This new aesthetic combined traditional African forms with revolutionary songs and slogans as well as elements of the Black Aesthetic developed in the U.S.-based Black Arts Movement (BAM) and Augusto Boal's Theatre of the Oppressed (TO). Such multi-cultural exchanges resulted in unprecedented creative experimentation and the *pungwe*.

The word *pungwe* describes something that goes on all night long. During the liberation war (1966–1979), political meetings between freedom fighters and villagers in rural Zimbabwe not only lasted all night long, but also amounted to political performances. In fact, the *pungwe* was a political process in itself. This means that, in addition to raising political issues, the *pungwe* theatrical performance was actual political activity because it directly participated in the liberation struggle. Conteh-Morgan contends, "The [avant-garde] theatre is the politics. It is politics in the way it is practiced, organized, and conceived."[8] In this sense, the *pungwe* is consistent with "the aestheticist or avant-garde orientation of African "radical theatre."[9] In terms of form and content, the *pungwe* marks a complete break with both dominant traditional and Western theatrical conventions of the time. While it followed the structure of a political meeting, the *pungwe* was an amalgam of meetings, song, dance, slogans, political teachings, and dramatic skits that thrived in sequestered spaces, out of reach of colonial security agents. The need to perform in out-of-view sites and the pragmatic adaptation of theatrical forms will be characteristic of future anti-establishment performance forms.

Although it is celebrated as the most inventive Zimbabwean theatrical model and as largely built out of indigenous performance forms and conventions, the *pungwe* also shows evidence of international ideological and aesthetic exchanges with other foreign traditions. Like Peter Brook and Augusto's Boal's avant-garde theatre, the *pungwe* took audience participation to a whole new level, the use of live music very much paralleling Brecht's epic theatre, particularly the adaptation of Christian hymns into liberation war songs. What was the inspiration for this? Freedom fighters who trained outside Zimbabwe in Russia, China, Tanzania, Mozambique, and Zambia brought back with them aesthetic and ideological conventions from other cultures, including the socialist and communist slogans that became an integral part of the *pungwe*.

Regardless, traditional indigenous performance forms clearly provided a more stimulating inspiration than international theatrical conventions. Whatever the liberation fighters incorporated from the outside resonated strongly with local performance traditions and philosophies. Socialist slogans, for example, recalled Zimbabwe's traditional *ubuntu* (humanism) belief system rooted in communalism, and the call-and-response structure of war slogans found strong resonance with the audiences' cultural and philosophical experiences. Due to its commitment to change and the future, and its effective hybridizing of the local and the foreign, the *pungwe* theatrical tradition remains foundational to almost all avant-garde creative endeavors in Zimbabwe ever since.

Zimbabwe's freedom fighters found an attractive model of radical art – and the power of an avant-garde that is rooted in both the new and the old, the high and the low – in the Black Arts Movement and Boal's Theatre of the Oppressed. The BAM's social, political, and aesthetic principles had a profound influence on theatrical practice during the liberation-war era. Popular avant-garde figures like Amiri Baraka, Larry Neal, Sonia Sanchez, and others crafted ideas about aesthetics, culture, nationalism, history, diaspora, and performance that facilitated intense ideological and aesthetic exchanges between Africa and its diaspora.[10] In particular, Baraka's criticism of the black experience in the U.S. appealed to blacks oppressed under similar racist colonial and apartheid conditions in Zimbabwe. In Zimbabwe, traditional cultural performance partnered with the liberation movements in the same way the BAM partnered with the Black Power movement in the U.S. Through these transatlantic ideological and aesthetic exchanges, African theatre artists adapted to African-American culture as part of an age-old diasporic continuum. In addition, the work of Baraka and others provided African artists exposure to the work of Artaud, Brecht, and others, as well as a way of imagining those avant-garde artists' work in relationship to indigenous traditions.[11]

Complementing the BAM's techniques were Augusto Boal's revolutionary Theatre of the Oppressed, including forms like Forum Theatre, Invisible Theatre, Image Theatre, and Newspaper Theatre. The Boalian tradition encouraged a direct translation of stage action into revolutionary action.[12] Like Paulo Freire's notion of praxis, which emphasized a dialectical relationship between theory and practice based in a continual process of self-reflection, Boal's concept of rehearsal for revolution regards theatrical performance as a process of action and critical reflection that should ultimately lead to social transformation.[13] This kind of *theatrical* experience provided a new *social* experience which not only redefined artists and audiences as political activists but also took the intervention of theatre in politics to a whole new level. Together, the BAM and TO helped Zimbabwean artists to effectively merge and exploit "the moral energy of social causes and the spirit of artistic exploration,"[14] giving birth to a boundary-pushing theatre which continues to be adapted to changing contexts and deployed in contemporary struggles for rights and democracy.

Post-independence leftist ideological mobility and exchanges (1980–1991)

In 1980, the attainment of political independence and the advent of democratic rule in Zimbabwe brought with it the democratization of theatrical forms, themes, and spaces. Performance spaces were desegregated and artists were free not only to explore broader themes like politics and race, but also to experiment with revolutionary traditional and international forms previously banned and censored under colonialism. Independence also opened up Zimbabwean artists to new, international theatrical experiences they were previously denied due to United Nations sanctions that effectively isolated the country from the rest of the world for more than a decade. Theatre companies like Zambuko, Amakhosi, Batsiranayi, Taako, Savannah, Rooftop, and Over the Edge started to break new ground, transforming both the content and style of their productions. Similarly, upon returning to Zimbabwe, theatre scholars and practitioners who had lived in exile or studied in other countries also impacted the emerging postcolonial avant-garde trends. After studying theatre at Nigerian, American, and British universities, Stephen Chifunyise, Thompson Tsodzo, and Vimbai Chivaura introduced the still-cutting-edge styles of theatre luminaries like Constantin Stanislavski, Erwin Piscator, Vsevolod Meyerhold, Artaud, Jerzy Grotowski, Brecht, Brook, and Boal. Formerly exiled theatre artists, scholars, and activists like Micere Mugo, Kimani Gecau, Robert Meshngu Kavanagh (aka Robert McLaren), and the late Ngugi waMirii made Zimbabwe their home. Their experiences with radical experimental theatre in Kenya, South Africa, and Ethiopia added another pan-African aesthetic and political dimension to Zimbabwean theatre.

Ideologically, the liberal-leftist orientation of these artists and scholars resonated well with the state's nationalist-cum-socialist inclinations, allowing them to form national theatre organizations and associations. During the 1980s, Zimbabwe became the Mecca of revolutionary theatre. The Zimbabwe Association of Community Theatre, National Theatre Organization, Zimbabwe Association of Theatre for Children and Young People, and National Drama Teachers' Association became vanguard organizations not only in the construction of appropriate forms, but also in the transformation of the larger society. These national theatre bodies not only represented various interest groups such as workers, students, the unemployed, the disabled, women, children, farmers, and Christians, but also the various trends and approaches that existed in Zimbabwean community theatre at the time. Although these organizations had different memberships and objectives, they all shared a commitment to revolutionary social transformation. As a result, Zimbabwean artists and audiences quickly embraced international trends that, unlike the liberation war era, were not an aesthetic and ideological match to their own traditions, whether avant-garde forms born in the liberation war or indigenous traditions, rituals, and ceremonies. The ability to mix and match international aesthetic and ideological trends while retaining a strong indigenous sensibility not only made the Zimbabwean avant-garde of the 1980s unique, but also provided an attractive model for other postcolonial regions and nations.

The anti-apartheid struggle and the rise of the agit-prop avant-garde (1984–1994)

In Zimbabwe, critical historical moments often serve as an arena for experimentation and creation of new theatrical content and staging methods. Specific historical moments in Zimbabwe necessitated the birth of new forms and sites of theatre and performance. A genealogy of this "avant-garde of necessity" in Zimbabwe includes the *pungwe*, Theatre for Development, Hit-and-Run Theatre, Urgent or Panic Theatre, and Agit-Prop Theatre, the last of which I'll discuss here.

Although Zimbabwean performance has pushed boundaries and expressed anti-establishment sentiments since antiquity, the liberation war ignited the modernist passion to break free of the past. Many theatre artists attempted to break free of the past in both the theatrical and political senses. As part of the Frontline States engaged in South Africa's anti-apartheid struggle,[15] the nationalist regime in Zimbabwe encouraged the use of theatre not only to mobilize, but also to conscientize the nation, region, and the world. This reflected South African scholar and theatre activist Robert Mshengu Kavanagh's view that, "[i]f our aim is to bring about revolutionary transformation through our work in theatre (or the other arts), the theatre we create and perform must be revolutionary in function."[16] Between 1984 and 1994, anti-apartheid agit-prop theatre flourished in Zimbabwe not only as a solidarity gesture, but as part of a regional effort to end a system of institutionalized racial segregation. For many Zimbabwean theatre artists and audiences, the shift from the *pungwe* to the anti-apartheid agit-prop was a natural one, given that the latter very much resembled the former. Just as with the *pungwe* performances, audience involvement was a key feature.

At the height of the Cold War in the 1970s and 1980s, agit-prop served as the dominant form of socialist theatre. In Zimbabwe and the Frontline States, agit-prop not only facilitated much-needed ideological mobility and cross-fertilization among the socialist nations and revolutionary parties, but also attacked capitalist institutions and establishments in both Zimbabwe and South Africa. This ideological cross-fertilization gave birth to a vibrant workers' theatre movement championing workers' rights in Zimbabwe. Zimbabwean theatre companies such as Zambuko/Izibuko and Chevhu-Ndechevhu embraced the agit-prop form. Robert Mshengu Kavanagh, who had worked with Experimental Theatre Workshop 71 in South Africa, has lived in exile in Zimbabwe since 1984, where he founded Zambuko/Izibuko. Coupled with his role as a theatre professor in the University of Zimbabwe's Faculty of Arts Drama Program, Kavanagh's work with Zambuko/Izibuko enhanced and consolidated the informal cultural exchanges that had always existed between Zimbabwe and South Africa (from the 1960s, South African theatre, music, and dance companies like comedian S'dumo, Mahotela Queens, Soul Brothers, and Ladysmith Black Mambazo often toured Zimbabwe and commanded large followings). In Zimbabwe, Kavanagh continued with the experimental tradition of Workshop 71. Zambuko/Izibuko's hugely successful productions such as *Katshaa! The Sound of the AK* (1985), *Mandela the Spirit of No Surrender* (1990), and *Samora Continua* (1988) incorporated elements of testimonial theatre, socialist theatre, story-telling theatre, and agit-prop. But there was also a connection to the past; many Zimbabwean theatre artists, activists, and audiences viewed Zambuko/Izibuko's use of symbolism, slogans, placards, dance, military drills, live music, audience interaction, various "poor theatre" techniques, and the transformation of public spaces into stages as a continuation of the *pungwe*. Zambuko/Izibuko also introduced multi-racial casts and multiple languages and accents, which not only added a realist dimension, but also helped to desegregate Zimbabwean theatre. Finally, the African National Congress (South Africa's most prominent liberation movement and now the country's governing party) sent its Cultural Ensemble to tour Zimbabwe regularly in the 1980s and boosted the aesthetic and ideological material exchanges between the two countries. Like the *pungwe*, the Cultural Ensemble aimed at political education, conscientization, and mass mobilization in the struggle against colonialism and apartheid – and like the *pungwe*, incorporated both the new and the old, the indigenous and the alien.

The post-independence theatre for development avant-garde (1980–2000)

The period preceding the attainment of political independence in Zimbabwe saw a shift from politically committed performance practices to theatre dealing mostly with non-political social issues. Alternatively referred to as Community Theatre in Zimbabwe, Theatre for Development (or TfD) became one of the most potent weapons used to educate the civic population about prevention, counseling, and caring for the affected in the fight against HIV/AIDS. With HIV/AIDS wreaking havoc, it became necessary for the theatre to educate, mobilize and conscientize about the pandemic. Besides the HIV/AIDS pandemic and apartheid, national development, reconstruction, and unity also became major thematic preoccupations in Zimbabwean popular theatre. However, the question of audience wasn't entirely settled – nor was the issue of aesthetic sources. Unlike conventional theatre, TfD emphasizes community participation at all levels. Though inconsistent in practice, TfD in Zimbabwe, as elsewhere, was understood as a process involving the wider community in the theatre creation process.[17] Typically, the TfD process involves research, data analysis, scene breakdown, rehearsal, performance, post-performance discussion or evaluation, and follow-up action.[18] However, some TfD practices exclude the community in the crucial conception, creation, analysis, and performance stages. Such approaches amount to top-down hegemonic development and educational models. In addition, according to David Kerr, "There have been two major sources of Theatre for Development: the colonial tradition of theatre as propaganda and another, more radical tradition of community theatre."[19] To an extent, the theatre lost its political and ideological zeal as it focused on the more objective facts of HIV transmission and prevention. However, as a global performance practice found in many developing countries such as Brazil, Argentina, Nicaragua, Jamaica, Bangladesh, Nigeria, Philippines, Pakistan, Uganda, Kenya, Ghana, Sierra Leone, Botswana, Malawi, Swaziland, Zambia, and many others, the TfD movement in Zimbabwe also facilitated international material and aesthetic exchanges.

Appealing to those who have always been avant-garde out of necessity, the TfD process is not a universal formula, but can be adapted to changing contexts, making room for improvisation and experimentation. Post-independence Zimbabwe's unique political and socio-cultural terrain and exposure to foreign performance trends gave birth to groundbreaking TfD practices for several reasons. First, there was the challenge of creating new expressive forms and educational discourses in keeping with fast-changing social relations and contexts; this required cross-cultural exchanges and constant experimentation as artists searched for ideal forms. They also faced the daunting task of breaking away not only from the old colonial and nationalist autocracies, but also outdated, oppressive, traditional cultural practices. Paulo Freire views such repressive traditional practices as "limit situations" that constitute "fetters and obstacles to freedom."[20] For example, certain topics such as sex and human anatomy are considered taboo in Zimbabwe and cannot be mentioned or discussed in public. This makes it difficult for theatre artists to deal with sensitive issues like HIV/AIDS, gay and lesbian rights, female genital mutilation, and rape. By respecting traditional communication forms and speech registers while pushing aesthetic boundaries, theatre artists in Zimbabwe gradually succeeded in opening up public discussions of culturally sensitive topics.

In one of their most experimental productions, *Hakuna Matata* (No Problem, 1995), Sunduza Dance Theatre used the concept of a soccer game to depict how the HIV/AIDS virus is passed from person to person and what can be done to stop the spread. Sunduza combined song, drumming, dance, movement, choreography, ball juggling, drama, and dialogue to find new ground and create a cutting-edge dance-drama. Similarly, in *Hoyaya Ho* (1997), Amakhosi Theatre used giants, ninjas, ogres, and dragons found in tales throughout the world to portray the universal dangers associated with HIV/AIDS. As a musical that verges on a dance-drama, *Hoyaya Ho* experimented with a combination of children's games, masks, puppets, dragons, music, dance, and audience involvement to come up with a unique production. In *Hakuna Matata* and *Hoyaya Ho*, Sunduza and Amakhosi conformed to the avant-garde tradition of combining the exotic and the familiar. In true avant-garde style, Amakhosi and Sunduza managed to show that it is possible to break with tradition and invent culturally acceptable styles to publicly discuss sensitive issues like sex and HIV/AIDS.

However, TfD dealing with HIV/AIDS, national unity, and development hardly attacks the state or hegemonic power in its analyses and cannot be considered anti-establishment. These represent some rare moments when avant-garde theatre artists and the state are in total agreement. However, divergences have emerged, particularly in the 1990s. For example, Kavanagh and waMirii spearheaded radical organic or bottom-up approaches to TfD based on their respective experiences in South Africa and Kenya. Kavanagh's play *Simuka Zimbabwe* (Arise Zimbabwe, 1994) and waMirii's *They Were Better* (1995) both critique the nationalist regime's blind acceptance of structural adjustment programs that resulted in severe job cuts and impoverishment of the civic population.

As has so often been the case during the post-independence era, Zimbabwean artists actively incorporated styles and processes from other cultures, though far more than before. Artists and audiences embraced Western acting and directing styles as well as play-production processes associated with avant-gardists like Meyerhold, Brook, Grotowski,

Artaud, Brecht, Baraka, and Boal. In particular, the ways in which these avant-gardes sought to connect with and actively involve audiences had strong resonances with participatory Zimbabwean performance traditions. This raises some interesting questions. While Harding and Conteh-Morgan argue that what is considered avant-garde in European art is often African in essence, scholars like Sandra Richards argue that the notion of influence is a two-directional process.[21] This means that aesthetics shared between African and Western cultures get transformed, adapted, and appropriated as they travel back and forth. However, both views emphasize intercultural material and aesthetic borrowings and exchanges between Africa and the West. My analysis shows that such reciprocal interactions are even more salient among African nations.

Vibrant cultural, ideological, and aesthetic exchanges among African nations date back to the pre-colonial era. Even in post-independence Africa, one of the key vectors of the radical connected African nations to each other, not Africa to Europe. For example, at independence, the new socialist state in Zimbabwe encouraged exchanges with radical theatre movements in African nations. The Kenyan popular theatre movement, particularly its Kamiriithu theatre project, stood out as an attractive model for the new socialist regime in Zimbabwe.[22] Kamiriithu Theatre's all-inclusive approach, which encouraged people from different social, educational, and economic backgrounds such as professors, teachers, students, professionals, peasants, workers, and amateurs to work together, resonated with the socialist ideals of the new state. Thus, avant-garde theatre in post-independence Zimbabwe is a confluence of African tradition; pre-colonial, colonial, and liberation war theatrical performances; and radical Western theatre traditions.

Avant-garde theatre challenges traditional nationalism (1984–1994)

Before apartheid ended in 1994, Zimbabwean theatre artists had already started questioning the nationalist regime's commitment to the socialist ideals it had championed during the liberation struggle. For example, Gonzo H. Msengezi's *The Honourable MP* (1984) and Amakhosi Theatre's *Workshop Negative* (1985) critiqued the black ruling elite. Among the earliest post-independence experimental theatre productions, they defined a new approach to critical theatrical art. *Workshop Negative* used multi-racial casting, multiple languages, martial arts, stage fighting, and military drills to break known theatrical conventions. Both plays experimented with a fusion of dialogue, mime, song, dance, slogans, and political rally techniques in a fashion reminiscent of the *pungwe*. These two served as vanguards for the radical, anti-establishment theatre that flourished in the 1990s and 2000s.

Although postcolonial avant-gardes in Zimbabwe have found it necessary to partner with the state to reject traditional stereotypes, stigmas, and myths and to promote HIV/AIDS awareness, national unity, and development, ideological and socio-political divergences always emerge when they challenge corruption, nepotism, bad governance, and rights abuses. Postcolonial political theatre in Zimbabwe has criticized the failure of the nationalist leadership to deliver promises made at independence, as evident in such ironic titles as Gonzo H. Msengezi's *The Honourable MP* (1984), Raisedon Baya's *Two Cheers for a Patriot* (2001), Cont Mhlanga's *Workshop Negative* (1987), *The Members* (1993), and *The Good President* (2007), Raisedon Baya and Leonard Matsa's *Super Patriot and Morons* (2004), Edgar Langeveldt and Raisedon Baya's *Pregnant with Emotion* (2008), and Stephen J Chifunyise and Raisedon Baya's *The Two Leaders I Know* (2008). This confirms John Conteh-Morgan's claim that "[i]t is this leader-as-messiah/father model of politics…with its almost inevitable slide into paternalism and authoritarianism, that is rejected by the postcolonial avant-garde."[23]

The question of balancing formal and thematic innovation is critical in contemporary Zimbabwe, where there is no tolerance of dissent. Reflecting its long familiarity with the politics of theatre, the state regards all radical theatrical productions as propaganda or outright politics. This means theatre artists risk being labeled as opposition politicians. For example, the state considers theatre artists who criticize those who fought the liberation war as unpatriotic or even as traitors working in alliance with former imperial powers to recolonize the country. Thus, anti-establishment theatre artists can be charged with treason, which carries a death sentence. Besides the Zimbabwean state's legally constituted censorship board, secret agents, military, and police, together with the ruling party's youth militias, war veterans, and vigilante groups constitute the nationalist regime's censorship machinery. Inevitably, experimentation and innovation become a necessity for artists who constantly find themselves searching for creative ways "to wrap and smuggle political goods across social boundaries policed by repressive and unintelligent state censors."[24]

Anti-establishment theatre artists live in constant fear of the regime's censorship machinery, which is notorious for not only practicing warrantless surveillance, but also for wantonly torturing, arresting, intimidating, beating, abducting, and even murdering opposition political activists and artists. Ironically, the nationalist regime has revived the restrictive and repressive colonial-era censorship laws. This necessitates that most radical theatre artists and activists abandon traditional theatre spaces, conventions, practices, and techniques and create new spaces and strategies to communicate with their targeted audiences. This dire need to interact with hard-to-reach audiences links the politically turbulent and repressive epochs of colonial and post-independence nationalist dictatorships, necessitating not only the birth of new forms but also the rejuvenation of older avant-garde traditions. Whether operating under repressive and authoritarian regimes or in restrictive and oppressive cultural traditions or environments, theatre artists must seek to break new ground as they create and widen their range of themes, styles, conventions, and techniques. The Zimbabwean scenario clearly shows that reaching back to one's tradition is not sufficient. Besides engaging in creative experimentation with new trends and practices, constant involvement in inter- and intracultural aesthetic and ideological exchange yields radical and cutting-edge performances.

Avant-garde of the crisis decade: challenging autocracy (1999–2009)

What has come to be known as the crisis decade (1999–2009) has produced the most inventive and cutting-edge theatre. For the past ten years, Zimbabwe has been mired in a political, humanitarian, and economic crisis of unprecedented magnitude. With Zimbabwe gradually becoming a *de facto* one-party state, the formation of a formidable opposition political party – the Movement for Democratic Change (MDC) – in 1999 to challenge the Zimbabwe African National Union (ZANU-PF's) domination marked the beginning of the crisis. While ZANU-PF bases its legitimacy on the history of the liberation struggle and an affirmative view of the controversial elections of 2000, the MDC claims legitimacy from its origins in trade union organizations and a negative view of the stolen elections of 2000. As the political impasse between the two power blocs deepened, ZANU-PF took advantage of its incumbency and control of the armed forces and resorted to killings, abductions, arrests, and torture of opposition party supporters. Theatre artists and activists producing anti-establishment theatre have not been spared.

The relationship between the state and popular theatre artists in Zimbabwe has always been characterized by alliance and discordance, loyalty and rebellion, as well as cooperation and interference. In a bid to stay in power, the Robert Mugabe regime has killed, maimed, persecuted, tortured, detained, and harassed anyone perceived as opposed to it. Such violations not only provided raw material for artists but also catalyzed the antagonistic relationship that now exists between popular theatre activists and the state. For example, plays such as Amakhosi Theatre's *Witnesses and Victims* (2000) depict the violence and rights violations associated with state-sanctioned invasions and expropriation of mostly white-owned commercial farms under the guise of land reform. Other popular theatre activists have focused on the rights of prisoners to food, access to healthcare, and decent accommodation, while others have highlighted state brutality, torture, and the violence associated with elections. For example, Savannah Arts's play *Decades of Terror* (2007) and Amakhosi's Theatre's *The Good President* (2007) discuss the culture of violence associated with election campaigns in post-independence Zimbabwe.

In the context of state censorship and surveillance, many theatre activists pursue the art of resistance through the subterfuge of entertainment and comedy. Political satire, in particular, became an important component of the crisis decade. For example, Rooftop's political satires such as *Ganyau Express* (2000), *Waiters 4* (2002), and *Rags and Garbage* (2002) are not just simple comedies, but are coded critiques of the post-independence nationalist regime's failures. These political satires came to be known as Panic Theatre or Urgent Theatre because, in attacking the establishment, they not only called attention to the regime's vices and follies, but also highlighted the urgent need for international help and intervention to redress the crisis. Panic Theatre amounts to satirical avant-garde performance in the manner in which it criticizes not only the political establishment, but also various phenomena in economic life, religion, and many other aspects of society – including censorship itself.[25] As Panic Theatre, this avant-garde also amounts to a call for help under critical circumstances.

It also continues the tradition of blending indigenous and international styles. Panic Theatre or Urgent Theatre derives from the *kurova bembera* public performance tradition in Zimbabwe which is intended not only to appeal for public help in emergency situations but also uses circumspection to name and shame perpetrators of any social ills. Joy Wrolson locates Panic Theatre in Zimbabwe's *nhimbe* tradition where communal or cooperative work gangs jestingly expose and castigate socially deviant behavior through indirection.[26] Panic Theatre's strength lies in its ability to use both popular or traditional and unconventional protest forms to capture and depict the ever-changing stream of the country's contemporary geo-political and economic context.

Satire in Zimbabwe escapes censorship because it exposes, ridicules, and attacks the failures and follies of the nationalist leadership, public figures, and society in general through irony, wit, metaphor, and indirection. Since satirical devices like these can lend performances to misinterpretation, Panic Theatre's political critique relies on the audience's ability to decode the hidden transcripts and to recognize its "ghosts" just like the *nhimbe*.[27] However, given a long tradition of Zimbabwean satire, avant-gardes can be fairly confident that audiences will understand the political implications of their work within their given contexts. James C. Scott describes such modes of protest performances as "a politics of disguise and anonymity that takes place in public view but is designed to have a double meaning or to shield the identity of the actors."[28] Political satire can successfully evade censorship when subordinate audiences are keyed into the cultural codes and meaning frequencies which exclude the dominant nationalist elites. Audience relations thus continue to play a key role in Zimbabwe's avant-garde theatre. Indeed, artists must calculate and manage the likely responses not only of the state but also of their audiences; most Panic Theatre plays are double-coded not only because practitioners fear state reprisals, but also because overt political criticism makes the targeted middle-class audiences nervous.

In addition to double-coding, the ability to adapt traditional satirical oral performances rooted in gests, trickster stories, innuendo, rumor, gossip, and jokes to suit the modern stage makes Panic Theatre artists part of the evolving avant-garde movement in Zimbabwe. Both satire and traditionalism enable avant-gardes to transform into what might be called liminal activists in order to evade censorship, surveillance, and persecution by vacillating between political activism and playful entertainment, the contemporary and the traditional. As a result, it is difficult for the Mugabe regime's censorship machinery to define these satirists as political activists. Due to their mixed cultural identity and coded play, these avant-gardes can easily claim that they are mere harmless comedians, jesters, clowns, or entertainers out to make people laugh rather than activists bent on inciting people.

Hit-and-Run Theatre: an anti-dictatorship avant-garde of the 2000s

As with so many of Zimbabwe's avant-gardes, Hit-and-Run Theatre is a historical necessity born out of a specific context; in this case, a repressive political and socio-economic environment in which dissent is muzzled and views opposed to the state are not tolerated. Abandoning the trickster aesthetic of Panic Theatre, it has emerged as an alternative medium to openly and provocatively address the most volatile and pressing issues of the day following the banning of independent and impartial media in Zimbabwe.[29]

James C. Scott and Michel de Certeau have identified protest forms that are reliant upon either sequestered spaces or coded language to critique the establishment, and I have discussed many critical theatre forms that have depended upon either a secret language system or a strategic withdrawal from public sites in order to elude state censorship. However, while Scott and de Certeau emphasize the linguistic and spatial modes of resistance, and these modes have dominated Zimbabwe's history, I would argue that time-based approaches are equally effective. Indeed, Hit-and-Run Theatre constitutes a third strategy that depends on time instead of just language and space. It seeks to convey its message within the shortest possible time to allow artists to get away before authorities figure out what they are doing and who they are.

Extreme censorship and surveillance from the ZANU-PF vigilante groups, youth militias, liberation war veterans, and police loyal to the Mugabe regime compel popular theatre artists to devise new performance strategies to avoid arrests, abductions, assaults, and torture. In addition, the autocratic regime either denies space to perform outright or the artists themselves deem it too risky to do so. Hit-and-Run Theatre derives its name from the idea of running away from a crime scene without necessarily identifying oneself. During shows, performers are constantly on the look-out for the ubiquitous state security agents and ruling party militias and vigilante groups. This means vigilance is part of the performance. Preparation involves establishing escape routes. A get-away car is always on stand-by, and artists are prepared to terminate their routines and vanish in case of any danger. Artists try to remain anonymous and travel light to make their escape. In the eyes of the autocratic regime, Hit-and-Run Theatre amounts to what Scott terms the "fugitive political conduct of subordinate groups."[30] Thus, the name Hit-and-Run aptly describes the combative aesthetic and pedagogical philosophies behind this new theatrical form.

Hit-and-Run Theatre artists perform in the face of unjust and totalitarian authority, their shows often disguised and embedded in everyday life, taking place in crowded public spaces such as streets, storefronts, flea markets, public commuter buses, and shopping malls. It is not publicized to avoid drawing any attention from local authorities. In some cases, it takes a while for both audiences and authorities to realize that a show is going on. In order to attract crowds, Hit-and-Run artists either use music and dance or simply fake a fight. For example, they might incorporate a blind singer who fakes ignorance of the performance and picks a fight with the performers, arguing that he/she does not discuss politics. They might ask the growing crowd for arbitration while the artists use the opportunity to improvise and steer the dialogue. As terse performances, the plays focus on specific issues and quickly hit their message home. This makes Hit-and-Run Theatre message-driven performance – and part of the tradition of agit-prop – that deals mostly with current issues affecting the civic population. For example, the Amakhosi and Savannah theatre companies have dealt with such sensitive issues as political violence, corruption, human rights abuses, and bad governance.

Like the *pungwe*, agit-prop, and TfD, Hit-and-Run Theatre relies heavily on improvisation – always a useful tool for these avant-gardes of necessity. Though each Hit-and-Run performance is essentially ephemeral, it can easily be adapted to changing contexts. For instance, audience involvement is necessary to draw attention to the performance, but it can also be costly in terms of time. Thus, artists must quickly steer the dialogue back to the central issue and disappear as soon as the performance is over. Unlike other anti-establishment performance practices in Zimbabwe's history, post-performance discussion is discouraged or minimized in Hit-and-Run Theatre. As the avant-garde of the dictatorship era in Zimbabwe, Hit-and-Run Theatre rejects old aesthetics, conventions and traditions, but does so as much out of necessity as out of any particular political or aesthetic position. Aiming to be the vanguard of change and the avatars of a more democratic future in a seemingly desperate and hopeless political context, Hit-and-Run Theatre represents not only the tenacity of Zimbabwean artists but also their unwavering commitment to change and values of a peaceful and democratic future.

Conclusion

Modern scholarship has a tendency to read African avant-garde theatre as an appendage or imitation of European models. Such an approach fails to be cognizant of parallel experimentations in Zimbabwe with age-old traditions both within Zimbabwe and across the African continent. Marvin Carlson supports a similar view in his analysis of avant-garde theatre in the Middle East, where he writes, "Theatrical activities very similar to those claimed as their own by European avant-garde in fact can be found in many theatrical cultures, where they were generated and developed with no thought of European artistic concerns."[31] Since the attainment of political independence in 1980, Zimbabwean theatre artists have striven to engage in a give-and-take cultural understanding and exchange with progressive world cultures in order to expand and enrich its cultural practice.

When cultures meet on an equal basis, opportunities for enrichment, experimentation, and innovation are boundless. Transnational aesthetic and ideological exchanges between the West and the rest of the world – but also among those outside the West – fuel avant-gardism in various global contexts, including Zimbabwe. The avant-garde theatre movement represents the culmination of international material, aesthetic, and ideological exchanges going full circle. This means African avant-gardes imitate Western avant-gardes imitating African avant-gardes. However, it is important to bear in mind the fact that each specific time and place shapes its ideological and aesthetic materials. Conversely, as different aesthetic and ideological materials travel across the globe, they in turn also shape their contexts. In short, aesthetic and ideological materials are adapted, transformed, and recast in a new light as different world cultures interact, experiment, and hybridize to produce new dramatic forms, styles, and thematic concerns.

Notes

1. Antonys Gyltzouris, "On the Emergence of European Avant-Garde Theatre," *Theatre History Studies* 28 (2008): 131–146, 136.
2. Joachim Fiebach, "Avant Garde and Performance Cultures in Africa," in *Not the Other Avant-Garde: The Transnational Foundations of Avant-Garde Performance*, ed. James M. Harding and John Rouse (Ann Arbor: University of Michigan Press, 2006), 69.
3. Claudia Orenstein, *Festive Revolutions: The Politics of Popular Theater and the San Francisco Mime Troupe* (Jackson, MS: University Press of Mississippi, 1998), 25.
4. Ngũgĩ wa Thiong'o, *Moving the Centre* (London: Currey, 1993), 13.
5. Jane Plastow, *African Theatre and Politics: The Evolution of Theatre in Ethiopia, Tanzania and Zimbabwe: A Comparative Study* (Amsterdam: Rodopi, 1996), 113.
6. For more details on UN sanctions, see Jeremy Matam Farrall, *United Nations Sanctions and The Rule of Law* (Cambridge: Cambridge University Press, 2009).
7. For more on the use of theatre during the liberation war era in Zimbabwe, see Kimani Gecau et al., *Community Based Theatre in Zimbabwe: An Evaluation of ZIMFEP's Experiences* (Harare: ZIMFEP, 1991); Ross Kidd, *From People's Theatre for Revolution to Popular Theatre for Reconstruction: Diary of a Zimbabwean Workshop* (The Hague, Netherlands: CESO; Toronto: ICAE, 1984); Preben Kaarsholm, "Mental Colonization or Catharsis? Theatre, Democracy and Cultural Struggle from Rhodesia to Zimbabwe," in *Politics and Performance: Theatre, Poetry, and Song in Southern Africa*, ed. Liz Gunner (Johannesburg: Witwatersrand University Press, 1994); and Plastow, *African Theatre and Politics*.

8. John Conteh-Morgan, "The Other Avant-Garde: The Theatre of Radical Aesthetics and the Poetics and Politics of Performance in Contemporary Africa," in *Not the Other Avant-Garde*, ed. Harding and Rouse, 99.
9. Ibid.
10. Gene Jarrett, "The Black Arts Movement and Its Scholars," *American Quarterly* 57.4 (2005), 1245.
11. Mike Sell, *Avant-Garde Performance and the Limits of Criticsim: Approaching the Living Theatre, Happenings/Fluxus, and the Black Arts Movement* (Ann Arbor: University of Michigan Press, 2005).
12. Augusto Boal, *Theatre of the Oppressed* (New York: The Communications Group, 1985), 122.
13. Ibid., 96.
14. Theodore Shank, *Beyond the Boundaries: American Alternative Theatre* (Ann Arbor: University of Michigan Press, 2002), 3.
15. The Frontline States included Angola, Botswana, Lesotho, Mozambique, Tanzania, Zambia, and Zimbabwe.
16. R. Mshengu Kavanagh, *Theatre and Cultural Struggle in South Africa* (London: Zed, 1985), xv.
17. Don Rubin (ed.), *The World Encyclopedia of Contemporary Theatre: Africa* (London: Routledge, 1997), 308.
18. Ross Kidd, David Kerr, and Martin Byram developed this standard methodology in the 1970s and emphasized that it is not a rigid TfD formula but practitioners should adapt it to their different contexts. See Oga Steve Aba, *Performing Life: Case Studies in the Practice of Theatre for Development* (Zaria, Nigeria: Shekut, 1997).
19. David Kerr, *African Popular Theatre* (London: Currey, 1995), 149.
20. Paulo Freire, *Pedagogy of the Oppressed*, trans. Myra Bergman Ramos (New York: Penguin, 1982), 284.
21. James M. Harding, "From Cutting Edge to Rough Edges: The Transnational Foundations of Avant-garde Performance," in *Not the Other Avant-Garde*, ed. Harding and Rouse; Conteh-Morgan, "The Other Avant-Garde"; Sandara Richards, "Wasn't Brecht an African Writer?: Parallels with Contemporary Nigerian Drama," in *Brecht in Asia and Africa*, ed. J. Fuegi and M. Silberman, *The Brecht Yearbook* 14 (1989) (Frankfurt/Main: Atheneum, 1989).
22. Kimani Gecau, *Community-Based Theatre in Zimbabwe*, 1. For more on the Kamiriithu Theatre Project, see Ngũgĩ wa Thiong'o, *Decolonizing the Mind: The Politics of Language in African Literature* (London: Heineman, 1986); and Gichingiri Ndigirigi, *Ngũgĩ wa Thiong'o: Drama and the Kamiriithu Popular Theatre Experiment* (Trenton, NJ: Africa World Press, 2007).
23. Conteh-Morgan, "The Other Avant-Garde," 114.
24. Ibid., 98.
25. For more on censorship in Zimbabwe, see Praise Zenenga, "Censorship, Surveillance and Protest Theatre in Zimbabwe," *Theater* 38.3 (2008): 64–83.
26. L. Joy Wrolson, "Conquered Plans: Performance for the Artist's Sake, Panic Theatre in Zimbabwe During the Murambatsvina," African Studies Association, Chicago, IL, Nov. 13–16, 2008.
27. Ibid., 21.

28. James C. Scott, *Domination and the Arts of Resistance: Hidden Transcripts* (New Haven: Yale University Press, 1990), 19.
29. For extended discussion of Hit-and-Run Theatre, see Praise Zenenga, "Hit-and-Run Theatre: The Rise of a New Dramatic Form in Zimbabwe," African and Afro-Caribbean Performance Conference, University of California, Berkeley, Sept. 26–28, 2008.
30. Scott, *Domination and the Arts of Resistance*, xii.
31. Marvin Carlson, "Avant-Garde Drama in the Middle East," in *Not the Other Avant-Garde*, ed. Harding and Rouse, 128.

12
The Ians in the Audience: Punk Attitude and the Influence of the Avant-Garde

Graham White

Introduction

In the summer of 1976, the London rock band The Sex Pistols played two gigs, one on June 4, the other July 20, at the Lesser Free Trade Hall in the Northern English city of Manchester, concerts which catalyzed a musical movement in the UK – punk rock and its offspring, post-punk – that has since grown in influence and significance to become a phenomenon memorialized, anthologized, and critically mulled over in vast numbers of recordings, books, articles, and films. In the words of the music journalist Paul Morley, who was present at the first of these gigs, an "emotional revolution" began in these encounters between performers and audience.[1] In particular, one young man who saw The Sex Pistols that summer and who found in their music an aesthetic form through which to channel his own sense of alienation has attained iconic status in the thirty-plus years since. His reputation and the impact of his musical and lyrical concerns has been steadily growing since he found a form of martyrdom in an early death, and the significance of the emotive epiphany the gig seemed to embody for him has run on through a cultic set of myths enshrined on various internet sites and in movements dedicated to pursuing his musical legacy. He has become a figurehead for a generation of alienated young men, the hero of an international movement.

Ian Curtis, the lead singer of the chief band of the Mancunian "emotional revolution," Joy Division, committed suicide at the age of twenty-three and was at the Lesser Free Trade Hall to see The Sex Pistols on July 20. However, while Curtis fits the bill as a totemic figure, a martyr to that emotional revolution, he is not the man I'm writing about. He does, though, share a first name with my subject. Ian Stuart, formerly Ian Stuart Donaldson, has not, like Curtis, been featured in a biopic celebrating his significance (i.e. Anton Corbijn's *Control*, 2007), nor has his death (in a car crash rather than by his own hand) been analyzed as an act which might have some aesthetic unity with his life. However, I would suggest that this less well-known narrative of revolutionary beatification is at least as significant as that featuring Curtis, and that it provides an illuminating counter-narrative concerning the processes of aesthetic influence and the critical modeling of the same by academics and historians.

The Lesser Free Trade Hall and the mythologization of punk

The Sex Pistols' performances are widely mythologized by commentators as the catalyst for an enormous cultural leap. These Manchester concerts – in which a then little-known, but already controversial band performed their innovative brand of reductive and aggressive, Situationist-inspired music to an audience out of which emerged a large and enormously influential rock diaspora – are generally written about as "classically" avant-garde performances, genuine moments of inspirational ground-taking in what is wryly dubbed in much British music journalism as "the punk wars." These concerts are seen to share characteristics with a host of influential avant-garde events in performance, music, theatre, and the visual arts throughout the period of the so-called "historical" avant-garde, the period of Dada and Surrealism, events containing what Günter Berghaus describes as an "intimate bond of art and anti-art, destructive impulses and forward-looking visions" characteristic of the avant-garde in action.[2] There, in Manchester, are that same small band of initiates (thirty-two at the first gig), that same clandestine network through which knowledge of the subversive material passes, that same controversy surrounding the initial appearance of the group and their work, that same extraordinary opening up of aesthetic possibilities which the event seems to have passed to its audience, that same taking of these lessons and inspirations and the wielding of them across the field of culture as a consequence, and that same staging of a manifesto redolent of other influential avant-garde assaults on cultural norms (in this case, championing a "punk" attitude which said that music could be simple and complex at the same time and that musicianship mattered far less than the use of an art practice as a vehicle for what needed to be said).

A key element in this "classical" formulation of the avant-garde moment is that the gig or performance or exhibition or screening represents a predominantly progressive eruption of creativity, complexity, and inspiration, one which grasps a vision of the future and which, in distinguishing itself from a modernist concern to engage with cultural tradition, breaks for the new. However, given the subsequent and repeated assertion of an intentional artistic "seriousness" in the work emerging from a moment like punk, the widespread *détournement*[3] in conventional commercial cinema of the B-movie/trash aesthetic, and the burgeoning recognition in the 1980s and 1990s of a similar definable seriousness in comics, pulp fiction, and sci-fi – all variously benefiting from the postmodern leveling of cultural value – it is perhaps instructive to examine some of the grounds for the championing of this culturally and politically progressive purpose and utility, and to see where an under-examined aesthetic which also emerged from this moment might tell a parallel, but rather less progressive, story.

Commentators writing on the Manchester gigs – generally partisan enthusiasts for punk – articulate the moment of the concerts as foundational for a new aesthetic movement, with an audience comprising members of future bands such as Joy Division, New Order, The Smiths, The Buzzcocks, The Fall, and Magazine,[4] and with John Lydon (then Johnny Rotten), the lead singer of the band, operating like a "psychotic lecturer explaining to these avant-garde music fans exactly what to do with their love of music, the things they wanted to say and their unknown need to perform."[5] The catalytic impact of the concerts is generally represented as a focused, small-scale eruption which was an incalculably influential force for cultural *good*, for the widening of the possibilities of performance and popular music and for the shaping of an aesthetic sensibility which echoes through subsequent developments in British music, performance, visual arts, literature, television, and film. For example, Tim Etchells, of the highly influential British performance group Forced Entertainment, cites Mark E. Smith, attendee of the Free Trade Hall gigs and lead singer, lyricist, and controller of the band The Fall (which formed after the gigs and is still going thirty years later), as a key influence on his own sense of the possibilities of language and performance.[6] Smith's work also had a major impact on the dancer and choreographer Michael Clark, often tagged in Britain as a "punk" dancer, whose use of The Fall's music in performance was, perhaps apocryphally, permitted by Smith with the rider "as long as you don't take the piss out of it," showing both the suspicious, gritty, and serious self-belief of the punk movement, and its welding, as it matured, to a more conventionally modernist readiness for engagement with old cultural forms – as long as those forms were adaptable to the needs of the new. A recent book of short stories by young-ish British writers results from each taking a Fall song title as inspiration.[7]

However, claiming a progressive value for what came out of the moment of punk – its liberation of gender, sexual identity, class, wit, spite, and creativity, all components of Morley's "emotional revolution" – is not always easily aligned with political liberalism. Smith's own political views tend to be voiced in uncompromising terms which often leave liberal interviewers struggling,[8] and his enthusiasm for right-wing mavericks such as Wyndham Lewis suggests that his own original inspirations may indeed have been conventionally – though unprogramatically – modernist, seeking a freedom from the immediate ascription of political values to his work or indeed any clear engagement with a declared politics. The development of the band Joy Division, which produced two albums before Curtis's suicide in 1980, was always shadowed by a flirtation with monumentality in packaging, presentation, and naming which led to accusations of fascist sympathies, particularly when the survivors dubbed themselves New Order.

This apparent complication in the conventional story of the punk revolution as progressive is furthered by two other factors, both of which cast light on the awkwardness of reading this kind of avant-garde intervention as a liberating leap. The first is the sense within the movement surrounding the catalysts themselves, The Sex Pistols, that the avant-garde moment was to be self-consciously and ironically employed – to be seized and then discarded. The band were presented through a framework of Situationist ideas constructed by their manager, Malcolm McLaren, whose own version of Situationist guru Guy Debord's writings clearly registered the concept of "spectacular rebellion" – Debord's suggestion that, in "the society of the spectacle," rebellion is always already recuperated and in the process of being re-engineered and sold back to the hapless young urban revolutionary through the commodification of subversion as image rather than substance.[9] Sharply aware of this dichotomy, McLaren sought to have his band marketed as the ultimate in subversive intent, while aware that the key impact this would have was financial. In this sense, he was the Tin Pan Alley impresario of a new and more cynical age. His sense that the avant-garde group must necessarily self-destruct and his subsequent use of that self-destruction as a vehicle for cartoon idiocy and outrage (see the movie *The Great Rock and Roll Swindle*[10]) perhaps reveal McLaren's intention all along to have been to play the media landscape for maximum publicity. The puritan aesthetic of punk attitude, as reified in the myths surrounding the Free Trade Hall gigs, is undermined by the sense that their influence cannot only be claimed in terms of a disaporic cultural shift, but may also, bathetically, occur exactly along the lines of Debord's predicted recuperation of any anarchic spirit into the commodity landscape of contemporary popular art and culture.

A second strand of avant-garde influence emerging from this moment provides a further disturbance of the model of punk as a progressive irruption of cultural innovation. The Lesser Free Trade Hall gigs were not only attended by now-celebrated performers whose output has been influential on succeeding generations of musicians and arts practitioners, but also by another, more hidden musical catalyst, a figure whose counter-history shares a sense of the event as catalytic, but whose interest in "what to do with [his] love of music, the things [he] wanted to say," while still chiming with punk's aesthetic of providing a voice to the relatively marginal, led not to a progressive, liberal future, but to political and cultural totalitarianism.[11]

Ian Stuart Donaldson, from Blackpool, attended either the first or second of the Free Trade Hall gigs and took inspiration from the new performance aesthetic he saw on stage, an aesthetic which he went on to employ with his band Skrewdriver.[12] In an interview, Donaldson remarked:

> We were playing a lot of pub gigs, doing the circuits, and then we went to see The Sex Pistols in Manchester with Buzzcocks and Slaughter and the Dogs. We really enjoyed it cos [*sic*] we thought that it was fresh, new sort of thing, so we did a tape more on that sort of line, sent it to a load of record companies. Chiswick [a UK record label] asked us to come down and do a session in a studio, and we got a single deal out of that, and then once we done [*sic*] that single, they updated the deal to two singles and an LP.[13]

Skrewdriver were part of a wave of punk which Paul Morley's writing doesn't address, what might be called the "meathead" tendency, which had no attachment to an art-school model of modernist aesthetic experiment but was attracted to punk's brutality, aggression, noise, and lyrical simplicity. These latter often comprised, if ironically employed, a musical bedrock for much of the movement, a self-conscious exercise in reductionist style. However, taken literally, the aggressive simplicity of punk became merely brutal, and the approach of bands like 999, Sham 69, Skrewdriver, Chelsea, and so on became associated with a right-wing, skinhead, racist element, at times troubling those bands into attempts to disentangle themselves from such elements, at other times leading to a very deliberate use of punk to proselytize for a far-right political agenda.[14] This "meathead" form of punk, culturally marginal, subject to little critical analysis and few claims for its influential status or its progressive aesthetic agenda, we might label "bad punk" against the "good punk" of the supposedly enlightened model. In his study of the musics that emerged after punk, *Rip It Up and Start Again*, Simon Reynolds mentions one version of this "bad punk" in passing and catches a sense of its aesthetic identity: "the non-arty side of punk...a.k.a. Oi!: crude, macho, always up for a ruck, a sound stunted by inverted snobbery."[15] However, neither Reynolds nor, more surprisingly, David Nolan in his book on eyewitness accounts of the two Sex Pistols gigs, mentions Skrewdriver or Stuart's presence at the Lesser Free Trade Hall.[16]

Commercially unsuccessful, musically unsophisticated, and politically antagonistic to the left-liberal agenda of punk, Stuart, having dropped the Donaldson from his name, split from Skrewdriver in 1978. When he re-formed the band in 1980, he did so with an explicitly racist, neo-Nazi agenda which led him to found a music-based propaganda movement grounded in a bastardized version of punk and developed until his death in a car crash in 1993. Ironically, this movement, called "Blood and Honour," now operates according to all the classic do-it-yourself attitudes expounded by punk: self-publication, intimate word-of-mouth networks, gigs as moments of enactment and realization of community, underground signs of commitment, rejection of social and aesthetic norms, celebration of outsider status. Here, the "classical" version of avant-garde practice, of the infectious agent of the new spreading through the weakened culture via underground activities and attitudes, becomes the modus operandi of a group with a truly "revolutionary" ambition. In this case, however, the "good punk" sense of "no sell-out" (which would have led to the puritanical rejection of any band who signed with a big record company or who employed a long guitar solo in 1976) is replaced by a commitment to extreme fanaticism. If the current prominence of the movement as a web presence is to be believed, there is a large and growing community of such fanatics to whom the organization proselytizes through music and attitude. Indeed, Blood and Honour is credited as a key catalyst in the growing political influence of the neo-Nazi National Democratic Party in the northeast German state of Mecklenburg-Vorpommern.[17]

Stuart's own recorded commentaries on his music and its roots make explicit his opportunistic use of punk. In their early incarnation,

Skrewdriver were dogged by accusations of racist motives and attitudes, although Stuart wrote often to the music press to claim that his band had no political leanings and the new group he intended to form would not be aligned with any movement, communist or fascist. In actual fact, when he did re-form the group, it was with an explicitly racist agenda, driven by close association with the then-dominant nationalist organization in Britain, the National Front. The punk "scene" in which Skrewdriver failed to succeed was rejected by Stuart for its politics:

> Basically, because we got fed up with punk turning a bit left-wing, whereas before everyone came along and had a laugh and danced about, but then it got to the stage where it became high fashion, and people would just stand there seeing who had the most drawing pins through their nose. When it got to that stage, it got really silly. We had all been skinheads in the past, so we all just reverted, and a lot of our mates coming to the gigs were skinheads.[18]

In fact one of the influential legacies of punk – the cottage industry approach to making, recording, and distributing music, putting on gigs, and writing about them and the scene in self-authored, self-distributed fanzines like *Sniffin' Glue* – can be seen as a residual influence of the manner in which Stuart set about furthering his role as an active racist and neo-Nazi propagandist. As he himself said of the Blood and Honour movement, itself set up around a quarterly fanzine first published in the 1980s, the aim was a low-level spearheading, with music as the rallying point:

> Blood and Honour has took off [*sic*] so well because of its idea. There has been no other magazine that promotes the advancement of the White race and that does not tie itself to any political party. B & H is not tied to any party; it is mainly run by the bands. The bands are popular, so the magazine is popular. Its main achievement has been to get more people involved in the White cause and to push the music of the bands over to a lot more people than would be possible otherwise. Food for thought, that Blood and Honour has got at least five times the circulation of *Searchlight* [a British anti-fascist journal]. That's a fact.[19]

This is a model of propagandist practice employed elsewhere in Christian Rock, the British Rock Against Racism movement of the 1970s, the Red Wedge model of a left-leaning band package aiming to counter Thatcherite conservatism in the 1980s, and in activist campaigns and attitudes struck across Mandela Days and Live Aids, Live 8s, and Earth Days. In these cases, a broadly defined musical aesthetic is employed as a vehicle for political beliefs, with the recruitment of musical forms which might speak across a range of possible support being a key component. The striking fact about Blood and Honour is that, if its own rhetoric is to be believed, it is succeeding in turning its vanguardism into a mass movement, with its forms of musical expression functioning not only as a vehicle for its appeal but as the immersive and expressive embodiment of its political agenda. To rock for racism and anti-Semitism, for fascism and extreme nationalism, is to rock to a particularly loud, aggressive, simple, and cartoonish version of punk rock – punk on steroids – in which raging, guttural vocals and sheets of guitar hammer home an extremity of unease and vengefulness. This is intended to appeal viscerally, to cajole and compel, to use elements that are deliberately musically violent and unsettling to immerse the listener – primarily young, male, aggressive, and somehow aggrieved – in confirmatory abandon.

The British anti-fascist organization Searchlight alleges that the emergence of the right-wing movement headed by Nick Griffin, which later became the British National Party, has its roots in Rock Against Communism, an outfit in which Stuart had an influential role and which used Griffin's father's Suffolk farm as the location for some of its gigs. In establishing this link between the extreme, non-parliamentary face of neo-Nazism and attempts to regulate extremity through conventional party politics, Searchlight provides further evidence of the history of influence, precedence, and ideological proximity which enabled punk rock to gain adherents who hold a body of radically conservative and reactionary beliefs. Blood and Honour, the product of Stuart's path through punk and into skinhead music – the stripped down, aggressive, and cartoon version of the punk model – is recognized as a musical genre by the Anti-Defamation League's Hate Music watch site, where it is defined in detailed fashion. The ADL's main concern, however, is not with aesthetic niceties, but with the speed and success of the movement as a recruiting forum for young, violent fascists, whose use of the musical and performance template handed on by Stuart has led to a burgeoning international "scene." Here, Stuart's template, restrictive and self-policing like that of so many musical sub-cultures, is the key medium through which a message is conveyed. The ADL's guide to the movement describes Stuart as a white supremacist "icon," although one (happily) unaware of the transformation of his legacy due to the emergence of the Web after his death, a medium which "radically altered the world of hate music, making it dramatically more accessible, more global, more visible, and more lucrative."[20]

The aesthetics of fascist rock

In the period after 1978, as the first waves of punk ebbed and those bands which had not adapted, like the original Skrewdriver, became stranded, a new movement emerged which may have been even more influential than punk in spreading an avant-garde agenda, a movement in which a Left-influenced, Brechtian model of defamiliarization was a key component. While marginal in its moment, this "post-punk" movement has now become so influential that much of the "indie" and experimental rock of the past five years can be properly said to have its roots in its particular innovations in sound, rhythm, lyrical concerns, and song writing. This offshoot originated among a series of groups that relied on a distancing, alienating separation of lyric, music, and event in order to deconstruct the core values of "rock" and was particularly antagonistic to the ideas of reductive rock and roll and proficient musicality. According to Simon Reynolds, "The post-punks set forth in the belief that 'radical content demands radical form'" and made a point out of "the systematic ransacking of twentieth-century modernist art and literature."[21] The immersive tendency in popular musical form and performance was viewed with special suspicion. Post-punk performers sought to puncture the ritual event of the gig, carrying on the "good punk" ethos. The band formed by Sex Pistols vocalist and lyricist Johnny Rotten, Public Image Limited (with whom he reverted to his original name, John Lydon), used a deliberately sparse, disorienting combination of music and lyric and embraced some Dadaist techniques to gigging which aimed to wind up audiences to a destructive pitch. The anarchist collective Crass used their own version of an apocalyptically extreme form of punk to embody an anarcho-syndicalist message in which the lyrical content maintained a propagandist intent, but in which musical subversion and variation were also permissible and encouraged in the service of the political agenda. (At one point, Crass succeeded in the Situationist gesture of disguising radical content as commodity when their anti-marriage ballad appeared as a flexi-disc sold on the cover of *Wedding* magazine.) In the post-punk moment, the formal and performative disjunctions of the historical avant-garde are self-consciously engaged with and replayed, and the names, attitudes, and affiliations of the historical avant-garde are reinscribed, as indicated by the recent exhibition of avant-garde graphics at London's British Library, which drew parallels between post-punk cover art and record labeling and the graphic innovations of various historical avant-garde movements.[22] In post-punk, the Left-modernist aesthetic concept of defamiliarization is brought to bear on a mixture of popular and avant-garde musical impulses in a rich and influential burst of creative activity.

William Niven's essay "The Birth of Nazi Drama" identifies the mythologizing processes of the Nazi-sponsored "Thingspiele" in prewar Germany as working antithetically to such a notion of defamiliarization, imposing instead what Niven calls a "refamiliarization, a bonding of audience and performance in a ritualistic stage-action designed to develop an intense, cultish, communal experience." He quotes from the tenets laid down by one leading practitioner, Richard Euringer: "Cult, not 'art,' is the purpose of the ThingPlatz," the theatre site specifically designed for such ritual performances.[23] These two concepts, refamiliarization and cult, might be read as the principles with which Blood and Honour defines an aesthetic identity for its punk-inspired music, which builds on the cultish tendencies in all rock music to define and further a particular assemblage of image, attitude, musical form, and event.

In contrast to post-punk, the focus of the Blood and Honour aesthetic is towards confirmation, by sonic overload and extremity of image and rhetoric, of the cartoon ideologies and stereotypes of right-wing viciousness: calls to violence, discipline, and self-sacrifice; attacks on the usual litany of ethnic and political enemies; repeated, anthemic choruses which call for rallying, sympathy, and support or which particularize enemies; threats and calls for widespread subversion. The success of this merging of the aesthetic and the propagandist in Stuart's model can be seen as a parallel, if inversed model of the post-punk aesthetic. If post-punk is read as a true movement, a formal and performative glue shaping a number of contemporary musical impulses with a common deconstructive interest in fracture, disruption, and repetition, then Blood and Honour can also be read as a coherent tendency, though based on an aesthetic that unites common interests and promotes an immersive political radicalism in order to advance a political position.

In September 2007, photographs in the press of a young man arrested for his part in a series of neo-Nazi, anti-Semitic attacks in Israel indicated the prominence of the Blood and Honour movement, "Skrewdriver" being the word tattooed in Gothic script along the underside of his forearm.[24] A London *Times* article by James Hider identifies the "white supremacist insignia" which the defendants had tattooed on them, including the number 88, a coded reference to Adolf Hitler ("H" being the eighth letter of the alphabet, "Heil Hitler" the traditional salute of Nazis).[25] However, the musical reference is not discussed in the article. Ironically, all of the young men involved were identified as immigrants under Israel's Law of Return, meaning that they would have been classed as Jewish by the Nuremberg race laws laid down in Nazi Germany in the 1930s and thus liable to elimination in the Holocaust. The leader of the gang, Eli Boanitov, was heard, in one conversation recorded by police, to tell another member of the gang, "My grandfather was a half-Jewboy. I will not have children so that this trash will not be born with even a tiny percent of Jewboy blood."[26] The complexity of identity – geographical, national, ethnic, racial, historical, and familial – in this alarming gang of self-haters is overlain by a unifying element, the epiphanic immersion signaled in extremist music, a parallel to Morley's emotional revolution, an immersion in a wave of white power ideologizing. The medium, in this instance, embodies the message: racism, masculinity, aggression, rage, noise, and hatred are combined in an oppressive musical and political stew.

Avant-gardes, epiphanies, and martyrs

Given that the roots of Blood and Honour and Skrewdriver in the Free Trade Hall performances have, like the link to this music movement in the news item above, passed relatively unnoticed by scholars and critics, the question arises as to how and why this should be the case. The Lesser Free Trade Hall gigs are the subject – like Bob Dylan's Royal Albert Hall gig of 1966 – of a growing body of analysis and commentary. The problematic nature of this ongoing reconstruction of the Lesser Free Trade Hall gigs as signaling "the future of Anglo-American rock" has been discussed by Sean Albiez, who argues that the gigs have come to stand in for a body of other, related factors, both "local and national," which have contributed to a mythical belief in their role in recent cultural change.[27] He discusses the variety of responses to the event from those in the audience, and the ways in which the first and second gigs have been conflated in many accounts (at the latter, The Sex Pistols were supported by a local band, the Buzzcocks, formed in excited response to the impact of the first gig), including those of some of the participants (Albiez quotes in particular Mark E. Smith's faulty memory). It is clear from Albiez's chapter in Ian Inglis's *Performance and Popular Music: History, Place and Time*, and from those on other canonical rock gigs in the same, that this kind of event is highly attractive to editors of anthologies and writers of critical commentary. Such work communicates the cultural values of an educated, articulate, and often dissenting body of individuals whose leisure, recreational space, and educational opportunities – as well as their professional and cultural positions of influence – make such performances especially likely to be written, spoken about, narrated, and mediated as significant events, regardless of any objectively authenticable judgement on the true proportions of their cultural reach. Albiez's account is a revisionist one which smartly addresses some of these issues, yet he, like Nolan and Reynolds, neglects to mention Stuart or Skrewdriver amongst the various musical also-rans who represent the second wave of Mancunian punk.

The way in which the past and the problems of documentation shape our present perspectives, especially when we examine something which touches on existing lives, and the sense of the need to go back and testify to the significance of experience also perhaps contributes to the political domestication of the Lesser Free Trade Hall mythscape. This is something which Nolan's book, *I Swear I Was There: The Gig That Changed the World*, highlights effectively. His reliance on anecdote and first-person memory shows voices clashing, competing, boasting, and mutually undermining each other. Because part of what I'm interested in here is how such anecdotes contribute to the historical record, I'd like to lapse into anecdote myself. When researching a similarly influential moment of social drama, the trial of the British anarchist group The Angry Brigade at the Old Bailey in 1972, for a radio play, I found myself faced with a similar mass of odd and contradictory stories from witnesses and participants, ranging from the member of an interview panel who declared that he'd shared a flat with one of the members of the group and who professed his unease at his past now returning as a research topic, to another academic who recalled the group blowing up a campus shed containing exam papers, to other colleagues, acquaintances, and friends who variously played on sports teams or attended drama school with group members or who claimed to know for certain of their attendance at a training camp in Turkey organized by the Palestine Liberation Organization. In each case, the eyewitness seemed to sense the complexity of the process of reconstruction, especially how the specifics of their own experience was becoming currency for contemporary consideration. My conversations highlighted for me one of the key problematics of documentary reconstruction that seeks to evaluate moments of particular cultural resonance: the influentially partisan participant. The title of Albiez's book – *Performance and Popular Music: History, Place and Time* – affirms my sense of the danger embedded in partisan representations concerning the cultural reach of a significant moment. Working far beyond the material specificity of the event and encouraging a variety of versions, claims, insights, and embodiments of memory, such representations are deeply dependent on personally accumulated cultural capital.

A similar burst of recollection to that surrounding The Angry Brigade emerges from my discussions of punk with colleagues and friends: a colleague spat at from the stage of The Roundhouse by Joe Strummer, a member of the Mekons (though, of course, any member of the audience became a Mekon). Bands and attitudes are labeled, fractures and splinters and supporting timbers of the movement are anatomized and lionized, disinterred, and reassessed. This is typical of the field. In tracing the landscape of the avant-garde, commentary repeatedly returns to the logic and influence of aesthetic evidence; in the case of the "punk wars," to the battle over who came first (New York or London?), who ripped off whom (Ramones, Stooges, or MC5?), where the scene coalesced (the Roxy nightclub, the Screen On The Green cinema, or a Bromley, London, comprehensive school?), or, particularly relevant to my concerns here, over which was the catalytic moment that shaped both the impact of the revolutionary movement (among which, we might choose The Sex Pistols' *London Tonight* interview with Bill Grundy, their So It Goes performance for Manchester's Granada TV, or, my favorite, the news item in the *Western Morning News* outlining how far the band had gone to spread its sick message as SPOTS, an acronym for Sex Pistols On Tour Secretly, when it attempted to smuggle itself into the nearest big city to me, Plymouth, for a gig). In such ways, and with this influential access to a set of spaces in which such a discourse could be furthered, the cultural mythopedia of good punk and post-punk is always already complex and endlessly rewritten.

However, Blood and Honour is building its own counter-narrative of influences, aesthetics, and political "progress" on the worldwide Web. Complementing this production, the world of "bad punk" remains relatively unanalyzed by critics and scholars. The subversive intent of music which stages a contradiction between political radicalism and economic exploitation that would have horrified any Frankfurt School theorist is instead affirmed in the aesthetic influence of the "art school" end of the punk parade. Meanwhile, the far more insurrectionary and perhaps politically effective direct action of Blood and Honour disappears into the realms of hate-group monitors and the political and social sciences, into the hands of anti-fascist activists and students of the horrors of fascist art activities. Also ignored in dominant accounts of punk is the possibility that the kind of punk aesthetic employed and championed in such accounts is essentially conservative, anti-radical, and pro-commodification. Indeed, in its celebration of the punk gig as epiphany, those accounts curiously chime with Stuart's own accounts of the conversion he experienced at the Lesser Free Trade Hall.

A further trait in the dominant accounts of punk rock's origins can be seen to overlap with Stuart's work; specifically, the desire to identify a movement in terms of inspiration, if not messianic figureheads. The curious consanguinity between the two epiphanies – the good punk gig and the bad punk gig – can be further traced through the representations of Stuart as a martyr to a political and aesthetic cause. This presence, influence, and sense of loss is written and spoken of in terms which often overlap with and mirror those surrounding Ian Curtis, the self-destructive lead singer of Joy Division and another attendee of the first Lesser Free Trade Hall gig. The language of self-sacrifice circulates around the iconic Curtis. His life and wild performance style, seeming to embody the alienation expressed in both his lyrical preoccupations and the sparse intensity of his band's music, has been the subject of a critically celebrated independent film, *Control*, shot entirely in the familiar monochrome style of the director, Anton Corbijn.[28] Corbijn is a rock photographer who captured Joy Division as they emerged and whose images contributed strongly to the mystique of the band during their brief career. One of the most striking elements in the commentary on the film is the repeated exploration of the figure of Curtis as the leader/spokesman/representative of a deeply felt and resonant mode of masculine despair, the band's undoubtedly powerful music being understood as the repository of a form of resonant, poeticized truth which, while undermined and contextualized in the film as partial and also somewhat comic, somehow echoes all the more loudly in the moments of its most forceful inscription, the gig. In these moments, the likeable, flawed, irritating, self-centered small-town obsessive becomes a seer, a shaman, a speaker of dark truths for the post-industrial landscape against which he is so frequently framed.

That Curtis's bandmates are less readily poeticized, despite having lived the vital, volatile, and vain lifestyles of rock music pioneers through a landscape of success, failure, compromise, and artistic unevenness, stands as evidence of a tendency among critics and historians to create martyrs in the field of popular music, to identify both the emotive charge of performance and the aggression, tension, introspection, and reflection of the band-as-group as revelatory, in a pure form, of the historicity of the messianic avant-gardist. Antonin Artaud, Ian Curtis, Nick Drake, Sarah Kane, Sylvia Plath, and Fred Herko all exist as mythopoetic figures whose descent into madness and self-destruction reflects their intense and visionary comprehension of an essential truth concerning them and ourselves. Set against this myth, we might read a series of rather less "successful" suicides, such as the English novelist B. S. Johnson, whose self-destruction seems to come more from a piqued sense of failure or injustice, a lack of recognition, or a disappointment which is factually unsustainable. Indeed, in respect to the demise of the British singer-songwriter Nick Drake in the mid-1970s, it would seem to be possible to assign his demise to either camp – as the seer who could no longer bear the visions with which he was confronted (e.g. the accounts of Patrick Humphries or Ian MacDonald) or as the thwarted figure of overly high self-esteem, brought low when his diffidence and public indifference coincided to enforce his obscurity (e.g. the account of Trevor Dann). From this perspective, Morley's emotional revolution through punk may in fact be no more than a reinscription of the adolescent preoccupation with the self as uniquely suffering, notwithstanding claims for wider critical, political, aesthetic, and social impact.

The tendency to read a suicide as the advent of an emotional revolution and to sentimentalize and romanticize both the suicide's work and his end reinforces a narrative of a particular form of artistic practice, of leadership and renewal embodied in the individual who has seen further and somehow created an aesthetic which is more vibrant, intense, and truthful than those of the artists whose canons stretch on into repetition, unsuccessful reinvention, ageing irrelevance, or reliance on the aesthetic tricks of yesteryear. In the case of Ian Stuart, however, we seem to remain in the territory of the cultic; specifically, the reinscription of the pioneer through the ritual of replaying musical and political forms and attitudes which retain that sense of the moment of inspirational disgust, of rejection, of the artist's embrace of the taboo in order to rise above the mundane, the untruthful, the inauthentic. If The Sex Pistols ushered in an aesthetic and emotional revolution, perhaps it may be said that Ian Stuart reveals that the avant-garde invariably becomes fixed in the form assumed in the moment of its appearance, and its restaging becomes a sentimental attempt to hold on to a moment of revolution which has already, inevitably, become someone's nostalgia.

Conclusion

When the Free Trade Hall gigs surface in Michael Winterbottom's 2002 film on the Manchester music scene, *24 Hour Party People*, it is as a comically low-key rallying point, with the members of the audience literally reduced to those who will go on to form bands. In this case, the catalytic jolt of the avant-garde moment is rendered bathetically, although this doesn't detract from the film's veneration of the "emotional revolution" driven by the music that emerged from it. However, in the language of the Blood and Honour movement, influential gigs, which the movement claims to be key to spreading the aesthetic, are summarized as totemic in similarly sentimental, but far more monumental ways. The emergence of the National Democratic Party of Germany would suggest that this alternative legacy of the Free Trade Hall is not so open to comic re-telling:

> National concerts like the Violent Storm Memorial in March, St George's Day in April, Ian Stuart Memorial in September, and White Christmas in December have become international festivals beyond frontiers and national boundaries with hundreds attending from all around the white world, all adding to our domestic might and fight for our glorious cause. The quality, number, and professionalism of the bands have also grown. Our bands and music, from [their] humble beginnings within the shores of Great Britain, have spawned a global music scene and way of life, a movement giving hope, financing, and advertising the good fight.[29]

Debord's model of the already commodified rebellion, exemplified by the logical absurdity of a commercial rock band such as The Sex Pistols singing "Anarchy in the UK," would seem to indicate the impossibility of a politicized avant-garde in the postmodern era; further, that the only viable model for a revolutionary aesthetic is one that engages with the revolution of the imagination in the very moment which Morley envisages, in which, for example, a city's identity and psycho-geography is exposed and explored in a particular aesthetic form.

However, as the case of "Blood and Honour" shows, a model rightwing avant-garde that celebrates a fascist mythology of violence, intensity, masculine camaraderie, sacrifice, and destruction can benefit from the lessons of classic avant-garde entryism. As Edward Commentale suggests, the avant-garde may be essentially fascistic in its revolutionary zeal, seeking the sensual enjoyment of violence and asserting that war is "a form of affirmation responsive to the newly exploited subject; egoism for its own sake is transmuted into a rhetoric of vitality and sacrifice."[30] It may be that the "Blood and Honour" websites are home to a similar commodification as that which Debord describes, a holding up of a mirror to a like-minded community looking for scapegoats, rather than a significant political force. However, the rhetoric and growth of the movement suggests that the harnessing of a particular avant-garde arts practice to the militaristic paradigm of the self-sacrificing pioneer has created a frighteningly plausible model of activist politics finding a strong purchase on contemporary youth and emerging from the aesthetic interplay of music, performance, myth, and avant-garde "leadership." The emotional revolution and the growth of a cult around a dead hero emerging from the Lesser Free Trade Hall is in fact as powerfully forged and (frighteningly) influential in the case of Ian Stuart as it has been in that of Ian Curtis. Where Ian Curtis's cultural capital makes him a figurehead for the emotional revolution which Morley claims, it is Ian Stuart whose deification points to a direct merging of the cultic with the political which, while also more hidden, embodies a more directly and dismayingly revolutionary dynamism.

Notes

1. Paul Morley, "A Northern Soul," *The Observer Music Monthly* (May 2006): 28–37.
2. Günter Berghaus, *Theatre, Performance and the Historical Avant-Garde* (Basingstoke: Palgrave Macmillan, 2005), 39.
3. "Détournement" is defined as the "reversal" or "turning" "of pre-existing aesthetic elements. The integration of present or past artistic production into a superior construction of a milieu. In this sense there can be no situationist painting or music, but only a situationist use of these means." From Guy Debord and Gil Wolman, "Methods of Détournement" (1956), trans. Ken Knabb in Knabb (ed.), *The Situationist International Anthology* (Berkeley: Bureau of Public Secrets, 1981).
4. A website, freakeytrigger.co.uk, currently features a list of those who actually attended the "seminal Sex Pistol's seminal gig at the seminal Manchester Free Trade Hall." Claiming to be transcribed from a crumpled piece of paper, the list includes forty-five significant personalities. Alongside Howard Devoto, Morrissey and Mark E Smith, appear Lord Lucan, Thora Hird, Haile Selassie and Yul Brynner. See www.freakeytrigger.co.uk/ft/2007/04/the-sex-pistols-at-the-manchester-free-trade-hall-the-truth/ (accessed Jan. 5, 2008).
5. Morley, "A Northern Soul."
6. Tim Etchells, *Certain Fragments: Contemporary Performance and Forced Entertainment* (London: Routledge, 1999), 106–107, 109.
7. Steve Aylett et al., *Perverted By Language* (London: Serpent's Tail, 2007).

8. Mark E Smith, *Renegade: The Lives and Takes of Mark E. Smith* (London: Penguin, 2008).
9. Guy Debord, *The Society of the Spectacle*, trans. Donald Nicholson-Smith (Boston: MIT Press, 1995).
10. Julian Temple (dir.), *The Great Rock and Roll Swindle* (London, Boyd's Company, 1980).
11. "Decade in Valhalla," *Rock-o-Rama Records*, www.rockorama.com/ian-interview.htm (accessed Feb. 21, 2008).
12. Accounts and sources vary, as they do over which gig many who claim to be there attended. See David Nolan, *I Swear I Was There: The Gig That Changed The World* (Church Stretton: Independent Music Publishers, 2006).
13. "Decade in Valhalla."
14. Stewart Home's *Cranked Up Really High: Genre Theory and Punk Rock* contains a chapter on Donaldson and a pithy examination of the lumpen punk and white power stages in the music of Skrewdriver. See http://www.stewarthomesociety.org/cranked/content.htm (accessed Feb. 24, 2008).
15. Simon Reynolds, *Rip It Up and Start Again: Postpunk 1978–1984* (London: Faber and Faber, 2005), 21.
16. Nolan, *I Swear I Was There*.
17. Luke Harding, "German Neo-Nazis Set for Poll Victory," *The Guardian*, Sept. 15, 2006, http://www.guardian.co.uk/world/2006/sep/15/germany.thefarright (accessed Nov. 12, 2007).
18. "Decade in Valhalla."
19. Ibid.
20. See Anti-Defamation League, www.adl.org/main_Extremism/hate_music_in_the_21st_century.htm?Multi_page_sections=sHeading_2 (accessed Feb. 12, 2008).
21. Reynolds, *Rip It Up and Start Again*, xix, xviii.
22. *Breaking The Rules: The Printed Face of the European Avant-Garde 1900–1937* at the British Library (London, 2007) featured album sleeves from New Order and the post-punk influenced contemporary band Franz Ferdinand as well as from a compilation album, *Lipstick Traces*, which accompanied Greil Marcus's book of the same name (Cambridge, MA: Harvard University Press, 1990), and a Sex Pistols T-shirt. Particular attention was drawn in the exhibition to the influence of the Italian Futurists – certainly aligned with right-wing political sympathies – on the designs of Peter Saville, sleeve designer for both Joy Division and New Order, whose work has contributed to the aura of fascist flirtation which has tended to dog those bands.
23. William Niven, "The Birth of Nazi Drama," in *Theatre Under the Nazis*, ed. John London (Manchester: Manchester University Press, 2006), 54–95 (58).
24. James Hider, "Swastikas, Neo-Nazi Gangs and Attacks on Jews. Where? In Israel," *Times Online*, Sept. 10, 2007, www.Timesonline.co.uk (accessed Dec. 11, 2007).
25. Ibid.
26. Conal Urquart, "Israeli Neo-Nazi Ring Caught After Attacks on Synagogues," *The Guardian*, Sept. 10, 2007, www.guardianunlimited.co.uk (accessed Dec. 11, 2007).

27. Sean Albiez, "Print the Truth, Not the Legend: The Sex Pistols: Lesser Free Trade Hall, Manchester, June 4, 1976," in *Performance and Popular Music: History, Place and Time*, ed. Ian Inglis (London: Ashgate, 2006), 92–93.
28. *Control*, dir. Anton Corbijn (Weinstein Company, 2007).
29. *Blood and Honour: The Independent Voice Against Communism*, www. bloodandhonour.org/ (accessed Jan. 5, 2009).
30. Edward P. Commentale, *Modernism, Cultural Production, and the British Avant-Garde* (Cambridge, MA: Cambridge University Press, 2004), 66.

Afterword
The Avant-Garde and Vector Studies: A Roundtable

Alan Filewod, James M. Harding, Jean Graham-Jones,
Kimberly Jannarone, and Mike Sell

Mike Sell: I've invited Jean Graham-Jones, James Harding, Kimberly
Jannarone, and Alan Filewod to Indiana University of Pennsylvania
to discuss the implications and opportunities of the essays in this
anthology. I've asked these particular people for several reasons. For
one, each of them is expert in the history of theatre, drama, and performance. Secondly, each has been working, in their respective areas
of specialization, to call into question the way we think about the
geopolitics of theatre, drama, and performance. Jean Graham-Jones
studies Latin America and has a special interest in translation. Though
James M. Harding's primary interests are in modern European and
U.S. art, particularly the avant-garde, he has written one of the more
significant statements about the avant-garde and global studies and
co-edited a very important anthology on the subject. Alan Filewod is a
Canadian scholar of Canadian theatre, drama, and performance and,
like Jean with Latin America, is highly aware of the hegemonic power
of the U.S. and Europe in those areas; further, he was one of the contributors to the original "Vectors of the Radical" issue of *Works and
Days*. Finally, Kimberly Jannarone is one of the scholars who is pressing us to be more careful with how we think about the avant-garde
as an ideological formation. Finally, all four have played a shaping
role in my own development as a scholar of the avant-garde, material
exchange, and performance. I asked them to read all the essays in the
anthology, criticize them, and identify some implications they see –
or don't see – in them that might guide future inquiries.

James M. Harding: Well, to begin with, I'm interested in the mistakes and
failures of the avant-garde, the kind we find discussed in the essays by

Laura Edmondson and, to an extent, Cindy Rosenthal. Failure usually suggests something went wrong, but thinking about vectors of the radical and the concept of experimentation, we know that's not the case. In science, failed experiments are a valuable source of information, right? Which leads to another issue. When I look at the unwritten histories that many of these essays discuss or attempt to write, I'm reminded of Walter Benjamin and his notion that there is no history of the vanquished. The concept of vectors suggests a way into that history.

MS: Where do you see this playing into a material history of the avant-garde?

JH: You no longer have a forward-moving paradigm, you have a *project* where a blunder might allow for an artist or community to move in different directions, for ideas and objects to move outside of the linear, progressive model that judged the work a failure.

Alan Filewod: But even so, the discourse of the avant-garde is always the cultural script of imperialism, isn't it? This idea of a genealogy of failure doesn't escape that. As soon as you start talking about the Living Theatre, for example, as a group of Americans traveling around the world, committed to revolution, sincere in their efforts, sincere in their blunders, and blundering – well, that's just another version of U.S. history, to my mind. As I read Edmondson's piece, too, I was struck by the absence of a history of Western artistic interventions in Africa.

JGJ: An interesting counter-example might be Siyuan Liu's essay on the genealogy of the modern Western theatre in early-twentieth-century China.

AF: Yes.

JH: As much as I appreciate the comparison you're making, Alan, there's a problem. The agenda of the Living Theatre is anarchist, not a protection of economic interest, not the cultivation of new markets, and not cultural imperialism. The fundamental requirement to entry is a commitment to pacifism and some variation of anarchism. In that respect, the more apt comparison would be the global workers' movements.

JGJ: I'd like to expand on Alan's concern regarding the location of historiography. At times during my reading of the essays, I found myself yearning for more intradisciplinary exchange. For example, I thought Zenenga's analysis could be enriched by an engagement with the theories of coloniality and performance coming out of Latin American theatre and performance studies, and Edmondson struck me as struggling to find a term already in circulation: "coexistence in difference." I'd love to see the field in general embrace a metacritical theoretical vectoring equivalent to the artistic trajectories many of the essays trace.

MS: How about you, Kimberly?

Kimberly Jannarone: Two things I was particularly excited about were in Graham White's and Patricia Gaborik and Andrea Harris's essays. They both showed the effect of what might be called a "rehistoriography" of vanguard performance, a rewriting based in a material analysis that allows them to question received notions about specific performances. In one case, we rethink Balanchine as a figure of wholesomeness and innovation; in the other, we ask, "Isn't it possible that punk is open to every kind of angry young man who wants to thwart the system?" These scholars ask, "What does this make us think about the avant-garde? How do we interpret this moment through ideological frameworks, some of which we might not be aware? How is the event 'political' in ways we might not want it to be?"

MS: Kimberly, your recent work on Antonin Artaud shows the value of theatre history and performance studies for this kind of "rehistoriography." Looking at the essays, where are theatre history and performance studies playing a role?

KJ: In the case of Gaborik and Harris, they identify discourses about modern ballet and Italian Futurism. Then they go back and show what kind of movement strategies were used by the performers, what the relationship of the audience to the stage was. This kind of archival analysis, which includes both formal and archaeological analysis, can displace the ideological or theoretical wash that has been placed over events. They show that we can in some ways go to the event itself, in all its material detail, as much as we can reconstruct, and see how untidy the event was and how inadequate the narratives and interpretations we have are.

MS: So, event-orientation and material formation are two ways that we can open up ideological closure?

JH: Yes, but the issue's bigger than that. As John Rouse and I have written, when you look at studies of the avant-garde, performance usually isn't in the picture.[1] But the notion of performance is fundamental to the very definition of the avant-garde. So, I think theatre and performance studies are a point of departure for a radical redefinition of the avant-garde *across the disciplines*. It's within theatre departments that you find people who understand performance not just in the sense of performativity, but as something that occurs within specific spaces, with specific things, audiences, and so on.

MS: That's right. People in theatre and performance studies have always needed to be attentive to the ways that different kinds of materiality exist. The materiality of a theatre building, for example, is different from the materiality of a moving dancer.

AF: I'd like to complicate this a bit, though, because the concept of the avant-garde as an historical bloc or formation is inherently unstable. I noticed in most of the essays a reluctance to think about art markets, cultural economy, and valuation. There's no discussion of economy and power. This mirrors something larger in theatre history studies: the need to go to spectator-based approaches, to the viewing practices and receptive practices of existing people. There's also a reluctance in these essays to address issues of gender and power. The recurring language of militant aesthetics and the kind of inherent masculinism that goes with it aren't often called into question by the writers, Graham White being one exception.

So, if the avant-garde is a kind of historical conversation, and we're trying to intervene critically in that conversation, then the questions should be: Who's talking? Who's not talking? Who's in the conversation? And why is that conversation always drawn between Berlin, Paris, New York, and London, with side trips to Moscow? The farther the essays move from the metropolitan centers, the more varied the ground gets, the boundaries more and more blurred, and the writers more and more engaged with the artist in relationship to *things* than they are with *artistic practice* or *form*.

JH: The majority of theatre histories focus on large metropolitan areas. So, that's not something unique to avant-garde studies, is it?

AF: No, but it is more formative within avant-garde studies.

MS: And more contradictory, given this idea that the avant-garde has a global reach and seeks the *essential* techniques that will be *essentially* liberatory.

AF: And what one always finds is that there are no essential techniques, period.

KJ: The avant-garde isn't always trying to be liberatory, either.

MS: For sure. Michel Foucault taught us that the concept of liberation is linked to specific historical paradigms and specific understandings of how cultural action is efficacious. Further, there are radical right-wing movements whose understanding of liberation is very different from the Left's, a point Kimberly's made in her work on Artaud and crowd theory.[2]

KJ: I'd like to take a step back to the role of theatre and performance studies. What we're often drawn to with the avant-garde isn't so much polished works of art, but the impulse that animates them. There's not much pleasure in reading *The Gas Heart* by itself if you don't know about Dada. Like Alan, I've been thinking about the audience–performer relationship as one of the more engaging elements of avant-garde work. I think many of the essays here do the same. It's not so much the frameable object they're discussing, but the shifting ways that people communicate and whether they're giving or receiving, a topic that is often of interest in theatre and performance studies.

MS: Do we see differences in the criticism attempted in these essays – or in other critical perspectives not attempted, but suggested here – because they're focusing more on *how things move* than on *what things are*?

AF: Yes, especially considering that scholars tend to think that historical propositions are historical evidence.

MS: What do you mean?

AF: As I discuss in my section introduction, the workers' theatre movement, to cite just one example, and its history has become a kind of *de facto* historical phenomenon that we refer to as if it were just one thing, when in fact it was really a kind of subjunctive proposition, a whole bunch of things, a mobilization technique that created many kinds of effects. The proposal of a workers' theatre movement was a political strategy; historians now tend to see the proposal as proof of the thing proposed.

In the same way, artistic celebrity becomes historicized as evidence of the art. Think of Esther Kim Lee's essay on Nam June Paik. It's great to be a radical artist, but it's hard that no one wants to see him, and he becomes institutionalized as a state industry in Korea because it serves the interests of the state to rebrand itself as modernist. That process of reclamation is fascinating, but also destabilizes the way that art history about him has been written, because it draws attention away from the art practice and relocates our attention to who's commenting upon it, who's seeing it, why they are commenting on this and seeing it, who gets the ashes. The work is subjunctive, contingent, possible.

MS: It makes me think that what we're doing here is pretty old-fashioned, in some ways. Marx writes in *Capital* that the commodity is a mystical thing that always manages to obfuscate its origins and pathways. By looking at how objects are produced and circulated by the avant-garde, we can demystify the commodity – in this case, the avant-garde – and comprehend better the way things are produced and the social relationships that determine that production. As a consequence of that, we not only demystify the object of our analysis, but our analysis itself. In both cases, we recover the social relationships that constitute the avant-garde event.

JH: If you go back to Sally Banes's beautiful book on Greenwich Village,[3] the one thing that has always stuck with me is the passage where she talks about the United States' funding of the arts, which she pinpoints to the Kennedy administration and Cold War politics. The idea here was that the United States, as opposed to the communist states, allowed openness and dissent. So there were funds available for artists to do weird and socially unacceptable things because the tolerance of weird and socially unacceptable artists served the ideological interests of the United States. Therefore, the most dissident voice, the most radical voice, is already contained. And I think that's exactly what Esther is talking about with Paik.

MS: True, but we need to keep in mind that the dissidence that was funded in the 1960s and 1970s is best characterized as *formal* dissidence, because the moment that African-Americans, queer people, and women began to inject *social* dissidence into their art, the funding was withdrawn.

KJ: James, what you just uttered was basically a Situationist critique, the idea that innovation, especially if it's slotted in a linear model of liberation, is what capitalism thrives on. The avant-garde is always vulnerable to the machine, the spectacle, whatever. I think this is where vectors can be very useful because they're plural, they pluralize, and they don't imply a monolithic, forward-moving linearity. That's very useful if we're trying to disrupt this idea of the avant-garde as a mental construct of us Western critics or as part of an expansive Western capitalism.

This leads me to a question about the essays, which do an excellent job of tracing artistic and geographical vectors; specifically, geographical vectors. But can we talk about temporal vectors, too, about exchanges across time? The idea of temporal restructuring is implied in the idea of vectors, but wasn't prominent in many of the essays.

JGJ: Yes, the overall project assumes a spatialized approach – a vector moves through space – and this emphasis on spatiality is apparent in the three sections of this book: intersection, translation, and divergence. I'd encourage us to think temporally not only in terms of diachrony but of other times such as the synchronic or the simultaneous. Synchronous time, for one, is central to current Latin American cultural theories of the modern, and is certainly an element that will help us to understand critical vanguard performances, as Mike would call those under consideration here.

MS: The exception being Praise Zenenga's piece, which shows a variety of historical imaginaries in play simultaneously over the course of Zimbabwe's postcolonial history. Tradition is continually reconsidered and repositioned. Where the past fits is continually revised and the idea of modernity continually transformed as political regimes change. This is very much in the spirit of Richard Schechner's idea of the tradition-seeking avant-garde, for sure, but suggests further that the way time is imagined by these vanguards is itself changing.[4] That said, Jean's right: We don't see enough focus on the temporal in these essays, despite the concern we all have with writing history.

JGJ: An awareness of multiplicity, such as Mike notes in Zenenga's essay, would enrich most analyses I've read of various avant-gardes. What about movement as multiple, multidirectional, constellative?

AF: Paik and the many artists in Praise's piece raise an issue. We've done a lot in theatre and performance studies to challenge the notion of "frameable art," but perhaps we need to start talking about the "frameable artist." It's really interesting to see in so much of the history of the avant-garde that the value of the artwork is almost always proportional to the value of the artist. We have to remember that artists are complicit; they have lives at stake in this. And that leads me to think about the lack of value of anonymous art, at least until anonymity comes to be seen as valuable, giving us artists like Banksy.

MS: On the other hand, I'm very conscious of artists such as my friend Rosaly Roffman. She was a fellow-traveler with some of the key post-Second World War avant-gardes – those we associate with Yoko Ono, John Cage, M. C. Richards, Merce Cunningham, and so on. She played a not insignificant role in building intercultural exchange between Japan and the United States during the 1960s and 1970s. And she's a noteworthy poet. Though she is anything but vanquished, to recall Benjamin again, Rosaly is close to anonymous. And here's the rub: she long ago let go of the desire to be "historical," the desire to be "big." But she's had an impact in the *smallest* of ways through chance meetings, work in small publications, friendships, collaborations on local projects. Being a woman no doubt exerted negative pressure on the things she did – her friend M. C. Richards often talked with her about why she, Richards, remained anonymous, while long-time collaborators, community members, and colleagues like John Cage and Merce Cunningham became celebrities.

If there's something else we don't like to talk about when we talk about the avant-garde, it's things that don't have grand ambition. This is what I like about theatre and performance studies: we have a high tolerance for that which is here and gone. And we have a fair amount of patience for smallness. But the bias is still there. We want the theatre events we write about to be big, to have historical significance.

JH: But this whole notion of being big; it's not just the event itself. Mike, your argument in *Avant-Garde Performance and the Limits of Criticism* suggests that we're the ones making the event big, at least in part.[5] It's clear also that the exploration that you do there – of our relationship to these events, to these art works, to these texts – is an invitation to do more. Vectors are performative entities and our response to them will have a performative dimension.

Once you move into a global, materialist understanding of avant-garde gestures, you realize that the world doesn't move in uniformity, and the evolution of the avant-gardes is very jagged, moving along different trajectories. As a consequence, it's very possible that the same person who speaks of the avant-garde in terms of an historical movement of the past may, in the next breath, speak of the avant-garde in such-and-such a place as a vital, contemporary, performative movement. That's a source of vitality for critical vanguard studies.

KJ: But it's not just us who make claims that these artists are big. We are drawn to people who are already grandiose. In his essay, Graham writes about how people are drawn to the inspirational, messianic figure, the artist who self-sacrifices in the name of art or an aesthetic cause. There is a long list of artists – Ian Stuart, Artaud, Sarah Kane, Jacques Vaché – who are grandiose. We're drawn to that. So the avant-gardists who are part of the canon do tend to be people who believe art is a tool for reconfiguring how we live life or for reconfiguring the relationship between the individual and the world. Rosaly Roffman doesn't fit in that crowd.

JH: That reminds me. When I first started giving my paper on Valerie Solanas[6] – as grandiose a figure as the avant-garde has ever known – I knew I had discovered a goldmine. People would start arguing in the audience as soon as I completed my paper, and I would wonder, "Wow, what did I do?" People would stand up and point their finger at me and say, "You are aestheticizing violence." And my response to that was, "I am not aestheticizing violence. I'm a critic. I'm writing *about* somebody who aestheticized violence." And what I encountered there is the debate that we're having right now. But that raises questions. On the one hand, am I the agent here, the one who found Valerie Solanas and said, "You know what, I can fit this into the paradigms of the avant-garde and, as a consequence, do something that's quite provocative"? Or am I merely the recording critic who says, "Nobody saw that before; there it is"?

KJ: I would say that it's between the two. The worst you can say of us is that we're taking these avant-garde artists at their word and giving them the value – or at least some of the value – that they claim they have.

JH: And so my point is not so much about markets, but about a kind of impulse that seems to recur in avant-garde studies – what Alan talked about earlier as a hidden bias or fantasy among scholars for some kind of utopian hope.

MS: The essays do show how much the desire of scholars and critics shape our understanding of the avant-garde. For some reason, this gets me thinking about humor. The avant-gardes that have been the funniest have tended to be the avant-gardes that were most aware of their materiality. So, Fluxus, which always portrayed itself as a capitalist enterprise, selling little trinkets and toys, putting together ad hoc stores, was always about having a good laugh. There's also Mayakovsky, one of the funniest avant-gardists, even at his most radical.

KJ: Berlin Dada.

JGJ: And the playfulness of Tzara's *Gas Heart*, even down to the printed page, as Sarah Bay-Cheng makes beautifully explicit in her essay.

MS: For sure. All of these were highly attentive to the fact that they were a congeries of things, and all of them were highly conscious, to the point of self-parody, about their claims to be the vanguard. Why is there this relationship between an ironic consciousness of one's own materiality and an ironic consciousness of being vanguard? Perhaps Henri Bergson's theory of humor can help us here: We laugh at the moment we recognize the materiality of the human being, the fact that it is an inert and opaque materiality...

KJ: Which reminds me that the least materialist of them all – and the least ironic – was the utterly humorless Artaud.

MS: It seems that we begin to be self-reflexive when we recognize our attachments to objects. Artaud was terrified by the "thinginess" of the world, right? How did that play into his incapacity to reflect on himself politically and economically? In some ways, this raises Peter Bürger's theory of the avant-garde – the avant-garde doesn't achieve adequate form until it is able to comprehend how the art it creates is determined by the material and social structures that allow it to be bought, sold, and valued.[7] Not surprisingly, Dada is his favorite vanguard.

AF: There's another thing to consider here. In 1929, Erwin Piscator announced the death of political theatre. It doesn't work, he realized; it's not going to work because the audiences just aren't going to fall for it. In 1934, the Soviet Writers Conference killed – both literally and figuratively – avant-garde theatre for much of the Left. Throughout the twentieth century, things got worse and worse and worse for the avant-garde, the body count got higher and higher, and there's no end in sight. Ironically, in the midst of all this tragedy and hopelessness, radical artists found more and more that they had the power to shape the terms of their reception. Talk about irony! To gain control of your objects, but lose their significance.

KJ: That helps to crystallize something that's been nagging me: the idea that a liberal, agit-prop agenda equals, in some of the writers' minds, a true form of activist avant-garde theatre. But is this always the case? Certainly, if we're going to go and defend people who have been the victims of some kind of mass brutality or who are disempowered and don't have the means to rectify that or wish to give voice to people who aren't voiced, then we have to have an agenda and an agenda-driven plan. But that presumes that the audience is passive, a kind of object to be manipulated. Don't get me wrong – that kind of oppression and suffering needs to be addressed vigorously. But in terms of vectors, what we're talking about here presumes a kind of mass circulation for the avant-garde event, one that dehumanizes and homogenizes at the very moment it's trying to be most humane.

MS: Isn't that what Laura Edmondson discovered in Rwanda and Uganda?

KJ: There's maybe one person who's managed to do activist theatre in the manner that Brecht envisioned, in a way that didn't presume mass circulation: Augusto Boal. He created a theatre structure where people could ask questions and come to a new awareness of themselves, could think about power in new ways. Boal was very attentive to the hypocrisy of humane endeavors. The thing is, Boal's method only works in small doses. If you try to go in with an agenda on a mass-scale, then you're just another agit-prop avant-garde; you're dogmatically orchestrating space so that people are forced to the point of view you already have. How can you engineer on a mass scale individual thought, self-awareness, consciousness, self-reflexivity?

JGJ: It's interesting that you should bring Boal into this conversation, Kimberly. My section introduction discusses Boal not only to mark his recent passing but to emphasize my belief that no theatre practitioner has embodied the mobility of radical cultural exchange more than he. You use the term "method"; I think that, in systematizing Boal, many practitioners, translators, and scholars have lost sight of Benjamin's insistence that translation is relational, with the result that Boal's multifaceted, ever-changing, always translated practice gets solidified into a monolithic method. Not only does this solidification effectively erase Boal's radicality, it neatly ignores his experiments with staging contemporary and classical plays and operas and marginalizes his strong commitment to a modified form of Stanislavskian directing principles.

MS: I think that's a marvelous point, Jean. It underlines the fact that a vectors-based history of the avant-garde inevitably alters our understanding of the avant-garde itself. Going back to the question of mass-distributed vanguards, there are two other exceptions, Mayakovsky and Fluxus coming to mind again. The Mayakovsky I'm talking about is the guy who designed those wonderful consumer goods, posters, and other mass-marketed and -distributed materials that people could consume and, in that moment of encountering it, be part of an emerging economy that promised greater freedom of choice and self-determination. The same thing with Fluxus. You'd buy a little box from a Fluxstore and you might find a little card with a Fluxus event written on it or some kind of gag object, and there's that possibility of something unexpected, a moment of alterity. What makes the difference is, I think, respect for the audience's ability to choose, think, and act. To paraphrase the old song, "If you love something, let it go." It's not by accident that the fascist movements of the 1930s wanted complete control of their nation's economies.

KJ: So all this comes from the growth of free-market commodity networks.

MS: To a degree, yes, though there are different kinds of markets and commodity networks – alternative networks, "black" networks, local networks. Many of the activists we associate with the Black Arts Movement advocated a cooperative form of capitalism. But your point's well taken: We're looking at a way of investigating the avant-garde that seems pretty indebted to capitalism and its circulation systems.

AF: So if we're going to do critical vanguard studies, then one of the questions we ought to ask is, how do emergent technologies prod us to be more critical or to alter our understandings of avant-gardism? Most new technologies, after all, are about moving things. One of the functions of the avant-garde – and avant-garde performance – is to push the boundaries of what you can do with new stuff. In which case, that confirms that the role of commodity circulation, capitalism, marketing...

MS: Labor...

AF:...and labor are significant factors. Come to think of it, I'm distressed by the fact that the word "class" is rarely used by the writers. But my point is that there is a relationship, not fully understood yet, between emerging technologies of circulation and the kinds of critical perspectives that are available to us.

KJ: Whether we talk about rough edges or vectors, whether we ground that talk in technologies or performance strategies, we're able to move beyond a linear, monolithic, imperialistic avant-garde idea. We can begin thinking about the gives and takes between communities, aesthetic forms, structures of performance, and so on, so that it becomes impossible to locate the original source. As long as we're always thinking about originality and origins, we're thinking in a linear, imperialist way...

MS: And a sexist way...

KJ: Right, so if we get out of that mode of thinking – as your theoretical models help us do, James and Mike – the question becomes not, "Where does this come from?" but, "What are people doing with it?" Then we get to a new way of theorizing the avant-garde, one that sees it as a constant process of grabbing, reappropriating, getting grabbed, and that creates new forms for new moments. That may be Balanchine grabbing from the Futurists or right-wingers grabbing from the Sex Pistols. That is far more interesting and illustrative than only wanting to put people that we like into a line that we like.

JGJ: I'd propose a kind of "collision analysis" that works by bringing seemingly disparate elements into conversation with each other – a kind of critical-historical collage. We take a page from some of the vanguard artists themselves – cut-up poems, collage – and linger in the conflict without seeking resolution or simplistic binaries.

KJ: Right. If we recognize that influences are coming from places we're not comfortable with, either because of the nature of the influence or the way they got the influence, that makes us more mindful about what makes the avant-garde significant, which is not going to be covered by a neat, linear theory, because it's a bit of a mess.

MS: Thank you, Jean, Alan, Kimberly, James. You've helped me – and, I hope, our readers – understand better how we might build from these essays' insights and oversights. There's a "mess" here, for sure, but exactly the kind of mess that I think promotes critical perspective, critical methods, and the curiosity that drives future scholarly inquiry.

Notes

1. James M. Harding and John Rouse, Introduction, *Not the Other Avant-Garde: The Transnational Foundations of Avant-Garde Performance*, ed. Harding and Rouse (Ann Arbor: University of Michigan Press, 2006).
2. Kimberly Jannarone, *Artaud and His Doubles* (Ann Arbor: University of Michigan Press, 2010).
3. Sally Banes, *Greenwich Village 1963: Avant-Garde Performance and the Effervescent Body* (Durham: Duke University Press, 1993).
4. Richard Schechner, "The Five Avant-Gardes or… [and]… or None?" in *The Twentieth-Century Performance Reader*, 2nd edn, ed. Michael Huxley and Noel Witts (New York and London: Routledge, 2002).
5. Mike Sell, *Avant-Garde Performance and the Limits of Criticism: Approaching the Living Theatre, Happenings/Fluxus, and the Black Arts Movement* (Ann Arbor: University of Michigan Press, 2005).
6. James M. Harding, "The Simplest Surrealist Act: Valerie Solanas and the (Re) Assertion of Avantgarde Priorities," *TDR* 45.4 (Winter 2001): 142–162.
7. Peter Bürger, *Theory of the Avant-Garde*, trans. Michael Shaw (Minneapolis: University of Minnesota Press, 1984).

Index